HOW TO SAVE
YOUR MARRIAGE
FROM AN AFFAIR

HOW TO SAVE YOUR MARRIAGE FROM AN AFFAIR

SEVEN STEPS TO REBUILDING A BROKEN TRUST

BY

DR. RONNIE EDELL

KENSINGTON BOOKS

http://www.kensingtonbooks.com

KENSINGTON BOOKS are published by

Kensington Publishing Corp.
850 Third Avenue
New York, NY 10022

Kensington and the K logo Reg. U.S. Pat. & TM Off.

First Zebra Printing: 1990
First Kensington Trade Paperback Printing: February, 1995
ISBN 0-8217-4886-6

Printed in the United States of America
10 9 8 7 6 5 4 3 2

*The greatest debt is to all the people who have endured
the pain of an affair to keep the institution of marriage alive.
I dedicate this book to you with the sincere hope
that others will join your ranks rather than give up.*

ACKNOWLEDGMENTS

This might be the most difficult part of the book to write. I feel a deep sense of personal, creative, and intellectual gratitude to a few extremely significant people who had the foresight and belief to make this project a reality. I am indebted to many individuals whose talents and creativity have made this dream a wondrous reality.

A very special thanks to my literary agent, Peter Miller, who is a genius at his chosen field of endeavor and a very special friend. I want to thank my publisher, Bobbs-Merrill, and especially my editor, Barbara Lagowski, whose belief, sensitivity, hard work, and creative talents made this manuscript a reality. I appreciate Stephen Meyer's editorial suggestions, which I feel strengthened the book considerably. Steve Meyer, in working with me, created a unique spirit of creative talents on all levels. This project could never have reached the level of uniqueness without his exceptional talents. I want to thank Jan Boyd who brought forth a vim and spirit of tenacity in the compilation of interviews and other important data for the development of this project. I feel a tremendous sense of gratitude to Jan for penetrating the pulse of how people feel when confronted with their feelings regarding an affair. I want to make a very special acknowledgment to Dr. J. Calvin Leonard, whose magical knowledge, sensitivity, and skill were transmitted to me with love. To my inlaws, Lillian and Edward Bomes, who have given me the love and support that is so rare: you've endured with tenacity all my professional and creative efforts. I want to thank you from the heart for your most precious gift to me—Barbara, who is such a beautiful and supportive individual. I would like to say thank you to my wife, Barbara, who always stood by me, supporting every effort fully with love and understanding. A big kiss to our two beautiful children, Ricki and Sherri, and our family dog, Star, who have brought us great joy. Much gratitude to my parents, Philip and Florence, for their enduring love, support, and understanding throughout my life. An extra special thanks, Dad, for your direction and guidance during this endeavor.

CONTENTS

INTRODUCTION

Affairs. The pages of the yellow press are full of torrid revelations about celebrities who cheat on their husbands and wives. Soap operas dramatize the emotional turmoil of doctors, nurses, lawyers, and business people who seek fulfillment outside marriage. An affair can spice up a vacuous film script or add a gripping dimension to an otherwise tired plot in a novel. There is no question but that the breaking of marital bonds is a great subject of interest in our culture.

We are eminently monogamous people. We don't believe in harems, nor do we accumulate wives and husbands as we would household antiques. Even a ménage à trois seems daring and out of the ordinary. Relationships being what they are in our society, we simply don't have enough hours in a day to really satisfy two people's emotional needs at once. When we try—well, it simply doesn't work. Yet statistics show that an affair occurs in one of two marriages today in the United States. That's a lot of infidelity, which creates a lot of sensational headlines but which, I assure you, creates great emotional turmoil in a lot of marriages.

There are a number of reasons why you may be reading this book. Perhaps you had an extramarital affair, are having one, or are thinking of having one. Or perhaps you suspect your spouse of past, present, or future infidelity. Whatever your reasons, you no doubt have a problem in your marriage. Deep emotional conflicts may be eroding your relationship, and overcoming them may require confronting issues that frighten you terribly. Or your problems could be caused by superficial misunderstandings that result from incomplete communication. In either case, *How To Save Your Marriage from an Affair* contains valuable information that will help you and your spouse restore harmony in your marriage.

The first section of the book is explanatory; essentially it lays out before you what happens when a marriage is disrupted by an affair. We will discuss warning signs (Chapter 1), the various forms of marital erosion that are symptomatic of the underlying tension caused by the affair (Chapter 4), and the consequences of the affair's disclosure (Chapter 5). Chapters 2 and 3 will discuss a number of problems that either come up in adulthood or are rooted in childhood and can predispose someone to seek extramarital fulfillment.

The last two sections provide structural guidelines that allow the reader to overcome the trauma of an affair. In Reconstructive Dynamics (Chapters 6, 7, 8, and 9), both partners will be encouraged to confront their own problems together and work to "reconstruct" their marriage. This is the real core of *How To Save Your Marriage from an Affair*. The degree of your commitment to Reconstructive Dynamics will determine how successful you will be in reuniting with your spouse.

The answer to saving a marriage from an affair may seem obvious to you; the partner having the affair has to stop seeing his or her lover and become a faithful husband or wife again. This solution, however, provides no guarantee that another affair won't occur soon afterward; nor does it ensure that either partner will be happy.

The word "save" in the title of this book is carefully chosen. This is not a book about "perpetuating" marriages. Its goal is not just to get husband and wife back together again, any more than the goal of making love is merely to copulate. The word "save" in the title means not just ending the affair but bringing back vitality, spontaneity, and love to your marriage. Without these things, there is no point in living together. When you finish Reconstructive Dynamics you and your spouse should be deeply in love with one another, and you both should be extremely eager to get on with your lives in a spirit of unity and common purpose.

Hard to believe? I'm sure it is. But I think for a moment of all the junk, all the emotional garbage that is literally piled between you and your spouse. If you are having an affair and your spouse doesn't know about it, you are lying to her (or him), and every move you make is made with considerations about your guilt or about whether you are giving yourself away. You are a phony; you lack all spontaneity; you are not "alive." If you suspect your spouse is having an affair but you refuse to say anything, your situation is as bad if not worse. I have known couples who go on "living" like this for months, even years, with the unfaithful partner's false behavior creating emotional garbage on one side, the faithful partner's denial mechanisms creating more of the same on the other. This emotional garbage poisons marriages, creating resentment, anger, insecurity, guilt, grief, pain, and even physical ailments related to emotional stress.

Now think for a moment what would happen if you removed all that accumulated emotional garbage. What would be left? Just you and your spouse. Just two people who got married years ago because they loved one another.

I don't pretend that all marriages can be saved. Sometimes people get married for the wrong reasons and have such radically different personalities that they can never fulfill one another. This book is not for them. It is for people who are willing to take the courageous steps necessary to reopen the channels of communication with their spouses. It is for people who, deep down, really love the person they married years ago and want their marriage not just to survive but to evolve and grow.

Following the guidelines offered in Reconstructive Dynamics will not be easy; the process of reconstructing a marriage requires that you confront yourself more rigorously and with deeper commitment than you ever have before. The unfaithful partner may discover that in having an affair he was merely acting out a "life script," a destructive pattern of behavior dictated by his own fear and insecurity. The faithful partner may be shocked to discover that she is not a blameless victim but that her own behavior prior to the affair contributed to her spouse's infidelity. As often as not, during the affair itself the unfaithful partner goes through as much emotional turmoil as the faithful partner. Furthermore, the deep emotional conflicts—rooted either in childhood or in current life situations—which may have caused the unfaithful partner to stray, are often much more complex and painful than those of the faithful partner.

So the first thing you must realize when you attempt to save your marriage from an affair is that there are no simple, black-and-white answers. There are no good guys or bad guys. An affair is the *result of* conflict in a marriage, not the cause. Simply labeling either partner as a bad person because he hurt his spouse totally ignores the real problem, which can only be identified after each partner has confronted his or her own role in creating marital discord. It takes commitment and courage to face the truth about yourself, but doing so could give you back your marriage. That's what this book is about.

Part One

COMING TO TERMS WITH INFIDELITY

Chapter 1

THE WARNING SIGNS OF AN AFFAIR

The days of "lipstick on your collar" are over. Today's warning signs are much more subtle and mysterious than they were twenty or thirty years ago. Affairs often go on for years before a partner suspects anything. Extramarital activities are so well disguised, in fact, so skillfully concealed, that it almost takes an undercover agent to dig up the evidence of a partner's infidelity.

But most of us wouldn't want to hire an undercover agent to expose our partner. Contrary to what some of the media stereotypes may lead us to believe, an affair is not always an insensitive, foolish, or flagrant violation of a marital bond. Nor is it usually indulged in for sexual reasons. It is a sign that there are serious problems in one's marriage, problems both partners are not taking a good enough look at.

As for what those problems are, we'll take a look at the possibilities in Chapters 2 and 3, on the causes of affairs, and in Chapter 7, on how to identify the cause in one's own situation. For now, suffice it to say that before we can look at the problems, we want to be able to answer the question: Is my partner having an affair?

If you strongly or even mildly suspect your partner of being involved in extramarital activity, then this chapter is for you. It will give you the tools to confirm or disprove your suspicions and will give you an understanding of how to react if you should be right, how *not* to react, and what steps to take next. It will also alert you to the fact that you may be denying your suspicions for any of a number of reasons I'll describe.

For those of you who already know your partner has had an affair, or is having one, I suggest you read this chapter anyway, as it will help you better understand what the warning signs were in your own situation and will give you further insight into the causes when we deal with them in the following two chapters.

As you read these warning signs, it's important to understand that if you do notice something unusual in your partner's behavior, you should not jump to conclusions or make rash accusations. This is especially true if you are by nature a jealous person—or if you begin to notice little signs of flirtatious behavior or talk in your partner. If you do jump to conclusions, your finger-pointing attitude could very well create an affair where none existed before.

At some time in your life you've probably read a list of the symptoms of a few serious diseases. As you read the symptoms you felt you had every disease in the book! This may happen to you as you read the warning signs—you may feel your partner surely is having an affair. First, keep in mind that you cannot go on one warning sign alone. Nor can you go on a few isolated signs here and there. What you are really looking for is a *pattern* of strange, unusual, or extreme behavior, behavior that does not fall within the range of what is normal for your relationship. You are looking for a combination of signs that add up to sudden, drastic change in your partner's usual routine.

If you recognize these warning-sign patterns in your partner, and there are strong indications that he or she is having an affair, it's important that you do not make the person feel guilty, wrong, or unjustified for what he or she has done. Affairs don't just happen. There is always a cause. Chances are your partner is not intentionally trying to hurt you by having an affair; he is only expressing a need that he is too afraid to confront you with. She is reaching out for help and understanding, and since she doesn't know how to reach out to *you* for that help and understanding, she reaches out to someone else.

And the truth is that most people who have affairs want to get caught. They're too afraid to take responsibility and face their partner with what needs of theirs are not being satisfied in the relationship; they prefer to be forced into a confrontation in order to get their feelings out.

Don't use these warning signs to point an accusing finger at your mate, to punish him or her, or to demand a divorce. Don't use them to say, with what you feel is utter certainty, "Aha! *You*, my dear, are having an affair!" The last thing I want to do is make you overly suspicious of your mate or wreak havoc in your marriage or relationship. These warning signs are intended only to alert you to what *could* be happening. They are meant to awaken you to the *possibility* that your partner is involved in an affair. They are not absolutes but merely potential indicators.

When it comes to spotting the signs themselves, you don't need any special or technical knowledge. You don't have to be a psychologist or a Sherlock Holmes. Though these signs are very subtle, they are all around you. All you do need are your intuition and a few guidelines. I'm going to provide the guidelines; it's up to you to use your intuition—but it will become more "tuned in" as you begin to really understand the patterns that are possible.

* * *

I find that an affair usually gives rise to signs in one of seven main categories. Let me start with the easier ones first, tackling the progressively harder ones as we go along.

1. Work.

Perhaps the most classic sign that something is wrong is when a husband or wife begins working later than usual on a consistent basis and for no apparent reason. In general, any sudden or drastic change in work patterns is suspicious, but only if it is out of the realm of what's normal for that relationship.

For example, if your husband has always put in long hours or lots of overtime, a few more hours here and there are consistent with his pattern. If he's a workaholic and you've learned to accept that, you'll always know where to find him—call him at work if you're ever in doubt! If your wife gets a promotion or lands a big account, you can expect her to be putting more hours in for a time.

But what makes any change in work pattern a potentially powerful warning sign is if the person continually makes excuses for his or her added activities. If your husband says to you, "We've got an important new project underway, and I've got to work late for a few weeks," and he feels no need to explain further, chances are you have no cause for suspicion. But if he constantly makes excuses for coming home late, even though he's already told you why the new hours are necessary, he may be covering up something. "Damn it, honey, that new secretary messed up my files, and I had to stay an extra four hours to straighten them out!" If he is having an affair, his excuses are an attempt to cover up his guilt about it.

Strange, vague, overly detailed excuses, an unending stream of excuses, or just a tremendous need to always explain the reasons why one had to work late—these are what can make the difference between a normal change in work habits and a suspicious one.

Many jobs require a lot of travel and involve conferences and seminars in distant cities. It's normal to feel insecure when a spouse is jaunting around on a business trip 3,000 miles away from home. But the frequency of conferences and trips falls into a certain pattern after a while. If your partner suddenly begins going to many conferences or starts seeking out opportunities to go away on business trips, you may have cause for concern. Again, it's the sudden, drastic, unexplained change in patterns that indicates something is going on.

2. Sex.

Sex within a marriage or relationship is a very intimate form of communication. Over the years partners get to know each other's sexual likes, dislikes, patterns, and rhythms so well that any change is likely to be noticed.

One of the more obvious potential warning signs of an affair is when a partner starts bringing new and unusual techniques into the couple's sex life. Of course, the person could have learned these techniques from a book, a movie, or a friend's description. But if a technique or an act is something out of the ordinary for that person or something he or she has always been opposed to or considered wrong or distasteful in the marriage, then there may be valid cause for suspicion.

If new and different sexual technique is a more obvious sign, lack of interest in sex is a more subtle, corrosive one. If your partner avoids sex totally or habitually makes excuses for not having sex with you, it could be the result of any of a number of problems in your marriage. Such statements as "I'm feeling down about work; business is off"; or, "I have my period and I'm having migraines"; or, "The kids are having all kinds of problems and I can't relax" may be legitimate reasons for not having sex—or they may be symptoms of other conflicts in the relationship. Certainly the avoidance of sex is an immediate indication that something is wrong. But if your partner *is* having an affair and avoids sex with you, either the "other woman" or "other man" is keeping your spouse well satisfied sexually, or your spouse is totally dissatisfied with you because you don't fulfill his or her needs and just doesn't want to face having sex with you. Beyond that, it's difficult to generalize. And this illustrates well the point I made earlier: that you cannot go on one warning sign alone; you must look at the bigger picture in your marriage.

3. Money.

When family resources start to dwindle down mysteriously and an excessive amount of money is being eaten away, that could be a sign of a spouse's affair.

Generally, if the man is having the affair he'll start to spend money on his affair partner. This will put a subtle drain on the budget. In fact, many times when a man is having an affair he'll tell his wife to cut down on expenses and on her use of credit cards—so that he can have more to spend on his "hobby." If he has a business, he'll attempt to disguise the spending by writing everything off as a business expense— "Lunch with client," "Business trip to Las Vegas," "Meeting with sales rep in Palm Springs," and all those other clever excuses.

A woman having an affair will tend to spend more money on clothes and items to increase her attractiveness and desirability. She'll go on buying sprees, fix herself up, go back to school, and try to use whatever time she feels may be left in the relationship to create a "package" for herself.

If your spouse writes all the checks, there won't be any way for you to know what's going on with the family money. If *you* write all the checks, of course you'll be the one in control of the financial situation. But if you both have a hand in family finances, you'll be in the unenviable position of being able to tell when something funny is going on. The changes are always hidden, but they'll surface somehow if you're in touch with the finances.

One other area involving money is when your spouse starts

buying you a multitude of gifts and has never done so before or normally does so infrequently. This is what I like to call "appeasement bargaining." Your partner is trying to relieve his or her guilt by "buying you off." The gifts are intended to prevent you from suspecting that something might be going on behind your back.

4. Children.

Since affairs tend to happen well into a marriage, most married people who have affairs have children. And children, unfortunately, are always caught in the middle of marital conflicts, no matter how careful the partners try to be. A child can be the object of an unfaithful spouse's guilt, frustration, anger, and stress. If you begin to notice your partner acting strangely with your children, that could be a sign of infidelity for several reasons.

Many times an unfaithful partner will target anger at his children because he can't cope with the feeling that his marriage may be coming to an end. He'll be short-tempered, overcritical, and hyperemotional with the kids because of the stress he's under.

A partner having an affair usually feels a tremendous amount of guilt when she sees and interacts with her children. She senses the impending loss of her children should the marriage fail, and it tears her apart. What will happen if my children find out? she thinks. Whose side will they take? And that's a valid fear, as children usually do take sides.

One way the unfaithful partner will try to compensate for his guilt is to spend more time with the children, be extremely nice to them, and try to do everything he or she didn't do for them before the affair. So if you begin to see any unusual change in your partner's dealings with your children, that may be a signal that the person is having an affair.

5. Personal Habit Changes.

These include changes in grooming, dress, day-to-day activities, and general attitude.

If your partner begins to dress in a radically different fashion, that can be suspicious. An example would be if he normally dresses in a shabby way and suddenly starts wearing suits, sportcoats, and dress slacks all the time; or if she's usually a formal dresser and begins wearing more casual or sporty clothing—jeans and such.

Your partner may begin putting a lot of cologne or perfume on at all times during the day or may devote an excessive amount of time to cleanliness, such as teeth-brushing or bathing. If your spouse begins taking more showers than usual, he or she may be trying to erase the evidence—the telltale perfume, cologne, stray hairs, and personal odors of his or her lover. On the other hand, if your spouse suddenly begins bathing less frequently at home and doesn't seem any worse off for it, the person may be taking his or her showers somewhere else!

Any drastic change in day-to-day activities is reason to be wary. Your partner may begin to get involved in sports, exercise classes, jogging, and other health-related activities during the day, or may take a number of adult-education classes out of a desire to become more knowledgeable. These could be harmless—even beneficial—exercises in self-improvement, or they could be sophisticated coverups for "extracurricular fun." When a person starts to devote an extended amount of time to such hobbies, it appears a bit strange. If the children are all grown up and leisure time is abundant in the marriage, investing a lot of time in such activities may be the normal thing to do. If not, the person will have some explaining to do, especially if he or she has previously been inactive and lacking in interests and now suddenly has many interests. These interests could very well be of the "indoor" persuasion.

6. Social Behavior.

If your spouse constantly wants to socialize or is overly "lovey-dovey" with you at social events—and isn't normally like that—he or she may be trying to cover something up. This kind of behavior is designed to allay your suspicions that anything is wrong and show the public at large that things are fine in your marriage. Again, guilt is the underlying drive that causes any kind of covering up. Your spouse's constant attentions to you in public creates the illusion for you that everything is okay and prevents your peers from pointing a finger at the two of you and saying, "Look at them—they've got some problems."

When a partner has an affair, he or she is often exposed to new social activities. Obviously, if your spouse suddenly begins taking you to new restaurants, museums, and night spots and knows a great deal about them or is well known by people who work there, you may think something's a little fishy. Any new social or cultural interests your partner exhibits that were never a part of his or her life before are potential signs of an affair.

Imagine this scene: You and your spouse are at a restaurant you've never been to before (but your spouse has, with his lover). A waiter sidles up and says, "Ah, Mr. Jones, welcome back! I see you have another ladyfriend with you this time." Sound ridiculous? It happens!

For these very reasons, many people who have affairs are afraid to socialize—they're afraid of getting caught red-handed. They fear being seen with their spouse by others who have seen them with their affair partner. If your mate suddenly begins to make a variety of excuses for not going out, you may have cause for suspicion—barring any other kinds of social fears, like the fear of going out after a personal trauma (a mastectomy, for example).

Another potential sign is when a spouse alternately humiliates and compliments you in front of others. One minute it might be, "Why are you wearing that piece of junk? You look terrible!" and the next it might be, "You look so wonderful tonight!" or, "Darling, you look great in anything!" The desire to humiliate you is out of the person's anger at you for not fulfilling his or her needs. The swing back to compliments is out of insecurity that he or she will lose you.

Finally, friends can be a powerful influence on a partner, and if your partner spends a lot of time with friends, it could mean trouble—especially if one or more of those friends has had an affair recently. You can be sure your spouse will get some peer pressure here and there to "think about it" or "try it out."

It works the other way, too: the partner having an affair will look for "co-conspirators" among his or her friends—sympathizers who are also having affairs. These friends all band together and justify what they're doing, and your partner becomes just another one of "the boys" or "the girls."

7. *The Emotional Atmosphere of the Relationship.*

I've left this, the largest, most important category for last, as it's the one that shows its symptoms in the most subtle ways imaginable. What I mean by the "emotional atmosphere" of the relationship is the complex web of emotions you and your partner feel for each other—the freeness of the communication between you, the level of trust you have for each other, the depth of love, the intimacy, the passion and the romance. If these elements are not present, or if they are only present in small amounts, your relationship could be an easy target for an affair. By the same token, if whatever bonds of love, trust, intimacy, communication, passion, and romance you *do* have in your relationship are shaken or broken in any way, that can create all the necessary ingredients for infidelity. Let's look at a few examples.

Probably the most subtle sign of all is a general tension in the air. A breakdown in communication (or a total lack of communication), a general constrictedness, feelings of uptightness around your partner, a lack of touching or physicalness between the two of you, paranoia in one or both of you—these are all signs of conflict in your marriage. Again, marital conflict comes about for many reasons; but if your partner is having an affair, that can cast a deathly silence over your relationship and create an impending sense of doom. A vague sort of uneasiness overtakes you, and you can't quite pinpoint the reason.

But being in close contact with your partner's emotional patterns means you will be tuned in to any change in those patterns; and it's exactly those changes that can clue you in to his or her involvement in any extramarital activity.

One sign is when your partner begins to indulge in escapism through various means, such as going to bed early, sleeping much more than normal, overeating, overindulging in alcohol, or taking tranquilizers.

Another sign is extreme tension or moodiness. These develop from stress that builds up—the stress of not wanting to be found out and the stress of wanting to live out the affair to its bitter end, whether that means the end of the affair itself or the end of the marriage. An unfaithful partner is always afraid of losing his spouse or his lover or both. Add to that the stress of constantly having to cover up and lie about one's activities, and you can see the tremendous pressure that can build up. (Imagine what it's like to have to remember all your lies and cover all your tracks—one mistake and it's all over!)

The partner having an affair has to live a lie and try to keep two worlds going. Most people can't handle that. The result is strange behavior, emotional ups and downs, and explosiveness.

Your partner may begin to avoid you for no apparent reason. If you've had very healthy communications and a very active sex life together, and that suddenly stops, something is obviously wrong—especially if it's not related to business or anything else that's visible. If he or she is having an affair, the avoidance may be an attempt to punish you, or it may just be because the person has no need for communication, touching, or sex from you.

Your partner may begin to experience vague depressions. This is one of the more subtle signs of an affair. Such depressions come about because the person is denying the reality of the damage the affair will do to the two of you. He doesn't want to look at the inevitable conflict between the affair and his marriage and what will come out of that conflict—turmoil and loss. Depression is also anger turned inward—anger your spouse feels at you for not making him or her satisfied in the marriage.

One way these depressions will break is for the anger the person has kept in to come to the surface. That anger will explode in outbursts at you or, more often, in petty criticisms of you—"Why didn't you clean the house today?" "Why don't you ask for a raise already?" "Why did you do this? why didn't you do that?" Your partner will start to belittle you and put you down in an effort to make you feel worthless. And once she's convinced herself that you *are* worthless, she'll use that belief to justify continuing her affair: "He's good for nothing, the jerk! Any woman with a husband like that has a *right* to have an affair!"

The other way a depression will break is in unexplained moments of tremendous sadness and closeness. For no particular reason and at any time during the day, your partner will suddenly hold you close and cry in your arms. In this case he's going through a tug of war inside. He wants to rid himself of the affair partner in his mind and return to the "splendor in the grass" that the marriage once was. Yet he feels the end of the marriage coming on and the end of everything that goes along with it—the children, the years spent together, the good times, the sharing—and a terrible sadness comes over him.

This tug of war your partner experiences can cause him or her physical symptoms and difficulties such as headaches, tension, insomnia, or fatigue. If you begin to see any of these symptoms, be aware of what they could be saying.

*　*　*

As you can see by now, most warning signals involve a little bit of knowledge and a lot of common sense. The signs are subtle, but they're all there if you know how and where to look.

Many people don't want to look, though. The signs can be staring them right in the face, yet they'll indulge in one of the most pervasive and damaging behaviors of all: denials.

DENIAL

Denial is the refusal to admit your suspicions about your partner's involvement in an affair because the pain of admitting them would be much too great. It's an escape mechanism used by people who do not want to cope with what is happening right in front of their eyes.

Simply put, denial is a way to avoid pain. When you deny that your partner may be having an affair, despite the fact that all the signs are pointing in that direction, you are running from reality. And you're only postponing your pain until later—for it will eventually catch up with you.

Most people know when their partner is having an affair. And if they don't know, they at least have some kind of inkling. So why would anyone turn the other cheek and deny that an affair is really happening? The answer can be summed up in one word: fear. Fear that the relationship will break up. There are other feelings involved, of course. There's the humiliation of the affair, the betrayal one feels because of the break in trust, the hurt from the realization that such a strong bond has been torn asunder, and the insecurity of, What do I do now?

But basically, people deny a spouse's affair out of fear that the marriage will end. They prefer to hide in a self-made emotional sanctuary and not have to deal with the conflict. Denial is nothing more than a form of self-preservation and self-protection against the slings and arrows of potential divorce.

First and foremost among the fears associated with denial is that of facing the world alone. When a woman suspects her spouse of being involved in an affair, it's not uncommon for her to ask herself all of these questions: If I open my eyes to this, what's in store for me? Will he leave me? And is it worth it? Is it worth going out into the world again? Is anything out there any better than what I have? Why not just live with it, bury it, and put it aside? Unfortunately, as we'll see later on in the book, you can't just live with it, bury it, and put it aside. Many, many people believe that if they just leave things alone the problem will go away. That *never* happens.

There's a tremendous fear involved in the thought of facing the world alone. The lack of emotional support, the burdens and responsibilities, the loneliness of the singles world—all these realities contribute to a general dread of confronting one's partner about his or her affair.

In a class by itself is the fear of losing financial support as a result of a confrontation and subsequent breakup. Many people stay in relationships against their will strictly because of finances. The thought of having to financially support themselves again—or for the first time—is enough to make these people put up with any conflict in their relationships in order to feel financially secure. With today's troubled economy, one can't blame them for feeling the way they do. It's difficult enough for families with two working spouses to make ends meet. It's extremely difficult for a single person to "make it," and for the single parent with one or two or more children . . . well, good luck.

In today's more equalizing times many women have careers and can support themselves; yet there are still a great many who are financially dependent on their husbands. These women don't have the training or the skills to survive on their own, let alone to support children as well; so the prospect of being thrust out into the world to fend for themselves is understandably frightening.

This fear creates a tremendous sense of imprisonment for the woman who does not have such skills. Questions such as, How long will my spousal support last? How in the world will I make the house payments? and What will I do without a car? course through her mind, and because of her tremendous fears she sees no other choice but to deny her husband's affair. Financial incompetence is indeed a terrifying feeling.

I'd like to digress for a moment to state that I feel women should develop their skills so that they are marketable and can support themselves if they should ever need to. To know that you can take care of yourself financially in a crisis is to be far ahead of the game; and the feeling that goes along with that knowledge can prevent a lot of the fears and turmoil that arise whenever a marriage is threatened by any sort of conflict. In particular, it would allow you to confront your partner, with strength and on an equal footing, should you suspect him of having an affair—and it would allow you to resolve the difficulty.

As her children grow older, a woman can get back out into the world, take a job or learn a skill, and have the sense of appreciation and satisfaction that comes from such activity. It will only strengthen her marriage and prevent her from being totally at the disposal of her husband and his wants and needs.

The third major fear associated with denial is the fear of hurting or losing one's children. Many people are terribly afraid of harming their children with any kind of marital conflict. They'll deny any suspicions of a partner's affair in order to protect the children. They may think to themselves, I don't want to do anything about this affair because I know what happened to me when my parents divorced, and I don't want the same thing to happen to my kids. Or they may reflect on how a friend turned out after his or her parents got divorced.

The truth is that marital conflicts don't take effect on children until they are in their teenage years. But regardless of the child's age, most parents won't want to have the child caught in the crossfire of marital conflict, having to make a choice between which parent is right and which is wrong. (And, as I stated before, children do take sides.)

The fear of losing one's children is even stronger than the fear of hurting them. In the past, custody would almost always go to the wife after a divorce; it was the husband who worried most about losing his children. Nowadays, though, with the changing laws, the wife doesn't automatically gain custody. Consequently, women now tend to be just as fearful as men that they will lose their children.

There are other reasons for denial. One is to avoid humiliation. A common concern, particularly among women, is, What will my friends think if they find out? That may be a valid fear, too. If the partner having the affair is bitter and angry because his needs are not being fulfilled in his marriage, he may go around telling everyone about it, in an irrational way. And then friends *will* find out.

Another concern of the suspecting partner is that his or her suspicions may be dead wrong. Indeed, what if you *are* wrong? What if there are already problems in your marriage and you make an unjust accusation? You run the risk of opening a Pandora's box of torture and torment should your partner resent your lack of trust. (Fortunately, the Reconstructive Dynamics outlined later in this book will give you the tools to know how and when to approach your partner with your fears and tell you how to open communication and avoid any pain if your suspicions turn out to be wrong.)

If you are engaging in denial you may experience physical symptoms such as headaches, nausea, diarrhea, aches and pains, all due to nerves being on edge. These symptoms come about because of your inability to express what you are feeling, to speak up about your suspicions for fear that the ultimate truth may be, yes, he or she *is* having an affair. But this creates a vicious circle: your reluctance to communicate your feelings creates tension in your relationship, and this tension and lack of communication gives your partner all the more reason for continuing the affair—or going out and having one if she isn't already. Thus, in your refusal to relate to your partner, you push him further and further away from yourself and more and more toward the affair partner.

The denial game has its rewards and penalties. The main reward is temporary escape from conflict and fear. By denying your suspicions, you can continue living your life as though nothing were wrong, and you can maintain a temporary peace of mind.

The main penalty is what happens to you inside. Deep down a volcano of anger, frustration, and fear begins to build and build. The mental energy it takes to hold back this volcano is enormous. It will build to a point where the body and mind can no longer take the punishment, and the result will be emotional eruption.

Chapter 2

THE CAUSES OF AFFAIRS, PART I

The causes of affairs are many. There are probably as many causes as there are relationships. As every individual has his own quirks and fancies, so every affair has its own peculiar set of underlying circumstances. Some causes are visible, others deeply hidden; some are simple, some complex.

In these next two chapters I'm going to deal with the causes of affairs as they fall into two main categories: those that stem from conflicts in everyday adult life, as well as from natural and unavoidable imbalances in the relationship; and those rooted primarily in childhood that are brought into adulthood, creating conflicts in the relationship in the here and now. Of the causes in these two categories, those in the former tend to be more visible and easy to identify, while those in the latter tend to be more hidden and complex in nature.

CONFLICTS IN ADULTHOOD

The trials and tribulations of adulthood are never ending. Frustration and disappointment abound from all corners of our adult lives. Whether the conflicts we experience as adults come from inside or outside our primary relationship, they can all potentially drive us into an affair. A husband caught in the grip of financial pressures may look outside his marriage for the understanding and support he doesn't feel he is getting at home. A wife discontented with her sex life may give up on her mate and decide to take on a lover. Two partners who cannot communicate with each other may slowly drift apart and seek outside emotional contact, their marriage thus becoming a shell of what it could be.

The key to understanding causes of infidelity that stem from purely adult conflicts is in the concept of *unfulfilled needs*. Basically, any need that goes unfulfilled in a marriage will seek its expression elsewhere. Whatever a person is not getting at home he or she will strive to find on the outside—whether that striving takes place unconsciously or consciously. And an affair is one of the most attractive ways available to fill a marital gap, as it seems to promise so many wonderful things.

A curious thing you'll find in many people who have affairs is that they fantasize about having their affair partner move in with them and their spouse—in a sort three-way, live-in relationship. This fantasy is unrealistic—and downright bizarre! But the fact that it is so common only goes to show how powerful and tempting unfulfilled needs can be and what irrational thoughts and behavior they can drive us to.

In my years of experience in counseling couples, I have found that the causes of affairs stemming from adult-related conflicts fall into roughly five main categories.

Sexual Conflicts

Sex is one of the primary ingredients in the success or failure of a marriage. Though two people may remain formally bound to each other for many years, if their sex life is not balanced and fulfilling, the seeds of discontent will grow, and an affair can become a most viable option.

Affairs are often thought of as being purely sexual in nature. Nothing could be further from the truth. For every sexual yearning a married partner has, there is generally an emotional component that goes along with it, whether it's a desire for more communication, more closeness, more intimacy, more understanding and support, more flexibility, or more passion and romance.

Yet the physical and emotional aspects of sex itself are often at the root of an affair. There are certain unavoidable realities we must face when it comes to sex: different people have different sex drives, different sexual backgrounds, different sexual wants and needs, and different sexual limits.

Let's take a look at some of the most common sexual conflicts that can cause infidelity.

Unfulfilled Sexual Needs

Frequently, at some point in a marriage, one partner begins to develop a desire for an act that falls out of the realm of the couple's standard sexual repertoire. Examples of such variations include oral sex, anal sex, intercourse in different positions, the use of sexual toys, fantasy role playing, the use of obscene language during sex, mild spanking, and some of the more serious variations such as fetishism, bondage, dominance, and submission. These desires usually don't surface until both partners have established a high degree of comfort and trust with each other sexually.

Secret sexual needs start out in fantasy. If a partner is courageous, at some point he will tell his spouse what he would like to try. In many cases his partner will try the variation once or twice in an effort to please him and then lose interest in it. If he feels guilty about continually having to ask his partner to satisfy him, he'll tend to forget the whole thing and let his desires fall by the wayside.

More often, however, he never gets up enough courage to

tell his spouse what he wants in the first place. In either event his desires remain in the realm of fantasy and just keep getting stronger and stronger.

Let's take the case of a husband who would like his wife to perform oral sex on him. Suppose he constantly thinks about it while he's having sex with his wife and wishes she would take the initiative to satisfy him orally. Perhaps he's told his wife of his desire and for certain reasons she can't fulfill it for him. Maybe she doesn't enjoy oral sex—she finds it distasteful or considers it "dirty." Maybe she's afraid of it—she may have had an unpleasant experience with it earlier in her life. Perhaps a teenage boyfriend once forced her to perform it on him, and from that point on she found she could not enjoy the act.

Whatever the reasons, the husband now experiences an unfulfilled need and as a result feels sexually rejected by his wife. What can he do with his desire? It won't just go away. What tends to happen is that he begins fantasizing about having oral sex performed on him by *another* woman—often while he's having sex with his wife. The fantasy builds to such a point that it becomes an obsession. If he cannot achieve any kind of understanding with his wife on the matter, he will eventually turn his focus from fantasy to reality—he'll look for and find a woman who will satisfy him orally. He may go to a prostitute, or he may have an affair.

Sexual Boredom

Whereas unfulfilled sexual needs tend to involve specific desires that go unanswered in one partner, sexual boredom is a larger problem that affects a couple's sex life as a whole.

When a couple first get married they generally experience a fantastic and varied sex life because of their youth, their energy, and the freshness of their love. Their lovemaking is full of passion and romance; it often seems they can't get enough of each other. But as the years go by, the freshness wears off, and the two tend to fall into a pattern of routine lovemaking. They have sex the same way, in the same position, over and over again. All the creativity, spontaneity, passion, and romance they once knew are gone, and what they are left with is rigidness, uptightness, and a lack of any real pleasure.

At some point such a couple begins to indulge in fantasy during their lovemaking. Their fantasies range over a wide variety of sexual variations and often involve other people. The movies of their minds take over, replacing the reality of each other's emotional presence. Sadly, the partners never share their private love scenes with one another—yet these imaginings become the major focus of their lovemaking.

What results is a kind of mutual masturbation—two robots having sex with each other, using each other as means of achieving orgasm. Their fantasies provide the emotional stimulation, their bodies provide the physical stimulation. Nowhere is there any intimacy, sharing, or communication. And when that happens, each partner is essentially having an affair in his mind. This often goes on for so long that it's only a matter of time and circumstance before these mental affairs develop into real ones.

Unfortunately, too many couples give up when sexual boredom sets in. Rather than attempt to deal with it by communicating with each other and making a joint effort to get past their fears and anxieties about sex, they'll take the easy way out and say to themselves, My partner just doesn't do it for me; therefore, I'm going to go out and find someone who will.

Sexual Inexperience

Inexperience in the bedroom can create both unfulfilled sexual needs and the more general problem of sexual boredom. If one or both partners in a marriage never had sex before getting married, then all they brought to the marriage was a very narrow sexual background. Their knowledge of sex will be limited to what little advice they were given by their parents and the questionable information they picked up from their peers. This translates into a terribly dull and uninspired sex life.

What often happens here is that several years into the marriage one or both partners become sexually curious and don't know quite how to take it from there.

For example, a husband walks into a bookstore and picks up an erotic magazine. He reads a story about an unusual sexual variation and is intrigued by it. It stimulates in him a vague fantasy he has never acknowledged before. Or, he is just curious and would like to experiment with this new and strange idea he has just read about. But he thinks to himself, I can't try this with my wife; she'll think I'm a pervert! He feels it would be acceptable to try this variation with someone else but not with the one he loves. So he goes out and experiments, either with a prostitute or by having an affair with someone he feels is sexually "free" and uninhibited.

Another way sexual curiosity gets stimulated is through hearing about the experiences of others. For example, you'll be sitting around the fireplace with a group of couples—all friends of yours—laughing and joking about sexual positions. Suddenly, someone says to you, "We've tried such-and-such position—have you?" Faced with such a question, you may begin to wonder if you haven't been missing something in your sex life. That opens the door to fantasy, again, and to a strong need to go out and experiment with someone other than the one you love, if you are too embarrassed about the activity to try it with him or her.

What often happens with sexually inexperienced partners is that after some years they reach a stage where they open up and want to try *everything* sexual to make up for the time they lost being "locked up" and inhibited. If their spouses cannot keep up with them, or if they feel too guilty about their own desires to open up to their spouses about them, they will look outside for the opportunity to fulfill their need to experiment with sex.

Sexual Frequency Differences

It's rare that two people will have the same sex drives or the same frequency of need for sex; yet couples generally achieve some kind of balance over a period of time. If a couple cannot achieve such a balance, or if the partners are by nature so imbalanced that they simply cannot reach a compromise in their sexual cycles, there again results an unfulfilled need for sex. The unsatisfied partner will go wanting and will look outside the marriage for satisfaction.

A classic illustration of this problem occurs in the Woody Allen movie, *Annie Hall*. In one scene, Allen, seen on one half of the screen talking to his psychiatrist, tells the doctor of the problem in his relationship with Annie Hall, played by Diane Keaton. "We hardly have sex at all," says Allen. "We make love three times a week."

On the other half of the screen, Keaton tells *her* psychiatrist what the *real* problem in their relationship is: "We have sex all the time," she says. "Three times a week!"

Sexual frequency differences can come about for a number of reasons. Our bodies are regulated in different ways, and the strength or weakness of one's sex drive may depend on both physical and emotional factors.

Certain forms of illness and stress decrease sex drive. Kidney and bladder infections, hypoglycemia, yeast infections—these can all affect desire in a negative way. The birth control pill often lowers one's drive.

On the other hand, high sex drive can be caused by strictly emotional factors such as a lack of touching and affection in early childhood or the need for physical release from tension due to stress.

Virility Strivings

Though "virility strivings" is a term that refers primarily to men, men and women alike experience a phase in middle age in which they get the urge to go out and try a new sexual partner—the "seven-year itch" (or twenty- or thirty-year itch, in most cases!).

Many men experience a tremendous depression at some point in their middle years; some call it "male menopause," or the "midlife crisis." It's usually associated with a desire to go out and test one's virility. A man in this stage of life will want to see if he still has that "old black magic," and is still masculine and virile; he'll want to know that he can still attract and be attracted to younger women—still "make it" with one. It's my last chance, he'll often think to himself. Once before I go I want to try something new.

Often a man's virility strivings have nothing to do with his marriage. On the contrary, many men who have such strivings love their wives very much. They just have the irrational (but normal) need to "light the fire" one last time before the flame goes out.

Sometimes, however, a man's strivings have *everything* to do with his marriage. Perhaps his wife is not allowing him to feel virile and sexy. Perhaps she has lost interest in sex or perhaps their sex life doesn't have the same old chemistry it used to. Maybe the passion and romance have gone, the frequency of their lovemaking has died down, or the lack of sexual creativity in it has resulted in boring routines. All these factors can stimulate a man to live out his virility needs elsewhere.

If she can face the challenge, a woman can satisfy her husband's virility strivings and keep him happy. If not, she can expect him to at least *think* about having an affair.

Women experience a similar phenomenon to men's virility strivings. Many times after menopause or a hysterectomy a woman will feel tremendously sexual. She'll experience a newfound sense of freedom now that she need no longer be afraid of getting pregnant. Her sex drive may increase tremendously. She may want to go out and test her attractiveness and sexuality with other men. If her husband cannot satisfy these heightened needs, or if their sex life is bland and lackluster, she will go out and find satisfaction elsewhere, generally with a younger man.

Impotence and Frigidity

This is an unfortunate problem that of course doesn't come to light until after a marriage has begun, because few people will marry a person they know is impotent or frigid to begin with.

Most men experience occasional bouts of impotence, but chronic impotence is something else entirely and is a crippling thing both physically and emotionally.

If a man develops an impotency problem so serious that he is absolutely unable to have sex (and this happens more often that one might think), his wife would understandably reach a point of frustration should the problem persist over a long period of time, and she may seek out a lover. If she is patient and willing to work with him to help him overcome his problem, that can save their marriage. Yet if she does work with him and his situation still shows no signs of improvement, she will reach a point of no return and will have no other choice but to find sexual satisfaction elsewhere (unless, of course, she has no need for sex). To save the marriage in this case, the man must be strong enough and willing enough to seek out the professional help he needs. (Some men steadfastly refuse to do this.)

Frigidity is a bit easier to disguise. If she's a good actress, a woman can fake enjoyment of sex and go on for many years without her husband suspecting a thing. She'll exaggerate her sexuality in order to hide her lack of enjoyment, hoping that in time she will overcome her dislike of sex. But it doesn't happen that way. And if her husband finds out at some point that she has been "faking it, not really making it," he'll feel tremendously cheated. His masculinity will have been violated in his mind, and he will be angry, hostile, and distrustful of his wife. How can he now feel like approaching her sexually if he doesn't know whether she'll give him the real thing or an

Academy Award performance? He won't, and that will under-
mine the marriage.

Sexual Trauma

Sexual trauma is something that can occur at any age, from
childhood on up through adolescence and adulthood. Unfortunately, we must still live in a world in which the problems of
rape, child molestation, and incest have not been solved.

A person who has been sexually molested at some point in
his or her life will generally feel very fearful of sex. For example, a woman raped in adulthood may experience sexual difficulties for a long time. It may take her many years to
overcome the trauma. She may try to run away from it and
deny it in her mind at first, but the sexual problems it causes
her will persist. If she refuses to deal with her conflict, or if her
husband is not patient and sensitive enough to help her deal
with it, their sex life will suffer, and he may just throw up his
hands in resignation and go out and have an affair. (To overcome her trauma, the woman must learn to accept what happened to her, express her pain and grief, and work to transcend
her fears of sex—and her husband must provide a supportive
emotional "cushion" in order for her to achieve these things.)

As far as earlier traumas go, the pattern is the same. What
determines the success or failure of a couple's sex life is how
willing they are to work together to help the traumatized partner overcome his or her difficulty. With patience, these things
can be resolved successfully. With frustration comes the tendency to look to an affair as the only solution.

Career and Financial Conflicts

Money and careers are constant sources of stress and strain in
a marriage—whether the conflicts involved are positive or
negative. For example, the news that you have just won the
Irish Sweepstakes can create just as much strain on your
nerves—once the initial euphoria has died down—as the news

that you have just been fired from your post as president of a large corporation. And in both cases you may be tempted to run out and have an affair—either for the sake of relieving the tremendous stress or for the sake of experimenting with a new life-style.

Career Failures and Financial Insecurity

Financial insecurity creates tremendous strain and pressure on a marriage and a family as a whole. The atmosphere in a financially struggling family is marked by an all-encompassing tension and an inability to relax. The feeling of always having to rob Peter to pay Paul casts a dark cloud over every aspect of daily life. Under the circumstances, one partner or both may be driven to seek the solace of an understanding, empathetic companion who can soothe these feelings of insecurity and make one feel instead like a "real man" or a "real woman."

Career failures of course primarily affect the family breadwinner. Such "failures" ("failings" would be a better word) can come from being fired, laid off, or demoted; from having a business fall through; from stagnating in a job; or from just not being able to make ends meet. If the breadwinner feels inadequate in his role, he will experience a terrific loss of pride and dignity. He tends to equate his self-worth with his success, and failure means, I am worthless. It's a very painful thing for a man to admit that he can't afford to buy his wife a new dress or his children a new pair of sneakers. And even though his partner may be very understanding, that won't take away from his feelings of having failed as a provider.

In the play *Death of a Salesman* by Arthur Miller, Willy Loman is the proverbial traveling salesman out on the road. He has an ongoing affair with a female supervisor at one of his stops in order to counteract his feelings of being a failure as a provider for his wife and two sons. He is lonely; he feels he has let his family down, and he cannot face them. The Woman, as she is called in the play, comforts his bruised ego, tells him what a great salesman he is, promises him she will see him through to the main buyers every time, laughs with him, and makes love to him. Too ashamed to face his wife, Willy always turns to The Woman for the comfort and support she provides him. To show his appreciation, he brings her stockings—stockings he had originally bought for his wife.

Sometimes a man experiencing career or financial failure will spend his last hundred dollars to create the opposite of the failure image. He'll find a woman who has no idea where he comes from or what he does—no knowledge of him or his past history—and he'll try to impress her in order to build himself up. "I'm such-and-such" (lawyer, accountant, etc.), he'll boast, "and therefore I'm a big shot!" He's simply trying to be what he would like to be but is not—confident about himself.

In many families where finances are under a strain, the woman of the house will go out and get a job. She'll often meet men in the work world who treat her differently than her husband does. She'll begin to recognize that she is attractive and desirable out in the world, and she may pursue an affair to explore these new feelings and to counteract any dissatisfaction with the way she is treated at home.

Emerging Careers and the "Quick Success" Syndrome

Often when a man first starts out in his chosen career, he must work his way through a substantial number of years of school, be it medical school, law school, business school, or what have you. Many times his partner will support him financially through those years by taking on a job herself and becoming the breadwinner. The image of the young struggling couple is a classic one; and the struggle creates a close bonding between the partners and a very tightly knit relationship. This is a very common occurrence among young professionals and was immortalized some years back in a film called *Not as a Stranger*, with Robert Mitchum and Olivia de Havilland.

Having completed his schooling, the young professional then begins his career. Several years up the line he starts to become successful and makes a sizable income. At that point things change radically. Even if his success is moderate, the same transformation takes place: he begins to get a lot of attention from people he associates with in his career, and he takes on an entirely new and different attitude about himself. He develops a new self-confidence, a feeling of emergence, and often an overinflated ego. He'll dress differently, buy a fancy new car, and act like a big deal.

Yet also as a result of this relatively sudden success he begins to grow further and further away from his partner—the one who so selflessly struggled to support him through those early years. His contacts in the career world cast him into an entirely different social milieu, and he loses the roots he had previously developed with his wife and family. He surpasses his partner who is unable to go along with him on his new adventure because she has not changed in the same way herself.

He now feels a need to project his new strength and power further out into the world. He feels he can attract a different kind of woman and pursue her. Certainly he will be more predisposed to an affair because it will be much more available to him in his new world. There will be many opportunities for it and many built-in excuses for hiding it.

It's a common cry: "I worked him through school, then he dumped me!" That's a pretty bitter pill to take. But success does that to people—yet it's not success that causes our problems; it is we ourselves.

A similar thing can happen to women who enter careers—especially nowadays, with so many women pursuing the high-powered professions that were previously closed to them. As she achieves success in her ventures, a woman may experience a freedom and self-emergence she never knew earlier in life or in other roles she has played. She'll outgrow the men in her life and begin to pursue relationships with her more high-powered contemporaries.

Jennifer D. was an attorney just beginning to achieve success in her career. At a certain point she started earning more money than her husband, Mike, a stockbroker. Mike became very threatened and intimidated by her success. His masculinity suffered greatly because of it. Jennifer became frustrated by Mike's stagnation in his feelings of inadequacy and wound up having an affair with a man more on her financial and emotional level.

Financial Security

Many people believe money is the solution to all their problems. What they don't realize is that big money means big problems—which means big stress. If you're not worrying about Uncle Sam lopping half your money off the top, you're concerned about how and where to invest it. And you *have* to invest it if you don't want inflation to erode it away to nothing in a matter of a few years. Fortunes are just as easily lost as they are made.

Whereas partners struggling to make ends meet often find themselves closely bonded by the common cause they are fighting for, a financially secure couple often find they have little or nothing in common and as a consequence wind up drifting apart from each other.

The moneymaker in a well-off couple often gets caught up in a game of power and more moneymaking, thriving on the ego-gratification his success brings. These people are often driven to workaholic extremes in their quest to expand their "kingdom." The other partner in such an arrangement will usually devote his or her life to spending the money that's made or languishing during the day in mindless activities. Having an enormous amount of leisure time, he or she will invariably devote it to shopping, socializing, or lounging at the pool or the club.

Such a separation of activities and interests, created by the freedom financial security brings, drives the two partners apart and virtually gives them both permission to have an affair. (As an interesting aside to this, at plush resorts you will often find wealthy husbands actually paying off gigolos to service their wives and keep them off their backs!)

Financial security gives you the ability to "buy" fulfillment of your needs outside your marriage. It does nothing to motivate you to confront your partner and try to make your marriage work. What you're not getting at home, you'll find elsewhere—and with your money you will cultivate the person you turn to. There are a lot of people out there you can impress by buying them fancy things and taking them places they've never been to before. You also have the freedom to run off whenever you want—*if* you can cover your tracks. And if there's one thing financially secure people have, it's the ability to afford the proper hiding places. A second condo, a rented apartment in another city, a cottage hideaway in the mountains—these are all pretty convenient, if you can afford them.

At the same time that you can buy fulfillment of your needs with someone else, you can "buy off" your partner by giving him or her money not to confront you with any suspicions about your having an affair.

Family Business

I want to touch on this dilemma briefly, as it is a common enough experience to warrant some discussion. The two most frequent situations involve a husband and wife going into business together or a husband or wife entering his or her family's business.

The problems of the husband-and-wife, or "Mom and Pop," business are fairly straightforward. Generally, if both Mom and Pop are actively involved in running the business, conflicts will arise when one feels the other is not pulling his weight or doing his fair share. The one feeling overworked will resent the other and become critical and accusatory. If this kind of behavior gets carried over into the marriage, it can mean trouble, and an affair on either end is a potential outcome.

A son or daughter going into his or her family's business is often asking for trouble because the total childhood environment is recreated in the business environment. All the same old childhood scripts, all the old feelings and conflicts are recycled—and the resultant emotional garbage is carried into the marriage. For the other partner, it's as if her spouse were having an affair with his family. He, being totally caught up in the business, devotes less time and attention to her. She is always included in the turmoil of the family business, however; and rather than having to compete with one person, as in a normal affair, she must compete with an entire family!

This is not to say that all family businesses are doomed emotionally, but if you do follow in a parent's footsteps, you'd better be prepared for the agonies as well as the ecstacies.

As for going into an in-law's business—well, that's *really* asking for trouble!

Conflicts Regarding the Children

Generally, any conflicts a couple experiences regarding their children will involve either disagreement on how to raise their children properly or the anger, guilt, and the pain they experience within themselves—and for each other—when they feel they have "failed" as parents.

A husband and wife may differ drastically in the way they approach the child-rearing process. Such differing views come about primarily because of the way the individuals were brought up themselves. For example, one partner might have been raised under the iron hand of a father who believed in strong moral fiber and severe discipline, while the other may have been brought up by parents who were more liberal in their approach to discipline and morality.

If child-rearing views are in severe enough conflict, the couple may be headed for trouble—especially if they are stubborn and unyielding in their respective beliefs. They may try to fight each other through their children. If the children decide to side with one parent (for example, a lenient mother in favor of a stern father), the other will feel he is losing them. He may then be driven to find someone who can give him the understanding and sensitivity he needs in the face of his dilemma.

Conflicts about being "failures" as parents generally arise in the wake of having to deal with a problem child. When a child is having serious behavioral or emotional problems, that can create tremendous stress for both parents and can lead to erosion in the relationship because of differing views on how to cope with the difficulty. One parent may want to turn his back on the whole thing and run away. The other may suffer greatly, feel tremendous guilt, and blame herself totally for what happened. Alternatively, one may be protective of the child and the other may insist, "You can't pamper him! You can't make it easy for him! We've got to handle this differently!"

Any of these options only adds to the stress the partners already feel. If they can't agree on a course of action in solving the difficulty, their disagreement will push them apart, and they will be forced outward to find support for their respective points of view.

Personal Habits and Quirks

Believe it or not, a person's annoying habits can drive his or her partner into an affair. If a husband eats like a slob, burps after every bite, chews with his mouth wide open, has poor hygiene, poor manners, or any of a number of other little idiosyncrasies, this may be enough to send his wife running into the arms of the nearest gentleman. If a woman walks around in curlers all day or goes to sleep with a mudpack on all the time or spends entire days clipping supermarket coupons to save a few pennies here and there, it can drive her husband up the wall—and into the arms of another woman.

On a more serious note, if a partner should develop a weight problem, that can create tremendous conflict in the marriage; and if the other person is not supportive and understanding—

and patient—he or she may just decide to give up on the over-weight partner and find satisfaction elsewhere.

Personal and Background Differences

Here I'm going to deal with the conflicts that occur between partners by virtue of the natural differences in their personalities and backgrounds. These differences might not be a problem for either individual when considering the two people separately; it's when these separate realities are brought together in a marriage that the trouble can really start.

Differences in Interests, Hobbies, and Activities

I find this to be a classic cause of affairs. Most spouses don't share exactly the same activities. Part of the initial attraction two people find for each other is due to their varying backgrounds and interests (though admittedly it's usually common interests that create the most attraction at first).

One partner may enjoy the theater, jogging, and writing, for example, and the other may go in for tennis, sailing, and backgammon. One may be an avid bowler, the other a devoted opera lover. Whatever their interests are, if they differ on too many of them they'll find themselves moving apart in many directions.

Opposites can attract—if you share your different hobbies and blend them in with your relationship, that can be a very rewarding thing. But if you keep your interests separate and refuse to share them with each other, or if one partner refuses to at least *try* to appreciate and take part in the other's hobbies, that creates a void in the relationship. And from that void springs a need to share your life with someone who is able to appreciate and take part in it.

If you come from a family that has a lot of cultural interests and many different hobbies, you will tend to have those same interests. If you then turn around and marry someone who is lacking in interests and hobbies, the environment becomes rather boring, because those needs of yours are frustrated. That may push you toward an affair. Your partner may be pushed toward an affair as a result of feeling rejected by not being included in your activities.

Educational and Intellectual Differences

Here again is a case where fate plays the major role but where the partners have a choice in adapting to the different hands that were dealt to them.

A husband and wife may have diverging educational backgrounds and intelligence levels. Now let me point out that education is no guarantee of intelligence, nor is IQ a measure of awareness. There are a lot of absent-minded professors in the world, and for all their brains they are often inept at understanding the ins and outs of everyday life. Some can't even tie their shoes in the morning, let alone successfully cope with their emotional lives.

But if two people who are otherwise reasonably healthy emotionally have different levels of knowledge and different intellectual abilities, that may cause problems. Again, interests can be at odds. If someone is into reading and discussing the classics or studying nuclear physics, politics, or higher consciousness, then that person is going to try to seek someone to express his or her intellectual needs and interests to. If the other partner is not on a similar level, even though he or she may be willing to learn, the more intellectually oriented partner will become frustrated. Often you will find that a teacher-student relationship develops between the two. But the teacher may not want to be a teacher any more than the student wants to be a student. A need is left unfulfilled, conflict results, and the teacher will seek out intellectual fulfillment from other people on a similar level. At that point it is often only a matter of time before an affair develops.

Again, these differences do not *have* to result in conflict. If neither partner feels the need to compete with the other, they both can experience a tremendous sense of intellectual freedom. Each can pursue his or her areas of intellectual interest and endeavor at his or her own rate and pace. Each can learn from the other. What creates conflict is when the intellectual interchange becomes boring and routine. The more gifted individual will then tend to seek nutrition for his or her mind elsewhere.

Social Class Differences

Frequently two people will marry across class borders, with love winning out over parental disapproval and any need or desire to be true to one's "breeding." For example, a woman from an aristocratic family may take up with a laborer, or an upper-middle-class professional may marry the "poor girl from the other side of town." These may sound like extremes, but they are not as uncommon as you think. And whether there is a minor difference in class or a sweeping one, the underlying principle is the same: deep down the partners know that they come from different "stock." How they choose to deal with these feelings makes the difference between acceptance and conflict.

Unfortunately, what most often happens is that the partner from the higher class feels superior to the other person, a notch above him or her, and the one from the lower class feels like the underdog. If the underdog feels like an underdog long enough, he or she can begin to resent it and may then seek fulfillment from someone on the same class level—in order to be accepted for who he or she is, without having to feel judged or ridiculed.

By the same token, the higher-class individual may seek out someone from the same social level because of strong values from his or her parents that dictate. You cannot go against what we want for you. We do not want you to be involved with this kind of person. Thus, the more well-bred partner will seek an affair to break with the other partner in his or her mind and fulfill the script imposed by his or her parents.

Religious Differences

This is a very delicate area and one that provides a great deal of opportunity for an affair to develop. Two partners who come from different religious backgrounds may have markedly different views about everything from marriage to child-rearing to sex to communication. If they cannot achieve some kind of agreement and harmony on these views, conflict will result.

Here again parental values may come into play. If the parents were disapproving of the marriage because of the differences in religion, that can be a tough burden to bear for both partners. Again they each may pursue an affair with someone of the same religion in order to, in their mind, appease their parents (or their own sense of guilt) and remain true to their church or temple.

Racial, Cultural, and Ethnic Differences

America being the cultural melting pot it is, there are many marriages that cross the boundaries of race, ethnic group, and nationality. Couples in such marriages can experience a tremendous enrichment and growth from the sharing of each other's various cultural heritages. But if they stay stuck in their respective systems, refuse to share, and insist on maintaining exclusive cultural links to the "mother" land or race, rifts will develop. This kind of rigidity about eating habits, worshipping practices, child-rearing philosophies, political views, and a general refusal to assimilate into the culture-at-large can create a great deal of stress, strain, and conflict in the marriage—and may drive one of the partners into an affair with someone of the same background.

Another factor involves underlying hostilities between the mother cultures or races of the two partners. For example, interracial marriages may be motivated by true love, yet deeply rooted prejudices can crop up at later points in the marriage, clouding over the purer feelings that brought the partners together initially.

Different Levels of Awareness and Actualization
This is a rather interesting dilemma in which two people have differing levels of emotional awareness and growth. It's rare that a highly self-actualized and independent person will marry an immature or emotionally unaware individual but a more common conflict occurs when one of two people who have the same relative emotional maturity begins to experience a tremendous surge forward in emotional growth. Self-development can occur through many different modes. Readings, contacts with influential people, counseling, psychotherapy, religious teachings, and metaphysical pursuits are just a few of the many ways such growth can be stimulated. If one partner begins to actualize and the other stays stuck and unaware, stagnating in immaturity, trouble lies ahead.

Once a rapid growth period starts for one person, it becomes very hard for the other to catch up. And the person who is growing then experiences many, many unfulfilled needs. A snowballing effect occurs; the growing party is thrust into a whole new environment of friends, people, and relationships, and what was satisfactory before becomes unsatisfactory now. He or she is then easy prey for an affair.

The nongrowing partner has his problems too. He will feel persecuted by the other's growth and will try to tear that person down with critical, castrating remarks in order to stabilize the relationship and hold the growing partner back. If he doesn't succeed, *he* may seek out a third party for consolation.

Chapter 3

THE CAUSES OF AFFAIRS, PART II

The causes we dealt with in Chapter 2 were those that arise primarily from conflicts occurring in adulthood—problems with sex, money, raising a family, and just putting up with another person who's so closely intertwined in your life every day of your life.

A vast number of other causes of affairs, however, stem from conflicts rooted in the childhood experience that then get carried over into adulthood. In these cases, the affair itself is the end product of much deeper conflicts in either one or both partners. For example, if a man comes from a family where there was very little communication or expression of feelings, chances are he will carry that noncommunicative pattern into his adult life. If he then marries a woman who is more outspoken and gregarious, she may become so frustrated by his fortresslike nature that she'll give up on him and find communication somewhere else. Alternatively, if a woman's childhood was characterized by neediness and dependency, and she takes that into her marriage, her husband may become so emotionally suffocated by her "clinging vine" attitude that an affair may be an attractive way for him to break free of that bondage.

Here again, the key concept is that of *unfulfilled needs*. The causes I'm going to deal with in this chapter stem from deprivations and "gaps" that were created in childhood and that as a result created strong unfulfilled needs that persisted into adulthood. Perhaps the best way to discover your own unfulfilled needs is to ask yourself, If I could have my childhood over again, what would I want that I didn't have the first time? For some it's touching and affection; for others it's attention, support, and understanding; for others it's the guidance of a good role model; and for still others it may be a parent they lost. Whatever we missed in childhood we tend to look for in adulthood, in other people—especially our mates. When we put such high expectations on our partners to fulfill what we didn't have as children, and they fail, it is tremendously disappointing to us.

LACK OF COMMUNICATION

Lack of communication in childhood is one of the most common causes of affairs because it invariably leads to a lack of communication in adulthood—and open, honest communication is the very foundation of a healthy relationship.

In many families there is sort of an unspoken code that you cannot talk about your feelings. You can't open up about what's really bothering you, you can't ask questions about the important aspects of growing up, you can't probe your parents and express curiosity about life and the world. "Children should be seen and not heard" is unfortunately a motto that many families live by to this day. You do what your parents say, you don't talk back, you don't ask questions, you just listen and keep quiet. A child is expected to learn how to live well and effectively strictly by absorbing everything around him and magically putting the pieces of life together. Essentially his parents say to him: You're on your own, kid. Figure it out for yourself.

Parents from such families are generally very uptight, rigid, internalized, and constrained in their show of any feelings. They do not exhibit emotions freely, and their children never feel they have permission to openly express their anger, fears, frustrations, and concerns.

A child from this kind of environment goes into the world very frustrated, inhibited, and frightened because he never acquired the skills necessary to cope with the world very well. He grows up to be very quiet and internalized. In extreme cases he grows up to be a "loner"—a social hermit or isolationist who cannot function with other people. If he ever has a relationship he will have great difficulty in maintaining it because his partner will feel she is living with a wall.

But most adults from such backgrounds eventually find a compatible mate and get married. Yet over the years their communication tends to be very superficial. They talk about mostly mundane things, like the weather or how work went that day or who's going to get the car fixed. They rarely engage in any truly meaningful conversation about how they feel in relationship to each other and to themselves.

This type of pattern leaves the marriage wide open to infidelity. Just because the partners don't communicate doesn't mean they don't have feelings. Those feelings simply go unspoken. Often, an internalized spouse will want her partner to read her mind and draw out her problems. "I wish he'd ask me how I was feeling and really try to find out what's bothering me so I could tell him," she'll say. When it's difficult for you to volunteer your own feelings, you tend to want others to pull them out of you. If this kind of thing goes on for a long time, and there is no true communication, it could lead one or both partners to seek out an affair.

The general pattern is this: If your childhood environment was very internalized and frustrated, you will probably have a hard time communicating and talking. That will frustrate your partner and make him or her feel rejected, thus driving the person into an affair.

Communication patterns can cause a lot of frustration in a marriage. Imagine having a spouse who hardly says a word and makes you feel as though you have to read his mind every time you want to know how he feels about something. A common complaint I hear from women is that their husbands often simply grunt or groan in response to any attempts to communicate meaningfully. If you come home from work, plop down in front of the TV set, and never say a word to your spouse all night, your spouse is going to feel somewhat lost in space. Why be married if you're married to a lump?

Then there's the person who has to finish saying what she wants to say before she will allow you to get a word in edgewise. No matter what you do, no matter how hard you try to break into her flow of words with a counterpoint of your own, she will totally ignore you and keep on talking until her point is made. This is extremely frustrating, for it makes you feel as though you are in debate or contest, with a timer, and you must wait until your spouse's time has expired before you can offer a rebuttal.

How long do you think you can live with such a person before you'd want to pull your hair out and run into another person's arms?

Communication patterns such as these are toxic and damaging to the relationship. Before good communication can be established, there must be a willingness to try to break these unhealthy patterns.

Good communication is the cornerstone of a healthy relationship. The ability to vent anger, frustration, fears, desires, needs, wants, and wishes is extremely important in a marriage. If a person doesn't have a sounding board and the ability to interact and share himself with another individual, whether that interaction be good, bad, or indifferent, then that person is having a major conflict. And if those needs are not met at some point, there is a tendency for the relationship to fall into a nonsupportive role. The partners are unable to be understanding of one another, and it's only natural then for the unfulfilled person to seek out a supportive individual outside the marriage.

Communication is a dynamic process of interaction that must get to the root of the partners' feelings. It must consist of a meaningful exchange of feelings rather than superficial small talk. It must come from the heart, not the head. Heart-to-heart communication is sincere, authentic, and satisfying. Heart-to-head communication is one way and very frustrating. Head-to-head communication is nowhere.

When communication needs are unfulfilled in a marriage, there is often a tremendous amount of censorship and oppression in the relationship. The partners' repressed feelings for each other tend to come out in peculiar ways, such as through petty, critical remarks. The imbalance in the communication leads to numerous unfulfilled needs, feelings of ineptness and inadequacy, incompleteness, and frustration. This builds and builds over a period of time. It may not be obvious at the beginning of the marriage and may take five, ten, twenty years or more for it to reach epidemic proportions. At that point the partners ask themselves, Where do we go from here?

LACK OF AFFECTION AND TOUCHING

Sadly, in our society affection and touching are sort of frowned upon and are often handled with embarrassment, restraint and shame. Many families are severely lacking in any expression of physical closeness and comfort. Just as babies need bonding, children of all ages need to be held and stroked, hugged, and physically protected. The comfort and closeness of a parent gives a child a sense of security and confidence that enables him or her to be strong and surefooted in the outside world. If we think of a child's environment as a supportive, living womb, a child without affection feels more like he is encased in a cold, dry coffin.

When a child grows up without the necessary physical affection and touching he develops a strong need for that in adulthood. He will want to be held, comforted, stroked, and caressed a great deal. If he then marries someone who is not prone to expressing a lot of affection, those early childhood deprivations can be recycled, and the needy spouse will want to find physicalness outside the marriage. (A common complaint among women is that men don't hold them or hug them enough. This is a combination of the fact that many fathers do not know how to express physical affection—or are not comfortable with it—and the fact that men as they grow up are conditioned to constrain their emotions and not to hold or hug others a great deal.)

Interestingly, the lack of physical affection in childhood often translates into a strong need for sex in adulthood. A person who shows these tendencies sees sex as a form of acceptance and love—sex equals love is the equation of his life. If his partner cannot fulfill those heightened needs, he may be driven to seek the affection through extramarital sex. This is ultimately the expression of an *emotional* need rather than a sexual one, however. (Most affairs, in fact, are rarely for sex at all, despite the image they have of being primarily sexual in nature. They are emotionally based in the majority of cases.)

In severe cases, lack of childhood affection and touching leads to promiscuity or the "Looking for Mr. (Mrs.) Goodbar" syndrome. The promiscuous person bounces around from lover to lover, searching desperately for affection and valuing the physical closeness far more than the actual sex. Yet the type of individual the promiscuous person tends to attract wants nothing more than pure sex; so she is denied the very thing she wants and winds up running in circles, never finding the love and affection she needs.

Barbara H. had a father who was ever distant and who rarely held her or touched her. She grew up to be very needy and went through an extended promiscuous phase from her late teens on up through her late twenties, when she finally married.

After some years her husband became less and less interested in the physical aspect of their marriage, though Barbara did her utmost to keep him happy sexually. Finally, he ignored her to such a degree that it recycled her earlier deprivations in that area, and she was eventually driven to seek the touching and affection she so desperately needed in an affair with a much warmer, more physical man.

LACK OF ATTENTION

Here is another area where tremendous neediness can arise from a sore deprivation in childhood. If a person was punished, criticized, or ignored a great deal as a child, he will tend to develop a tremendous need for attention, reinforcement, approval and ego-stroking in adulthood. A child who experiences a lack of attention often tries to get his affirmation through achievements in later life. This is where the "overachiever's" personality stems from. He strives and strives to make a name for himself or to accomplish some great goal, all for the sake of having people recognize him and tell him how great and wonderful he is.

Such a person carries these tremendous needs into his marriage and puts very high expectations on his partner to make him feel important and recognized. If she does not or cannot fulfill those needs for him, he feels cheated, let down, and insignificant, and he will seek the attention he needs so desperately somewhere else. (A man will often try to get these needs fulfilled where he works, from co-workers, secretaries, and those under his supervision. If that ego-stroking system breaks down, he next turns to his wife; and if she cannot stroke him as much as he needs, he turns to an affair.)

As in all of these areas in which a person experiences childhood deprivations, the man who didn't get enough attention as a child puts his spouse in the position of acting as his surrogate parent and tries to make her fulfill the role his real parents never fulfilled for him when he was a child. She will basically feel like a mother constantly feeding an insecure child.

I often encounter two particular areas where lack of attention in childhood gets recycled. One occurs when one partner in a marriage has a lot of interests and hobbies and the other—the one needy of attention—does not. The needy partner feels left out: "You spend all your time with your hobbies (or with the boys or the girls). You don't spend enough time with me." Instead of sharing the activities or hobbies with his or her partner, this person sits back and watches and feels bitter and cheated—and may turn to an affair for solace.

The other situation involves the needy partner complaining to his spouse that she spends too much time with the children: "You're too absorbed with them. You're always into their projects; you're always helping them with their work. And by the time you get done with them, there's no time left for me. They're more important to you than I am." The same dynamics come into play, the same bitterness and feeling of being ignored, and the same desire for an affair has the chance to arise.

UNRESOLVED ANGER

Many people unfortunately choose to hold in anger throughout their lives. The pattern begins in childhood and is perpetuated through adulthood, creating internalization, blockage, and suppression of a person's natural talents and abilities. This makes for a very inhibited life-style and a self-realization that falls far short of a person's true potential.

A child first learns to suppress anger because he is afraid to confront his parents with his true feelings. Either it is expressly forbidden to show anger in his family, or else he *feels* it is forbidden. He thus pushes the anger downward rather than venting it into the environment.

As the child grows, his internalized anger grows like a weed inside him and eventually branches out into other directions.

In adult life it becomes displaced onto innocent targets—one's wife or husband, one's children, one's boss or business associates. A young girl's anger at her father matures into anger at all men; a young boy's anger at his mother evolves into anger at all women. Of course, unresolved anger can develop in adulthood—it can be anger at an old friend, an old lover, a former spouse, or a previous employer—but for the most part it is rooted in the childhood experience.

You can think of unresolved anger as anger that is locked in a closet somewhere in a person's being. The adult with such anger tends to be a very frustrated person because no matter what they do the slightest bit of conflict recycles that locked-up hostility. For example, an everyday situation will get him all flustered, then the closet door will open just a bit, and some of the old anger will escape. It may not come to the surface directly or be expressed head on, but it will come out in frustration, short-temperedness, and distorted behaviorisms—such as quick, hostile remarks.

Depression occurs when the closet door is opened wide, the anger rushes out, and the person then forces that anger back into the closet and locks the door. Depression is anger turned inward—anger that is never ventilated but always forced back into the closet. And people with a lot of unresolved anger will have a strong tendency toward depression.

What does all this have to do with affairs? Basically, when a person with an unresolved anger blueprint gets married, that anger acts as a wall between him and his partner, choking off a great deal of the communication between them. Picture this scenario: Helen D. was a woman who grew up with a great deal of internalized anger for her father. She married Dave, a rather pleasant man. Every time Dave would say something that got her angry, her old anger for her father would come out of the closet, and she would be stuck with it for days, unable to break through the wall it created and get back in touch with her love for her husband. Now if this anger were to stay activated for days, weeks, or even months on end—which is quite possible—how long do you think it would be before Dave (or Helen, for that matter) gave up in frustration and looked for love somewhere else? (But the difference is that Helen would recycle her anger with *any* partner, not just Dave.) When unresolved anger gets in the way of love, the results can be catastrophic. This is why it is so important for someone with unresolved anger to work that anger out, through counseling or through some other effective method.

DEPENDENCY

Oftentimes parents will raise a child by telling him what to do in life and totally guiding his path—sort of pushing and pulling him into certain channels without giving him a sense of independence or self-sufficiency or any feelings that he can make it on his own. This can create a tremendous dependency need in the child, and when he grows up he may seek out a partner who will act primarily as a mother image or father image to him. He'll want to find someone who will tell him what to do and pave his way so that he can maintain the feeling of protectedness he had in childhood. Paradoxically, he will resent any person who fulfills this script at the same time he seeks such a person out. Deep down he doesn't really want to be dependent; yet he can't help it—that's the only way he knows how to feel secure. What happens then is that his anger at being placed in a dependent role—something he created—multiplies, he feels emotionally suffocated, and in a rebellion against his partner's parental role, he breaks away and has an affair.

You see this a great deal in women who accept the role of housewife as a dependent role rather than an independent one. This is, they gladly fall into the pattern of staying at home, taking care of the children, and sitting around all day because they feel safe and secure. They become very lazy and fall into sort of a stupor. They may work very hard, but they do their work mechanically, without taking any interest or finding any meaning in what they're doing. As the years wear on they become stifled and frustrated, and at some point, in an effort to break away from the nest, they may decide to have an affair. "I've got to find myself! I've got to be me!" is their common cry. They unfairly blame their husbands for making them dependent and dump everything onto him. It all stems from the childhood imprint of dependency and the subsequent need to break out of that dependency and exert one's independence. An affair in this case is always rebellion against a life script that was started in childhood.

FAULTY PARENTAL ROLE MODELS

Here is a classic pattern that causes infidelity. Many times our behavior in adulthood is modeled after whichever parent we chose to imitate in childhood. If a boy models himself after his father, and his father has a strong masculine image, the boy will likely grow up to be a strong, self-assured man. If a girl models herself after a mother who is independent and strong willed, she will likely grow up to be independent and strong willed as well. But if we model our behavior after a parent whose role was a negative one, that could lead us into negative behavior patterns that are either identical to the parent's or exactly the opposite. In addition, if the parent was of the opposite sex, that could *really* twist around our behavior.

Jennifer R. came from a family in which her father was a very weak man who provided a weak image for his children. As an adult she chose to model his behavior exactly, and she sought a mate who was extremely dominant. The marriage allowed her to play the "baby doll" role and be the little girl she never was to her father. She put her husband in the role of disciplinarian and authority figure so that she could live out the life script that was unfulfilled in childhood. But by doing this she gave her husband the right to do whatever he wanted, and she let him walk all over her. This predisposed her to a lot of fear in the relationship. He, feeling he had free rein, embarked on a series of affairs with her full knowledge. He would sometimes bring the women over and sleep with them right in front of her, even demanding that she join in their sexual activities. This was quite humiliating to her, yet her need to be dominated was very strong. Eventually, realizing how destructive the marriage was, she got out of it. But you can see to what lengths a need from childhood can take a person.

Another woman with the same weak father image might have gone the other way and sought out a mate who was totally passive, just as her father was. *She* would take on the dominant role in the relationship. But that creates problems as well. It could cause frustration in her husband and the need to get out and find his own manhood, thus driving him into an affair. Or she herself could get bored with her dominant role and begin to demand that he stop being such a "pansy" and stand up and be a man! Yet because of her behavioral pattern, any time he would attempt to assert himself, she would emotionally castrate him and cut him down to size. The result: frustration for her and the need to seek out a more masculine partner.

Finally, Mark B. grew up with a very weak father and a very domineering mother. He adopted his father's passivity and sought out women who exhibited his mother's strength and dominance, eventually marrying one. Yet he had hated his mother and had rebelled against her domineering tendencies all through his childhood. He carried this same hatred and rebellion into his marriage, even though he needed a strong woman because that was all he knew and felt comfortable with. Thus, his need for strength in a woman conflicted with his hatred of it; the anger and rebellion won out. He broke away from his wife and had an affair.

COMPETITIVENESS

A child who grows up in a highly competitive family is a sure bet to be competitive in all of his adult relationships. When he marries he will experience great difficulty because the environment of his marriage will mimic the competitive environment of his childhood—his interactions with his spouse and his children will be very combative and bellicose. He'll compete with his spouse in everything he does; the tiniest thing will take on the import of a life-or-death struggle. This can be taxing on a person's nerves after a while. When everything you do in your relationship has a win/lose outcome, there will always be a winner and a loser. And when one loses often enough, she will seek the support she needs elsewhere. Thus, heavily competitive relationships are on dangerous ground.

Competition often has its roots in large families. Children from such families are always going to suffer—you can't equalize love among six, eight, ten, twelve, or more kids, no matter how hard you try. There will always be the "pet" child, the favorites, and those who are singled out as "bad seeds" or habitual failures. As a consequence, most of the children in such families will scramble and fight with each other for the few crumbs of affection that are thrown out to them. They then grow up to be competitors in everything they do.

Children from highly intellectual or academic environments also tend to be extremely competitive. They strive with each other to achieve success in the arts, the sciences, and other endeavors, always trying to outdo each other in their parents' eyes so that they will get the lion's share of the attention and accolades. They then carry this over into their adult relationships. Since intellectuals tend to be attracted to other intellectuals, they often marry each other. If two such partners start seriously competing with each other as they did in childhood, it won't be long before frustration sets in on one side, and the potential for an affair will increase.

THE "MILITARY BRAT" SYNDROME

Here is a cause that is strictly situational and a quite common one at that. (Statistics show that in 1980 there were close to three million military dependents in America.) A child who grows up in a family in which one or both parents are in the armed forces will be exposed to a lot of rootlessness, since such families tend to move around from place to place. This rootlessness and sense of wandering stays imprinted in the child. If, as an adult, the person then has to move a few times, for whatever reason, that can recycle the same old fears he had when moving as a child.

Dorothy J.'s father was a commissioned officer in the Navy, and was transferred around a lot when Dorothy was a child. She grew up and married Bill, a sales representative for a major pharmaceutical firm. Bill got transferred a few times on his job, and at one point they had to pack up and move twice in three months. That created a tremendous upheaval in Dorothy and made her terribly discontented. Twice in rapid succession she had to relive the traumatic moving episodes from earlier in her life—the break with friends, putting the kids in a new school, still not having any sense of roots. Just prior to the second move she had an affair with a close friend to combat her fears and find some kind of comfort. Fortunately, it didn't last, and she overcame her fears and made the move successfully.

DEATH OF A PARENT IN CHILDHOOD

This is another situational cause that happens frequently enough to be dealt with separately. When a parent dies, the child can grow up to be very much in need of love and affection from a substitute parental image of the same sex as the lost parent. For example, a man who grows up without a father to model himself after may seek out a wife who has "fatherly" tendencies. That creates an identity problem for him, and he will look for a woman to be both his mother and his father—just as his own mother was. Few people can live up to that expectation; thus the man may bounce from woman to woman in search of the one who will give him the sense of identity he needs.

Here again, the needs the child grows up with are based on a situation in childhood that is not along the lines of what a child would ordinarily experience. Thus, as an adult he develops *situational* needs that do not coincide with his true inner needs. His behavior is directed toward seeking out a partner who will satisfy the situational needs. He finds such a partner who will satisfy the situational needs. He finds such a partner but eventually the *true* inner needs assert themselves and come into conflict with the situational needs. Whichever needs are stronger will win out and will push him either toward his partner or away from her. It's the latter case that causes an affair.

PARENTAL VALUES AND EXPECTATIONS

Many parents convey their love for their children through the values they instill in them. Examples of values would be, "You should become a doctor (lawyer, etc.) when you grow up"; "You must succeed"; "You should have a career"; or, for women, "You should get married, have children, and forget about careers"; "Sex before marriage is a sin"; "A man doesn't cry"; and "Women don't play sports." (We'll take a look at religious values and sexual values as separate categories below.) Whether these values are openly stated by the parents or merely implied in their behavior and attitudes, the effects of them on a growing, developing child are the same.

The reason parents convey their love for their children through values is that many times they can't express that love directly. They either don't know how or they are just not capable of doing so. A child interprets these values as expectations that he must fulfill rather than as love. He thus winds up going through life trying to please his parents rather than himself. Of course, he projects that behavior into his relationships and may imitate his parents' behavior by conveying his love for his partner through the same values that were instilled in him. (For example, a husband may say, "I am the man and you are the woman. I love you, therefore you must stay home and keep house while I go off and bring home the bacon.") This is a poor substitute for authentic love, love that comes from the heart and has nothing to do with what you want or expect from your partner. Values are something outside of ourselves, something we learn. Love is a natural process, an intrinsic feeling you convey from the heart.

If two partners don't agree in their values and try to impose their separate values on each other, they will become adversaries—unless they are flexible enough to compromise and tolerate each other's point of view. For example, a man who believes strongly that he should be the breadwinner would go a long way toward achieving harmony with his wife if he allowed her to fulfill a need for meaningful work by getting a part-time job. A woman who places a great emphasis on material things would be demonstrating flexibility toward her husband if she were to sacrifice some of the finer things in life in order to allow him to spend more time with their children. If the partners cannot give in even a little bit, each will feel that the other is different, hostile, and lacks understanding, and the two will begin to grow apart. Conflict and repression will start to come between the partners, and at some point one or both may seek someone else out who will be able to understand and fulfill those needs for agreement and support.

Educational and career expectations are a heavy burden parents often place on their children: "You must be a doctor"; "You must go to college"; "You must go to graduate school"; "You must do what your father or mother did"; "What are you going to do with your life?"; "Hurry up and choose a career. You can't just be a bum the rest of your life!" It goes on and on. Years ago these things were understood and accepted. People chose careers and stuck with them, firmly committed to their choices. Nowadays it's much more difficult for young people to make a commitment, faced as they are with so many choices and so much uncertainty. This creates a great deal of pressure in a child. He feels he must fulfill his parents' expectations of him if he is not to be a failure in life. As a result he experiences a severe loss of identity, which he perpetuates well into adulthood, if not all through his life—and his spouse must deal with his lack of a firm identity all through their marriage.

Most children attempt to get reinforcement from their parents by doing what their parents say. But if a child is not allowed to evolve at his own rate and his own pace and is forced into choices he is not ready to make—even given ultimatums rather than choices ("You've got until your twenty-first birthday to make a decision!")—he will never develop a sense of his own self. That lack of identity will surely carry over into his relationships and can create a love-style pattern that is highly predisposed to an affair.

When such a heavy burden of expectation is placed on a child, he conditions himself into the role of pleasing his parents, gaining their approval by meeting their demands and expectations of him. Rather than having the experience of being loved for himself, he feels he is loved only for his achievements. He becomes very organized, methodical, controlled, and disciplined. He puts all his energies into achieving things and being successful so that his parents will accept him and approve of him.

Taking that behavior into a marriage, he strives to be successful to get approval and acceptance from his partner. If she doesn't fulfill that role by patting him on the back all the time and giving him the admiration he needs, frustration sets in, and he may be pushed into seeking an affair.

By placing a tremendous you-must-succeed expectation on a child—the "musterbation" syndrome—parents predispose the child to a lot of future-oriented anxiety and a whole host of neurotic fears. If as an adult the child doesn't fulfill his parents' expectations of him, he displaces much of the anger and hostility he feels toward his parents (for *making* those expectations in the first place) onto his spouse, creating nothing but doom and gloom in the marriage.

RELIGIOUS VALUES

This is a special category of parental values I'd like to deal with separately as it is so common and creates so much misunderstanding and pain.

Parents who instill their children with strong religious values often do so thinking that this is a way of reinforcing love. Yet religious values can entrap a child because they do not necessarily allow room for freedom of choice. They are again an imposition on the child to please his parents and meet their needs. Later on in the child's life this can cause problems in his sexuality and in his life-style in general, causing rigid, constricted behavior and making guilt the primary component of his emotional makeup.

This childhood imprint of religion is used to give a child a value system that will protect him from the evils of the world and give him high moral fiber. From the parents' point of view, that constitutes a healthy value system for the child. Yet from the point of view of the child's development among his peers, it is a constricted and narrow value system. It can create a tremendous sense of guilt for the child should he at any time desire to break out of the mold of those values. Thus religious individuals are always caught between what their religious values might be and what their emotions and intuition suggest they do. (For example, a child might feel very guilty about listening to and enjoying certain types of music if it is considered "evil" by his religion.)

Religion is a tremendously powerful force in the life of a person who was instilled with religious values as a child. The resulting guilt that occurs can infiltrate every aspect of the communication pattern of that person's relationship—emotionally, physically, and sexually. There can be a great deal of dormant guilt related to certain experiences in marriage, such as a spouse's business ethics—juggling taxes, for example, in a way that may seem unethical even though it is entirely legal.

As with any parental value, a child learns to continuously please his parents by adhering to their religious values in order to receive their continued acceptance and emotional stroking. Then, as an adult, the person transfers that training to his children, recycling the same pattern.

The problem in such families, I feel, is that too much of the family dynamics centers around religion rather than emotion. Religion is basically a philosophical system—a belief system. It does not generally allow room for originality of thought, for experimentation and experience. The religious person is not allowed to experiment with life; he must live it only according to a set of very narrow rules. Religion, in fact, filters out a lot of the experience that is necessary for really understanding one's self and one's life.

Because of the guilt and constricted communication pattern religion brings into a marriage, the religious partner may be driven by his own frustrations into seeking out an affair. The tremendous guilt he feels in having the affair can then only be relieved, in his mind, through confession. He thus winds up caught in a vicious circle of frustration and guilt. To outline the pattern once again, he is frustrated by the restrictions his religion places on his life and his marriage, he seeks out an affair, and he feels tremendously guilty for having broken the marriage contract. He then chastises himself for his breach, and that drives him further into a sense of frustration.

I want to point out that I am not criticizing religion; I only wish to state that if a parent transmits his love for his child primarily through religious values, it will hinder the child's ability to truly experience his world and develop and grow in a natural way. What he misses as a child he will then strive to make up for as an adult; and what he misses in his marriage— because of the rigid and constricted communication style his religious values brought to it—he will strive to find in an affair.

SEXUAL VALUES

Negative sexual values are another dire nemesis of a healthy marriage.

Sexual values are an explosive issue between parents and their children. Too often attitudes and information about sex are left unstated to a child. He is forced to formulate his sexual values around what he believes his parents want him to think, based on what he picks up in the environment—a distorted view, to be sure. As a result, many children grow up with tremendous guilt about sex. When they have sex the first time they feel the whole world knows it. They suffer terrible apprehension as well as an inability to relax. That certainly makes it difficult to experience sex as pleasurable and enjoyable.

If those early, guilt-ridden values about sex are perpetuated into marriage and are not expressed, there will be trouble. The couple's sex life will function at a bare minimum, with much left unspoken in the realm of fantasy, and will be characterized by tremendous uptightedness, rigidity, and awkwardness. At some point, one partner's awareness level will rise above the darkness, and he will do one of two things: either he'll attempt to tell his spouse what he wants—that more creativity, passion, and romance are needed—or he'll seek those things elsewhere because he feels his partner is not capable of changing in that area. On the other hand, if he does confront his partner and she cannot adapt, he will seek outside fulfillment.

As you can see by now, the common thread that runs through all these causes I've talked about in this chapter is that we take emotional garbage from our childhood and recycle it into the present, into our adult relationships. And that's *on top of* the garbage that has already accumulated in the marriage. So what we wind up with is a sort of double indemnity—two piles of garbage for the price of one. In order to effectively save one's marriage in this situation, the couple must first work through the garbage that exists between the two of them, then through the garbage each partner accumulated from childhood. The slate has to be cleaned completely. To what extent the partners have the ability to do that is based on how much love underlies the relationship, underneath all the garbage that has accumulated.

There are countless causes of affairs that stem from childhood imprints. It would take volumes to list them all and would probably require a duplication of the works of Freud. There's no need to do that, however. The ones I've listed here encompass most of the major causes, and they will give you a basic knowledge from which you can pinpoint others that might apply in your case or in the case of people you know. Once you have a feel for the underlying mechanism, you're on your way to being able to deduce the causes in a number of situations.

We're not finished with the causes of affairs, however. We'll be taking a look at them from another angle—that of common behavioral roles stemming from childhood and dominating our behavior in adulthood—in Chapter 7, under the "Identifying the Problem" section of Reconstructive Dynamics.

Chapter 4

BEFORE THE REVELATION—MARITAL AND FAMILY EROSION

In reality, the greatest strain put on a marriage by an affair happens before the affair is disclosed. Once an affair is out in the open, a volcano of emotions explodes to the surface. Everything that has been held back emerges, and all of it must be dealt with face to face. There can be no more hiding; the partners must confront each other directly and achieve some kind of resolution.

Before an affair is disclosed, however, all the information, feelings, fears, and worries associated with the activity are kept inside, and the result is tremendous stress on both partners. Of course, a husband and wife hide different things when it comes to an affair: The unfaithful partner hides the affair itself, along with his or her feelings about what's been wrong in the marriage; the other spouse hides—from himself or herself more than anyone else—the suspicion and possible knowledge that something is going on.

What comes out of this mutual hiding is an atmosphere of internalization and suppression that just refuses to quit. It continues until one of three things happens: the affair is disclosed; the partners just keep on living their lie forever, one having an affair, the other denying it; or the marriage steadily deteriorates and ends in either stagnation or divorce.

Let's examine the marital and family environment before an affair has been revealed. We can break it down into four distinct objects of conflict: the unfaithful partner; the faithful partner; the marriage or relationship; and the children, if there are any.

THE UNFAITHFUL PARTNER—THE STRESS OF LIVING A DOUBLE LIFE

The unfaithful partner's greatest conflict is that he must keep two separate worlds going—his marriage and his affair. It's difficult enough for most people to make one relationship work; but to keep two afloat is quite a sizable task. And the strain is tremendous. Put yourself for a moment in this person's shoes. He must keep one image up on the home front for his spouse and children and display another, totally different, image up for his extramarital partner. At home he's Joe Family Man, a devoted husband and father who would never dream of cheating on his wife, and with his lover he's a tormented, misunderstood soul who needs constant love and attention—or he's a con man who makes himself out to be much more important and successful than he really is. He must maintain two entirely different life-styles; he must uphold two different sets of standards.

It's extremely difficult to live this kind of lie because you always have to watch yourself and cover your tracks wherever you are—and no matter which relationship you feel will ultimately win out in the end. You've got to make sure you never slip and reveal anything about your lover to your spouse, and you've got to make sure you don't tell your lover anything about your spouse you don't want the person to know. As a result you wind up caught in a tug of war emotionally. And you get trapped in a fantasy world—some of your needs are fulfilled in your marriage, others are fulfilled in your affair; so you're really not rooted firmly in either relationship. You may fantasize about having *both* partners live with you, but in most cases you'd better forget about that one! Thus, you're left with no sense of stability or security, and you're kind of stranded between two shores. Which one do you swim to?

Other factors can intensify the stress of living the double life even more. If you're a religious person, then the fact that guilt and lying are against the tenets of most religions will make your affair more stressful than it would for the nonreligious person. The same holds true if you're a highly ethical or moral individual. Having to hide your affair in such a devious way will create conflict of a higher order for you, going as it does firmly against your ethics and morals.

But no matter what the level of a person's religious, ethical, or moral beliefs, there is a certain discontent he or she will experience in having to carry the weight of an affair around inside. And this discontent eats away at one's soul, both physically and emotionally.

Curiously, it is precisely because of the stress of the double life that the unfaithful partner keeps both his worlds going. His stress makes him feel insecure and fearful that he will lose one or both relationships. He doesn't want to miss having all his needs fulfilled, so he invests more energy into keeping both relationships going. This leads to a vicious circle of stress, striving to keep both relationships alive, stress, striving to keep both alive, etc.

A Trail of Clues

It's a peculiar trait of human nature that every person who has an affair always feels at some level he's successfully covering all his tracks. Nothing could be further from the truth. In 99 out of 100 cases the unfaithful partner is as transparent as can be, leaving clue after revealing clue (see warning signs in Chapter 1). Virtually no one is thorough enough to successfully clean up all the evidence of his affair. When you try to cover up what's behind you, you don't see what's ahead of you, and you don't realize what you are revealing in trying to cover up.

The truth is, most people who have affairs want to get caught. As I pointed out earlier, many unfaithful spouses actually leave a trail of clues on purpose (unconsciously, of course) in order to be found out. The reason is that they want to be able to get it out of their system and confront the issue finally—despite the fact that they may have all sorts of fears and trepidations that cause them to hold everything in. The clues seep out between the cracks in the woodwork. Getting caught allows a cheating partner to lift up the veil of guilt and finally speak to someone about what he has been doing.

Holding On to the Secret

Many people who have affairs tend to just keep to themselves and not tell anyone what they're doing. There's a payoff for this, and it's not a good one. When you keep everything in and refuse to talk about it, that blows up the importance of your affair, in your mind, far out of proportion. You begin to think it's the answer to all your problems. Your sense of adventure heightens. You give the affair far more value than it's really worth. When you share your feelings about the affair with someone—be it a friend, a family member, your partner, or whomever—the very act of sharing allows you to put your feelings into perspective. You come back down to earth and begin to see the affair for what it really is. Without any kind of outlet, you remain up in the clouds.

The unfaithful partner's urge to keep things in is caused by the guilt that underlies his covert behavior. When he's with his lover, he must put his guilt on the shelf. In most affairs, the "other woman" (or "other man") doesn't want to hear anything about her lover's spouse. This is often due to jealousy. "When you are with me," you may insist, "I want to be with *you* and you *alone!*" But there's another type of affair partner who wants to hear *everything* about her lover's spouse, in order to learn how serious the man is about leaving or not leaving his wife. This person wants to know if the affair holds any future for her or if she is just wasting her time in a meaningless interlude.

Keeping everything inside has a devastating effect on the partner having the affair. One result of this internalization of his feelings is that he will develop a sort of hypochondria— endless physical pains and symptoms that are outward, bodily expressions of the guilt and turmoil going on inside. These are the signs that mark the beginnings of a physical breakdown. The human body can absorb only so much stress and guilt before something starts to happen. Many people involved in an affair will complain about headaches, stomach pains, nausea, diarrhea, and other physical ailments in order to get their spouse to nurse them.

Getting sick is a great attention-getting device. It allows the unfaithful partner to express his physical and emotional despair in a way that is acceptable. If he confronts his spouse directly, she might leave him; but if he gets sick, she'll take care of him. This I'm-sick-take-care-of-me role is tempting for several reasons. If you're having an affair and you're sick, your partner's attentions will allow you to strengthen your marriage in your own mind because of the caring that person will give. The cheating partner wants his spouse to come to his rescue. He wants to see if there is still something in his marriage to hold on to, in order to counteract his fears about losing his spouse. Even if one partner feels an underlying anger and hostility toward the other, this will be set aside with the hope that out of the closeness of this "nursing" will come a breakthrough and a possible reunion.

Unfortunately, this rarely happens. The nursing partner usually winds up hurting even more because as soon as her spouse gets past his temporary symptoms of headaches, stomach pains, and whatever other variants of anxiety and stress-related illness he is experiencing, he will immediately go back to the same behavior he exhibited prior to the physical problems—namely, keeping *both* relationships very much alive.

Another way the unfaithful partner will try to find an outlet for his stress and internalization is to become absorbed in activities he wasn't necessarily interested in before. For example, he may take up tennis, golf, or racquetball in order to have an outlet through which to vent his anger and frustration. Any kind of release for the body is invariably a release for the emotions at some level. There's only one problem with this, though: the release of the emotions is only temporary; they're back the next day. And so is the stress on the body. Thus, taking out your frustrations with a good game of tennis only relieves you for the moment, then doubles your misery when everything comes back to hit you at once.

The degree of strain an unfaithful partner will experience—and the amount of lying and cheating he will indulge in—depends on how intense his affair relationship really is. Most people who have affairs tend to idolize their lovers. They blow the person up far out of proportion in their minds because of all the unfulfilled needs he or she is fulfilling. This makes it very difficult to let go of the affair, which only increases one's sense of guilt and frustration and in turn leads to physical breakdown and other symptoms.

Nothing Short of Heaven

A person having an affair may feel he or she is in blissful heaven because of it—he or she may feel "born again." Most of that is due to the novelty of the experience and the fact that, with two relationships going, many needs are being fulfilled at once. Additionally, in most cases the third party knows virtually nothing about the unfaithful spouse or his past. He can have been divorced six times, can have lost three businesses in a row, may have twenty kids floating around all over the country, and may be millions of dollars in debt. But no matter: he can project any image he wants to with his lover. He can live out his fantasy of who he wants to be without having to carry the burden of his past and the life history—good, bad, or ugly—that led up to the present.

That's a very strengthening thing to his ego. It gives him the motivation to develop in his career, mature emotionally, be really open and honest with his lover, and experience more of a naturalness, a fluidness, and an intensity in his affair relationship—something he may not have had with his spouse. It may even bring him the most satisfying sexual relationship he has ever had.

Bliss Dies Hard

But the unfaithful partner's days of heaven are short-lived. As his affair progresses, his marriage steadily erodes. And once the marital erosion reaches a point of breakdown, he no longer has the same magical feelings for his lover. This creates an emotional panic in him: what with his marriage falling apart and his affair losing its magic, both worlds seem to be slipping away from him.

Some people in this situation are pushed into a greater enchantment with their spouses. The security of knowing that there is someone for them to come home to intensifies their marital love and makes them want to salvage the marriage.

On the other hand, if the unfaithful partner's spouse begins to show signs of total indifference to his extramarital activities, he will become frightened of losing her and will once again strive to keep both relationships afloat. (You can well imagine that being pulled in all these different directions makes one rather weak emotionally.)

The bliss of an affair dies for a number of reasons. After a while the novelty wears down. The unfulfilled needs are fulfilled to a saturation point, and their intensity diminishes. Or something happens that even the unfaithful partner doesn't bargain for: his lover begins to lose interest in the affair and starts "weaning away" from him.

The Party's Really Over

When this hard reality sets in, the result is often a greater sense of conflict and loss than the cheating spouse had to begin with. He goes through a mourning period. In this stage he will experience a tremendous anger and hostility for his spouse and will blame her entirely for the loss of bliss in his affair. This blame, though unintentional, actually begins immediately after the newness of the affair wears down and reaches its zenith in the period of mourning. If it wasn't for *you*, he says to his partner unconsciously, I would still have this person in my life. This blame stays in the unconscious, of course, and is never expressed verbally (otherwise, he would be admitting his affair!) He is then faced with having to take a look at what's left in his marriage and actively salvage the wreck that's been made—despite the feeling that he may be headed down a dead-end street.

THE FAITHFUL PARTNER—CAUGHT IN A DENIAL SYSTEM

The greatest conflict for the faithful spouse comes about because of her denial of her partner's extramarital activities. Even though the affair has not been disclosed, she will sense at some level the funny business that's going on. I dealt with this in much greater detail in Chapter 1 under the section called "Denial." (The interested reader may want to go back and re-read this section as it will be much more meaningful to him or her at this point.) Let me stress here once again that this spouse labors under a fear of looking at the truth and thus denies any awareness of what is going on around her. She tends to go about life with a bunch of emotional lead weights hanging from her shoulders and feels persecuted and victimized to the hilt, without having the slightest idea why. Again, a great deal of the time people in this position know deep down what is going on; they just push it aside. They don't want to deal with the reality of the affair because of all their fears of what will happen if the whole thing comes out into the open—the scars of divorce, the financial desperation, the finger-pointing of others, etc.

THE MARITAL RELATIONSHIP—TROUBLE IN PARADISE

The combination of one partner's stress at having to lead a secret, double life and the other's suffering due to his or her denial of the affair is an explosive one that can wreak total havoc in the marital relationship.

Drifting Apart—the Crack in the Bond

The immediate effect these dynamics have on the marriage is to create a sense of alienation between the two partners and a tendency for them to "fake it, not really make it" with each other. They go through the motions of their marriage in a very mechanical way. It's very hard for the partner having the affair to really, truly "be" with his spouse if he's out in the world pursuing a relationship with another person. And it's difficult for his spouse to be really open and honest if she is living in fear or suspicion of his activities. Both partners tend to go through the daily marital rituals they have always gone through; but the difference is that whereas in the past these rituals might have been engaged in with mutual love and respect, now they are done very coldly and mechanically. And the only reason the two stay together at this point is out of a sense of obligation and fear—the fear of what it would mean to lose each other.

It's very difficult in this situation to go about your married life as if nothing were wrong. It's a strain on your nerves every day. But partners will tend to avoid each other and will communicate much less, if at all. The marital environment will be characterized by feelings of awkwardness, avoidance, internalized anger and hostility, fear, frustration, and hurt. (The intensity of these feelings will of course depend on the emotional makeup of the two individuals.)

Both partners will tend to escape into whatever activities they can—not so much into hobbies but into things like watching television more than usual, reading more than usual, sitting in another room and talking on the telephone for hours on end, or doing these things at inappropriate times. At different points in a marriage these are all natural activities to indulge in. But if they are taken to an extreme or done in a compulsive way, that's certainly an indication that one or both partners are trying to avoid each other.

What causes alienation? Avoidance, indifference, insensitivity, terseness, and mild annoyance or temper tantrums regarding tiny, insignificant things. "Why didn't you clean the house today?" yells one partner. "The hell with you! Why didn't you bring in the newspaper for me?" screams the other. Out of these little issues develop earth-shattering arguments, and a deep and constant anger fills the environment.

Breakdown in Trust

Once the initial alienation sets in, the next step is a gradual breakdown in further communication and trust. The intensity of the conflict and the inability to resolve that conflict worsen. Neither partner wants to take the risk of being vulnerable by sharing his or her feelings with the other because of fear of potential revenge or hurt. Thus the conflict intensifies, and the only way out at that point is to admit the affair and face the ensuing confrontation.

The breakdown in trust destroys any capacity for love because everything either partner states is regarded by the other with suspicion. The unfaithful partner will walk on eggs for fear that he may slip and give away his secret to his spouse. His spouse may continuously look for verbal and nonverbal clues that he's actually having an affair. The only kind of communication that generally exists at this point is the superficial kind surrounding issues that *have* to be discussed, such as food, money, bills, who's going to take the car in for repairs, who's going to pick up the kids, what time we have to be at the Joneses' party on Saturday night.

Dwindling Sex Life

The couple's sex life suffers terribly during this stage of marital erosion. If they have any sex at all, it's engaged in in a very mechanical way, without any real pleasure or sharing. The act amounts to nothing more than a physical release of tension.

Sometimes one partner will deny the other sex in order to punish him or her, either for a suspected infidelity or for not fulfilling his or her needs. More often, however, the unfaithful partner will make it a point to have sex with his spouse on a regular basis, in order to cover up what he's doing elsewhere. He won't want to give his spouse any sexual clues that he's having an affair. As we saw earlier, sex is the area that provides the most intimate and blatant warning signs of a spouse's infidelity. If a couple had a relatively good sex life and that were to suddenly stop, it would be a pretty obvious tipoff that something was wrong. Thus, the partner having the affair, in order to deflect any suspicions, will go out of his way to make his wife feel that everything's "hunky-dory" with their sex life.

Taking It Out on Each Other for the Kids' Problems

If the couple have children and they begin to see the effects of the erosion of their relationship on their children (I'll outline those effects below), they'll tend to blame each other. If you had done this, that, and the other thing, the argument goes, the children wouldn't be caught up in this mess! Each throws the entire responsibility for damaging the children onto the other, which only further destroys what little communication is left.

The Chasm Runs Deep

By this time things look pretty grim in the marriage. For the most part the corrosive, rusting process of this erosion is left alone by the couple. They try to ignore it, but it just keeps getting worse until eventually the relationship is hanging on by a mere thread of neediness, fear, and uncertainty.

Part of the fear of letting go of each other comes about because the partners think to themselves, What purpose would it serve to end this? The same mechanisms are at play here as underlie the faithful partner's denial spoken of earlier: fear of what's out in the world, financial insecurity, fear of loneliness, and the fear of being branded a failure by others—the "scarlet letter" syndrome.

Games Lovers Play

The period prior to disclosure of an affair is characterized by a number of manipulative and destructive emotional games both spouses will play with each other. I'd like to highlight five of those games here: "The Torture Game," "The Blame Game," "The Game of Emotional Indifference," "The Bitch/ Nice Guy Syndrome," and "The Brute and the Lady."

The Torture Game

In the Torture Game, one partner continually attacks the other verbally, torturing him or her with harsh, critical words. These attacks may be subtle, or they may be very overt. The Torture Game is characterized by put-downs, condescending remarks, and criticisms—anything designed to rub salt into the open emotional wounds of a partner's vulnerabilities and soft spots. The torturing spouse does his level best to make his partner feel stupid, inadequate, and incompetent—in anything. For example: A couple walks out of a movie and the wife says, "I really enjoyed that film," to which the torturing husband replies, "It figures you'd like that sentimental garbage! That stuff is made for idiots like you!" Or, a husband is trying to fix a leaky toilet; he fumbles and breaks a washer, and water starts squirting out all over. "Why don't you face it, Jack," yells his wife, "you were never handy at anything!" Criticizing, castrating remarks are the hallmark of this game.

When two partners play the Torture Game with each other, it can be likened to a furious tennis volley in which each tries to slam home the winning point. Back and forth, back and forth goes the ball, in a sort of point-counterpoint, each person trying to get the upper hand. But the result is a stalemate. Two-handed torture goes nowhere. It's merely a way of emotionally strangulating your partner and only worsens the marital erosion. If there are children involved, they'll get caught smack in the middle of this game.

The rationale for the Torture Game is twofold: for the partner having the affair, it's a way to justify his guilt for what he's doing; for his spouse, it's a way to fight back and survive her feelings of emotional "slippage" and insecurity.

The Torture Game can go on and on until the marital erosion reaches a point of no return. The only alternatives then left are disclosure, breakup, or a hollow existence as two people who happen to live together but share no feelings for each other.

The Blame Game

In the Blame Game, one partner blames the other totally and completely for everything that's gone wrong in the relationship. "It's all your fault!" is the battle cry. "You're ruining my whole life. You don't bring up the children right, you don't cook right, you don't sleep right, you don't dress right, you don't walk right, you don't talk right." In this game everything has a blaming, critical side to it; everything is based on criticism, in fact—and the criticism is never constructive, always destructive. The game basically functions as a way to strip your partner of his or her dignity and self-respect in order for you to fortify your own ego. It differs from the Torture Game in focus. Whereas in that game one partner attacks the other's flaws and weaknesses, in the Blame Game he or she attacks the other's whole being by making the person feel guilty for even being alive.

The Blame Game is a win-lose situation—there's always a winner and a loser. And any time you have a winner and a loser in a relationship, you have trouble. It's a sophisticated game, though, in the sense that it is often played without the couple's awareness.

The general pattern of the game is that the blaming partner treats the other as an emotional garbage can, dumping everything onto him or her. He then looks at the mess he has made out of his spouse and says, "I can't stand you! You have no self-respect!" That again provides him with the justification for taking flight into his affair.

If the "blamee" allows herself to get dumped on enough and absorbs enough shock, hurt, and pain, she may turn around and start blaming back at the "blamer." "You don't do this, you don't do that; what's the matter with you, anyway?" The result is another stalemate in which both partners just go along blaming each other for their problems and dissatisfactions with life and never really communicating. That's the number-one hallmark of all these games: There is no *real* communication; just bitter, hostile talk designed to destroy.

The Game of Emotional Indifference

In this game one partner plays it cool—acts sophisticated and aloof and attempts to give the impression that "this doesn't bother me one bit." The partner who plays this game totally avoids the conflict and doesn't show any kind of emotion—especially hurt or pain. This is a classic role you see quite a bit, usually played by one partner rather than both. It's not a coldness that the person gives off but rather a total indifference that says to the other, "I'm tough, I'm strong, nothing gets to me, especially this. I can handle it. No problem." This kind of behavior tends to make the other spouse feel needy and abandoned—a lost, drifting soul awash in a sea of uncertainty—and this neediness leads to a loss of self-respect. The end result is what we call "needaholism," or need addiction. The needaholic constantly bounces around in search of something that will fulfill his unfulfilled needs; but he's never satisfied. As soon as he fulfills one need, another one crops up to take its place.

When both partners play the Game of Emotional Indifference, they simply try to "outcool" each other and wind up totally avoiding each other. Since both are aloof and indifferent, there is no communication, no relationship, nothing—just two bodies existing in the same general quarters.

The Bitch/Nice Guy Syndrome

Here's a classic game based on two of the more traditional male-female sex roles. In this game the female is always crabby, moody, and critical. She never has anything positive to say and can never be supportive of her mate. Everything is negative from the word go. She vents strong hostility directly at her husband, who winds up essentially being castrated emotionally. He just takes it; he's Mr. Nice Guy: "Oh, just keep hitting me on the head, I'll put up with it. Do anything you want, it's fine with me." He plays the role of the passive, subservient whipping boy, smiling through it all as he's being pummeled in the face with emotional right hooks. "Everything's wonderful, dear." Mr. Nice Guy, of course, willingly takes on his role out of a desire to deny his own feelings—particularly his anger (at his spouse and at himself).

The Brute and the Lady

This is the flip side of the Bitch/Nice Guy Syndrome. The Brute is the male version of the Bitch: he dominates and controls his Lady with macho behavior. He's a highly demanding, manipulative, cold person totally out of touch with his feelings. The Brute is the "executioner" in the marriage; the Lady, his "victim."

In both the Bitch/Nice Guy Syndrome and The Brute and the Lady, whichever spouse takes on the underdog role experiences a tremendous loss of self-respect, dignity, identity, and self-worth. With this breakdown in sense of self and the resulting loss of emotional stamina comes an inability for trust to emerge in any way (unless these difficulties are dealt with, of course). Communication is nonexistent here, based as it is on artificial, learned roles rather than authentic, gut-level feelings. The result once again is a deepening of the marital erosion and a relationship that's about as meaningful as a leftover TV dinner.

THE CHILDREN—PAWNS IN A GAME OF EMOTIONAL CHESS

As we've seen, children are generally the innocent victims of any marital conflict. In the marital erosion that takes place before an affair has been disclosed, children are particularly caught in an emotional squeeze that can have far-reaching effects on their lives. This squeeze happens at a child's unconscious level and is created by the pressure and tension he senses between his two parents.

Alienation

The primary reaction a child experiences under these conditions is a profound distrust of his place in the family. The emotional bedrock on which his sense of security rests is shattered, and he winds up hanging from a precipice of fear and insecurity.

Without trust in one's family surroundings there is no capacity for love and intimacy. The child begins to feel isolated and detached from his family because he does not understand what is creating the tension in the environment. He experiences a sense of abandonment—which is an awfully powerful feeling for a child to have. He'll feel he has to walk on eggs around his parents and will tend to keep all his emotions inside.

Though children may not be directly aware of what is going on in the family environment, they have a certain intuitive understanding and are able to grasp the situation without having a concrete picture of what it all means. As a result a child will feel confused and frustrated and many times will question whether he or she is really loved. Children also tend to blame themselves for any problems their parents are having. They'll often wonder, Why can't Daddy and Mommy be nice to each other? Is it because of me?

To make matters worse, generally neither partner will be willing to discuss with or explain to the child what is happening. Neither wants to admit anything is wrong; neither wants to be the fall guy or the bad guy; or neither knows how to approach the child on the subject, and both wind up avoiding him out of fear.

Children are afraid to seek answers directly from their parents in this situation. And, unfortunately, when they do ask questions they usually get responses that are more harmful than anything else. "It's not your problem! It has nothing to do with you!"—these are typical replies to a child's probing. Such statements either deny that there is a conflict or blatantly admit that there is one without giving the child any kind of solution for dealing with his feelings of insecurity.

Neediness

A child will become very needy under these circumstances. He'll especially need to feel that his parents still love him and that he is *not* the cause of their difficulties. His feelings of abandonment will lead him to try to fulfill his unfulfilled need for love in negative, attention-getting ways. He may start to show behavioral problems, especially at school. He'll do this because he wants his parents to come to his rescue. But this tends to backfire. His parents will get frustrated, will become very strict with him, and he'll feel even more alienated. A vicious cycle of alienation, attention-getting behavior, punishment, and further alienation will be the result. Unfortunately, the anger the parents express at their child is often really anger they feel for each other that is displaced onto the wrong target.

The long-term effects of these feelings of abandonment and alienation on a child are subtle yet devastating. His social, sexual, and intellectual development will be terribly undermined. And what will happen then is that he'll develop the same unfulfilled needs that created his parents' marital conflict in the first place. Thus, neediness is handed down from generation to generation.

Social Awkwardness

A child who feels abandoned and at some level unloved feels ill at ease and unnatural in his world because of all the tension and continuous turning inward of his feelings. Whereas in the past his parents might have shown him a lot of caring, support, nurturance, and cooperativeness, he now feels they are no longer on his side—no longer the parents he once knew. Hence, socially he'll become awkward, shy, uptight, constricted, and embarrassed. He'll be too ashamed to talk to anyone at school about what's going on at home, and he certainly won't be able to talk to his parents; so there'll be no outlet at all through which to express his feelings.

Because of his tremendous shame and his fear of what will happen to him, his distrust for the family nest is projected out onto the whole world, and he loses his foundation for dealing with the world emotionally. He begins to feel isolated and detached from *everyone.* He loses his self-confidence, his ego-strength, and his ability to cope with his everyday life, and he winds up socially stunted.

The child no longer feels on an equal level with his peers and feels he has to cover up his problems just as his parents are covering up theirs. He loses the fun-loving, freewheeling, free-floating nature children have and instead mirrors the conflicts of his environment without understanding why or how.

Sexual Immaturity

The stage of marital erosion also affects a child's sexual development. The emotional insecurity he feels seeps into every aspect of his life and especially prevents him from maturing through the natural stages of sexual growth. For example, whereas a sexually precocious little girl might have always enjoyed bouncing on Daddy's lap, she won't now because she'll feel distrust from him. Does Daddy really love me? she'll wonder.

The child also begins to lose his ability to identify with whichever parent he has up to now chosen as his model. This again causes tremendous frustration and hinders the child's natural evolution through the various stages of sexual growth and maturity since a strong role model is so crucial to healthy sexual development.

Learning Problems

The child's intellectual curiosity is also greatly hindered by this erosion, for he no longer feels at ease in probing and questioning his world. That capacity has been cut off by the conflict his parents are having. If he probes and questions *that*, he may find out he is unloved; so better not to challenge anything in life, better just to play it safe and feel secure. Also, when a child holds in his emotions, they block his ability to learn and feed his mind. This leads to academic problems at school on top of any behavioral and social problems he may be having there already.

Intellectual curiosity is what allows a child to feel free and easy in his environment. True learning takes place through a free-flowing interaction with the world. It also comes about through a repetitiveness of actions and feelings. Yet when a child's intellectual curiosity is stunted, the only thing he learns to repeat is the tension, suppression, frustration, and anger he sees around him, in his parents. He also tends to copy the attention-getting behaviors the unfaithful partner may be inclined to use (such as getting sick). These become a part of him and will stay with him as he grows up.

Effects of the Games Lovers Play on Their Children

How do the various emotional games a husband and wife play with each other affect their children?

When a child constantly sees anger and vindictiveness tossed back and forth between his parents, his problem then becomes which role to identify with: that of the "victim" in the marriage or the "executioner"? Both roles are damaging; so either way he can only lose. And if both parents are playing the same role—as often happens in the Torture Game and the Blame Game—he won't even have a choice: he'll have to identify with the one, common role model. The only other alternative he'll have is to seek an outside role model—which is something a lot of children do. They'll identify with a TV character, a friend or playmate, or someone else's mother or father. To a child's unconscious mind, *that* is abandonment taken to its extreme. Imagine not being able to model yourself after your own parents! What a devastating feeling.

In a game in which two different roles are being played the child must always choose which negative role he will model and whose side he is going to take. For the most part, children tend to take the side of the "victim" in an affair. (I put that word in quotes because there is no real victim in an affair—one *chooses* to be a victim; one does not *have* to feel victimized.) They may, however, side with a favored parent regardless of which role the parent has played in the affair—the "victim" or the "executioner."

Once all of these convoluted emotions have been planted in a child's unconscious mind, they become very difficult to unwind and exorcise. In all of these areas of a child's growth—social, sexual, intellectual, and emotional—the destruction that's caused is absolute and permanent. And the child's ability to achieve closeness and intimacy with anyone as he gets older is depressingly slim.

It's a widely accepted theory that infants respond to hostility and tension in their environment by crying. Since our communication with infants is limited and doesn't allow us to read their minds, we must rely on studies to verify this. They do.

But when a child is at a point where he can talk and understand basic, concrete thought, he is at a point where he can grasp that he's severely affected by his parents' conflicts. And if that tension and those conflicts continue, he just might, during his preteen or teenage years, seek out partners who will fulfill the very negative roles his parents did—because that's the way he believes a relationship is formed.

When you refuse to admit your affair to your partner, or you refuse to admit your partner's affair to yourself, you allow the erosion on your marriage and family to reach a point beyond which there is no turning back. And the consequences can be most painful—especially when you begin to see your children living out your own negative life scripts.

Chapter 5

DISCLOSURE AND ITS AFTEREFFECTS

Whereas the period before the news of a partner's affair has been revealed is characterized by the suppression of emotions and the emotional rusting process that affects all family members as a result, the disclosure of the affair, and the period that follows it, is characterized by emotional upheaval. Disclosure opens a Pandora's box of intense feelings that range from anger to guilt to hurt and pain to depression to jealousy to vengeance and beyond. All the emotions both partners have kept inside for so long come bursting to the surface, and the result is nothing short of chaos. No one in the family is spared the effects of this chaos, either. Emotionally, both partners and their children are buffeted around like leaves in a high wind. Yet disclosure is ultimately the healthier route, for it alone leads to the opportunity to repair the wreck that has been made in the marriage and achieve harmony once again.

Unfortunately, most people approach the disclosure process in a very haphazard, unstructured way. They rely too much on impulsive feelings and not enough on clear objectivity. Their reactions, too, are impulsive and tend to lead to dangerous or destructive behaviors that are indulged in without any thought given to the potential consequences.

These are the things I'd like to deal with in this chapter: the haphazard ways in which an affair is revealed and the impulsive, destructive reactions that usually follow. Let's first take a look at the typically random and chaotic ways in which a partner's affair is disclosed.

DISCLOSURE

There are basically two ways a partner finds out about his or her spouse's affair. One is through discovery, i.e., either the deduction of the affair through visible warning signs or a tip-off about the affair from a third party. The other is through the unfaithful partner's direct disclosure of the affair. The first method is perhaps more frightening because you know something you're not supposed to know, and the second involves more fireworks because the news comes right from the source.

Discovery

Solving the Puzzle

One way of discovering a spouse's affair is by deduction— putting together the warning signs we discussed in Chapter 1. A few little signs begin to crop up here and there, and along the way you see a pattern form. The pieces of the puzzle fit together, and you realize what's been going on all this time, right under your nose. Your partner has been cheating on you.

Listen to Rena H. as she relates how she finally realized her husband, an aerospace engineer, was involved with another woman:

> John was working at the plant five days a week, but he was also trying to start his own business; so he was working nights too. One week he started coming home at ten or eleven at night—sometimes twelve. That didn't bother

me too much at first. Then he started coming home about three or four in the morning. Well, even that wasn't unreasonable for him because if there was something important going on at work he might stay that late. But then he kept doing this every night—and he'd get up and go to work the next day. I'd say, "God, John, you're going to kill yourself. You've got to quit doing this." I was really concerned about him. When it kept going on for two weeks and I saw he wasn't getting tired, I knew something was wrong. But the thing that *really* made me realize something was wrong was the fact that he'd get up in the morning and not take a bath or a shower before he left. "I don't have time!" he'd say. Then he'd leave, and I'd say to myself, That's kind of weird. Finally I realized he must be taking a shower somewhere else.

Several days later Rena found a note from John saying that he was staying with another woman and didn't know when he'd be home.

Monica Q.'s situation was a variation on a similar theme. Though she and her boyfriend, Mike, did not live together, they had been going steady for five years and saw each other almost every day:

Mike would call me at work and tell me he was going to go out with the guys that evening. Pretty soon I figured out that it was always on a Friday night. Then he'd call and tell me he was going to go golfing early Saturday morning; so I wouldn't see him at all Friday night, and I wouldn't see him until the afternoon on Saturday—then on Sunday he was always too tired to do anything. Pretty soon I began to put two and two together.

As we saw in Chapter 1, the warning signs generally involve extremes in behavior one way or the other. A partner will usually either overcompensate for feelings of guilt (by buying you gifts, calling you a lot, or making excuses, for example) or go the other way and withdraw totally (by refusing to communicate, have sex, or go out socially). There is also a middle ground where the person will try to maintain the status quo—keep everything the same—in order not to give off any signs.

Habit changes, things that are unfamiliar or unexpected, overcompensating behavior, attempts to cover up, changes in patterns, new and unfamiliar patterns, constant excuses—these are the ways in which people can begin to see that an affair is going on. Other tip-offs include, once again, spending an excessive amount of money, reducing the family budget drastically, changes in grooming, colognes and perfumes, and changes in dress, such as when a partner suddenly becomes very stylish. These are the signs by which you can immediately sense a difference.

Sometimes a spouse will discover his or her partner's affair by finding incriminating little notes, cards, or gifts around the house—a pocket watch inscribed on the inside cover, a humorous or intimate greeting card, etc. People having an affair often exchange little trinkets or notes. When confronted with such an item, the unfaithful spouse will try to toss it off with an excuse: "Oh, I bought it down the street at the gift shop. It was just a spur of the moment thing." Or, "One of the girls at work got it for me. It's just a joke."

Other items, however, are a little more difficult to explain away—and a little more embarrassing to discover. Jackie's husband Tom had had a vasectomy some years into their marriage, so from that point on she never had to worry about birth control. When she decided to have an affair with a man at work several years later, the issue of birth control came up again. She didn't want to take the Pill, and the IUD frightened her. Condoms took away all the pleasure, so she decided a diaphragm would be the best course. When she went to have herself fitted for the device the doctor told her she would have to leave it in for at least six hours after every lovemaking session. Since the only time she could rendezvous with her boyfriend was right after work, that meant that on those evenings after the two made love she would have to sleep with the diaphragm in and avoid having sex with her husband at all costs. (She could have taken it out before going to bed, but she didn't want to leave it around the house where Tom could find it more easily.) She decided to go ahead and use it anyway, as she was confident she could repel Tom's advances—she had always had the final say about whether or not they would have sex.

One evening, after a torrid, late afternoon lovemaking session with her lover, Jackie bowed out of sex with Tom with the excuse that she had a headache (yes, people still use this one), and husband and wife went to sleep. But Tom's frustrations got the best of him. He became terribly aroused in the middle of the night, and Jackie awoke to find him touching her. To his surprise he discovered the diaphragm. Unfortunately for Jackie, he knew what a diaphragm felt like, and thus knew right away what was going on.

Dealing with Denial

Most people know about their spouse's affair long before it is disclosed. If they are honest with themselves, they either know outright or have some sense of what's going on. Yet too often they will let the denial mechanism block them from taking responsibility and confronting the situation.

Listen to Monica Q. again as she takes her story a little further. (Her boyfriend was the one who went "out with the guys" on Friday nights and "golfing" early Saturday mornings.)

> I was afraid to confront Mike because I didn't really want to hear the truth; so I let it go on far too long. I'd get angry and try to make myself believe he really *was* with the guys all the time, and then when I believed him I'd get angry that he was spending so much time with them. It finally got to the point where I just couldn't blind myself to what he was doing anymore, and I confronted him. He admitted

he was having an affair. It was a really hard thing for me to deal with. When it all came out in the open I was pretty torn apart.

Third-party Tip-offs

The other method of discovery comes about through tip-offs from third parties—friends, family, co-workers, or even strangers. Essentially, someone takes you aside and says, "Listen, there's something I think you should know. Your husband (wife) is having an affair. Everybody knows but you." The message isn't necessarily transmitted in those words, but that's the general drift.

News travels fast through the grapevine. If you're seen galavanting around town with the same person in a number of different places, and that person is not your spouse, someone is bound to make the connection—and you can be sure your spouse will find out about it before you do. Even the biggest of cities have their small-town qualities. The same six hundred people you know go to the same one hundred places over and over again.

Most people who have affairs take their lovers to their favorite restaurants, night clubs, hotels, and fun spots because they get all the nice amenities and the personal service they're accustomed to. (Sometimes they'll even use their familiarity with the place to impress their lovers.) When you're having an affair, you basically do things similar to the things you would do in any relationship—including your marriage. No one wants to drive a hundred miles away to see a movie!

Thus, upon taking your lover to one of your favorite night spots or weekend retreats, you're bound to bump into someone you know. You can use all the excuses you want, but if that person spreads the word and others are on the lookout, you'll be found out before you know it. The news will get back to your spouse, and all hell will break loose.

Whispering campaigns can arise out of any situation. If you're walking down the street with someone in an intimate way—holding hands or with your arm around the person's shoulder—that alone can be viewed as suspicious by people who recognize you. And if you're not famous for being a warm, physical person who normally goes around holding hands with people or putting his arm around them, those who recognize you are going to wonder what in the world you're doing.

Of course, one such incident won't be enough to cause an uproar. Two won't either. But a pattern of such goings-on will. And you can bet the news will get back home to your mate.

(As an interesting aside, anonymous phone tips, though infrequent, do happen occasionally, and they usually come from someone at the cheating spouse's workplace. Sometimes— just like in the movies—blackmail is the motivation. Most husbands who have affairs make their secret calls from outside the home, generally from work. If a secretary or co-worker hears a woman's name over and over again and puts the pieces together, the news may somehow get back to the man's wife. If that person has some hostility for the man—bears a grudge against him or wishes to get back at him in some way—that's where the phone tip comes in.)

Upon hearing of a spouse's affair from a third party, most people will react with disbelief: "What! How can you say that? You don't know my Johnny (Joanie)!" Then the denial mechanism sets in, and if the faithful partner doesn't take the blinders from her eyes, she'll be doomed to walk around in a state of emotional shell shock while her mate continues to cavort at his leisure.

Direct Disclosure

Discovery happens by accident; direct disclosure is deliberate (though often somewhat sneaky and underhanded). In discovery you find out without your partner's knowledge; in direct disclosure you find out straight from the horse's mouth, so to speak.

The way an unfaithful partner discloses his affair is important, since it will determine the way his spouse will handle the whole situation. There's a right way and a wrong way. The right way can lead to reunion and healing; the wrong way can lead to impulsive behavior, retaliatory affairs, vengefulness, a desire to punish the cheating partner, or a cry for divorce. Most people disclose their extramarital activities in the wrong way.

The Breakdown

The breakdown is one of the most common methods of direct disclosure. In it, the unfaithful partner decides to let everything out into the open because he is no longer able to deal with all the guilt, the hiding, the games, and the insecurity. Many times, his confession is done in an impulsive way, which does more damage than good.

An excellent illustration of the breakdown occurs in the classic film *An Unmarried Woman*. In one scene Michael Murphy, as Jill Clayburgh's husband, breaks down in tears on the street and blurts out the news of his affair to his wife. Clayburgh's reaction is to stagger over the curb and vomit uncontrollably. This is a highly emotional scene—perhaps the most powerful one in the film.

The breakdown is an unloading of all the guilt and torment and is motivated by the unfaithful partner's fear of losing his spouse. He can handle the erosion no longer and is so afraid of losing his partner that he just blurts out the news: "I'm having an affair!" His confession is totally reactive and impulsive. He just wants to get it out and over with. He sputters it out in four or five words and then immediately walks away from it. Usually, there's no preparation whatsoever for his partner, who is caught totally off guard and is thrown into a state of emotional shock.

Often, the breakdown is caused by an emotional tug of war that takes place in the unfaithful partner's mind between his wife and his girlfriend (or husband and boyfriend, in the woman's case). He is caught in a vise grip emotionally and fears the impending loss of either one or the other—lover or spouse. He doesn't want to lose his girlfriend because of all the needs she is fulfilling; but he doesn't want to marry her because he doesn't want to give up his family. (In some cases, guilt over what he is doing to the family is the stronger motivating force for the breakdown; but the overpowering feeling is generally the fear of losing either his spouse or his lover.)

Many times the "other woman" will put pressure on him to get out of his marriage. "You've got to make a choice," she'll say. "It's either her or me!" This heightens the tug of war in him and often leads to physical symptoms, such as severe headaches.

Interestingly, if the girlfriend issues an ultimatum to the husband to make a choice, that will push him back toward his wife. The same thing happens the other way around. If his wife knows about the affair and tries to force him to make a decision, he'll swing back toward his girlfriend. Whichever partner pushes him—out of neediness—is going to lose. (The secret, then, is to not show neediness and instead let the girlfriend— or boyfriend—push.)

Forcing His Own Admission

In the breakdown, the unfaithful spouse is forced into a confession by his own conflicting emotions and his fear of losing his spouse (or his lover or both). Sometimes, however, his own *behavior* will force him into a confession, because it will compel his wife to back him into a corner and make him admit what he's doing. For example, a cheating spouse may close off all sexual relations with his wife at some point in his affair. He'll completely abstain from having sex with her. When his wife asks him what's wrong, he'll respond with excuses: "Well, I'm under a lot of stress; I have headaches," etc. Yet if this goes on for a long period of time, she will confront him and force him to reveal the truth—particularly if they have up until then enjoyed an active sex life.

If one partner is being denied a great deal over a long period of time, she will pressure the other into doing something about it. Thus, any extreme indifference or change in behavior compels the faithful spouse to corner the unfaithful one and make him confess his activities.

Religious Values

Here is another factor that forces a person to disclose his or her affair. An unfaithful spouse with strong religious values will often experience a great deal of guilt that he can't handle. Religious teachings stress closeness, family unity, and certain kinds of beliefs that followers must adhere to. If you do not adhere to those beliefs you are considered a sinner. In order to overcome the feeling of having sinned, along with the guilt that's caused by both the involvement in the affair and the erosion it is causing the family, the religious person will disclose his activities to his spouse. His confession acts as a sort of cleansing process. (Some people will go to traditional confession to relieve their guilt, then turn around and visit their lover the same day!)

The Counseling Environment

In my years in private practice as a human behavior specialist, I have found that an interesting thing happens in the counseling milieu. Oftentimes a woman will enter counseling when she suspects her husband of having an affair or if their marriage isn't working. (It's very rare for both partners to enter counseling at this stage. Usually one person comes in when she has an awareness that the other is being unfaithful or senses it through recognizing the warning signs.)

As she becomes stronger, through dealing with her own conflicts head on as well as those in the marriage, her growing emotional strength will threaten her partner. He'll feel he can't play his game out too much longer because he doesn't call the shots anymore. There's now a mediator directing the action; he won't know how to control the situation.

This causes a great deal of conflict in the unfaithful partner and in the marriage. The tug of war inside him between his wife and his lover will become very strong and reach a zenith. At this point one of two things happens: either his spouse will confront him—"Are you having an affair?"—and he, having run out of steam, will admit it; or he'll feel himself losing ground, and as a result will try to beat her to the punch by saying, "I'm having an affair" before she can even ask.

Telling Other People

Many people who have affairs eventually discuss their activities with someone else, generally a close friend. They're driven to unburden the intense pain and turmoil they're experiencing—and where else can you go with such feelings but to a friend? Besides, the unfaithful partner has a strong need to feel that he's right and justified in what he's doing—and friends will tend to support his point of view and take his side over his spouse's.

Often, however, this tactic backfires. The friend will take the Good Samaritan role and say, "You've got to get this out of your system; you've got to tell your spouse. I'll be there with you. I'll help you with it." This is a well-meaning approach, but a sticky one; for it is the friend's pressure and "encouragement" that then forces the unfaithful partner into confessing his activities to his spouse. He thus winds up reacting not out of his own impulses but because of outside pressure applied to him by people who are close to him.

The methods of direct disclosure I've listed so far are somewhat passive and reactive on the unfaithful spouse's part, in the sense that he is forced into a confession without his necessarily wanting it. He is at the mercy of either his own feelings and actions, those of his spouse (which are at bottom caused by his own), or outside influences, and he winds up being checkmated into a disclosure.

Other methods are more active, however, and they usually involve a high degree of manipulation.

The Baiting Game

In the Baiting Game, the unfaithful partner takes an indirect, roundabout approach in which he baits his spouse and tests the waters to see if the time is right for his confession. He lays the foundation for his disclosure by talking about the dissatisfaction he is experiencing in the marriage. "I'm not happy with the way we communicate," he'll say. "We don't seem to share the same interests anymore." It seems honest enough on the surface; but what his spouse doesn't realize is that he's testing her.

It's sort of a businessman's game of "leverage." The unfaithful spouse wants to see how his partner will deal with the news of his dissatisfaction and its specific reasons. He wants to see whether she will accept it or not. Many times his spouse will give in and acknowledge what he is saying because she senses that something is wrong and that this may mean there's an end to the problem in sight. "You know, you're right," she'll say. "I can understand what you're feeling, and I'm willing to look at these areas." But at that point the trap has been set. His spouse's acquiescence gives the cheating partner permission to unload his secret. "Honey, I'm having an affair, and now you know the reasons why."

"Here, Read This Book"

Another "baiting" type of approach an unfaithful partner will take is to give his spouse a certain book to read. The book will deal with affairs, relationships, "open marriages," and such—all relevant material that will enable him to gauge her reaction to the subject matter. (Alternatively, he'll ask her to watch a particular movie or TV show that deals with these topics or listen to a similarly relevant song.)

After she's read the book, he'll probe her: "What did you think about that?" If her response is favorable, and he feels the coast is clear for an admission, he'll pop the secret—"Guess what, honey? That's me they're talking about!" (One fellow I know underlined an entire book in a number of crucial spots, then left it right out in the open so his spouse would *really* get the message!)

This method allows the unfaithful spouse to give his partner the hint in a safe way. The indirect signs enable him to side-step a direct confrontation—something he is deathly afraid of. It's a way of "feeling out" his partner to see how she will re-spond; and if it looks as if he's going to get out of it relatively unscathed, he'll confess.

The Last Fling

This is perhaps the granddaddy of all baiting approaches and is a very common one. In this ploy the unfaithful partner gives his marriage "one last fling" before he calls it quits and tells his spouse about his affair. He'll take his wife away for a week-end or a week to some mountain retreat or vacation resort, and he'll try to have a wonderful time to see if there's anything worth saving in the marriage. He'll give it everything he has so that when he's convinced the marriage is hopeless he'll have an excuse for his affair. And no matter how good that one last fling is, he'll always say, "It's no use. The marriage just isn't working."

He may really enjoy the trip while he's on it, but he'll invari-ably miss his lover and may be tempted to call her at different points along the way. That comes about because he's afraid if he doesn't keep in touch with her he'll lose her. He'll be anx-ious to get back home and see his lover, but he'll try to cater to his wife and make the trip a pleasant experience for her. At the end of the trip he'll start to get indifferent to his wife, though. Then on the way home he'll have all kinds of anxiety and will just want to get back and get it over with.

Finally, when it's all over and they're home, he'll say to his wife, "Look, I'm just not happy. I've given it everything, I've tried everything, it's just not working." Thus, he uses an exter-nal event to justify the fact that the marriage "isn't right." He's given it one last fling, and now he's ready to give it up and go all out with his affair.

* * *

All of these baiting methods are manipulative little games that are used to see if the faithful spouse is going to take the bait and react. If she does react, and her reaction is favorable, the unfaithful partner will feel on safe enough ground to admit what he's doing. If she doesn't react, he'll feel justified in continuing his affair. Either way he saves face and avoids a confrontation. This is a very cowardly way to deal with the problem.

For the most part, what causes the unfaithful partner's disclosure is his inability to break off his affair relationship. It goes on and on, and at some point he knows he has reached a point of no return. If he discloses the activity, at least his spouse will know what he is doing, and he'll be able to find out where she stands on the issue. Then he can make his decision from there.

But the trouble is that all of the methods of direct disclosure, whether they involve baiting your partner or being pressured into an admission by forces, beyond your immediate control, are dangerous. They do not approach the situation in a way that allows a healthy releases of emotions and a proper resolution of the conflict. The proof is in the aftereffects of one of these impulsive, misdirected, or manipulative breast-barings.

The Shock of Finding Out

The news that your partner is having an affair—however it reaches you—often sends shock waves rippling through your mind and body. Emotions vary from horror to disbelief to anger to hurt to a sense of betrayal and back again. It's like having a knife stuck in your heart. The longer you've been married, of course, the more it hurts because you've built so much and have gone through so many things together. If you have children, there's an even stronger bond that makes the realization of the affair very, very difficult and painful.

An affair is a sort of emotional rape whose effects on the emotions are not unlike those of physical rape. One feels brutalized and violated. It's just a total shock to the system. The betrayed partner's immediate reactions range over a wide spectrum of possibilities:

Anger and Hurt

Anger is probably the most popular first reaction. "What?! Why you son-of-a-bitch. How could you do this to me? After all these years, after I've trusted you for so long! How could you betray me like this? And what about the kids? How could you do this to them?"

Then there's hurt and the fountain of tears that follow: "I can't believe you would do this to me. I'm so hurt. I'm so upset. You've hurt me so badly. I'll never be able to forgive you!"

Anger and hurt come about primarily because of the feeling that one has been living a lie for so long. One of the first questions the betrayed spouse will ask is, "How long has this been going on?" It's not all that uncommon for an affair or a series of affairs to last five, ten, fifteen, or more years. Imagine how horrible a feeling it is to think that everything you've done in those years has been false—a lie. Yet this is the betrayed partner's dilemma. She now feels that every tender, loving moment she shared with her partner was an act, a falsehood. Everything her partner did up until now was out of guilt or a need to make up for what he was doing. She feels used—a very painful thing to feel. And as a result her trust in her spouse completely evaporates. The foundation of the marriage is totally dismantled, and the communications system shuts down completely.

Disbelief

Some people defer the anger and hurt they will ultimately feel by refusing to believe the affair is really happening. "This isn't happening to me. I've heard about these things, but it can't happen to me. We have the perfect marriage. Sure, there've been problems, but we've handled them all together. We've been through so much together. How could this happen?" Here again we see the denial mechanism at work. The betrayed partner walks around in an emotional coma and sort of passes the whole thing by. There's always a delayed reaction: "No, it can't be true, it just can't be true. I just can't believe it." But when the truth hits, it hits hard.

Indifference

Indifference is another form of denial: "Oh, I don't care. You do whatever you want to do. I just don't care." This is a way of blocking out your emotions in order not to show the bastard that you're in pain. And, as with disbelief, indifference merely postpones the anger and bitterness that will result when the truth finally hits home.

Inadequacy

"I thought I did everything," is a common reaction. "I thought I really made you happy. You never told me anything about what you were feeling. You never shared with me what wasn't right or what you wanted that I wasn't giving you. I thought I pleased you. I thought I did everything for you. I thought I was the perfect wife (husband), the perfect mother (father)." Here the betrayed partner feels he or she has failed as a spouse and feels totally inadequate as a person. "It's my fault," she thinks. "I guess I just wasn't good enough for him."

Humiliation

Here the stigma of what others will think comes into play: What will the neighbors think of this? What will my friends and family think? How am I going to deal with this? Should I cover it up? Should I just pretend it didn't happen? What am I going to do? The conflict becomes whether or not to tell anybody what has transpired. Yet the temptation is to run to others for comfort, support, and validation—reassurance that you are not to blame and are worthwhile as a person. It's very difficult to keep everything to yourself in this situation. Thus the betrayed partner is caught between wanting to find comfort and support and not wanting to face the embarrassment of having others know her secret.

Insecurity

What happens now? is perhaps the bottom-line question after all the hurt, pain, and anger are out in the open. Where do I go from here? Thoughts of divorce run through the betrayed partner's mind, and the result is insecurity at the thought of having to face the world alone, survive financially, and give up what she has worked for so long to build—yet what has now turned out to be a sham. Once these feelings have sunk in, the betrayed partner will tend to respond with any of a number of impulsive, vengeful reactions. As in a physical rape, the emotionally violated person always wants to strike back. Once the fear, the denial, the disbelief, and all the other feelings come and go, you want to go after the person who cheated on you and "kill" or "castrate" him or her.

Some people will run to an attorney and immediately file for divorce. Others may close off everything—sex, money, communication—or use the children as weapons to punish the unfaithful partner. Some will threaten the betrayer: "Get out! Pack up your things and get out of here!" Or they may take the kids and go to their parents' house or to a friend's house. (For the most part, a betrayed wife will stay if there are children involved.) Some will run away, some will go out and spend money, some will flirt, and some will go out and have an affair themselves.

These reactions are all highly impulsive and spontaneous—strictly from the emotions, without thought. That's the trouble with chaotic, unstructured type of disclosure; it allows no room for contemplation or any desire to find out why the affair took place. It just produces thoughtless, blind, vengeful activity that's meant to strike back at and maim the unfaithful spouse. Here are just a few of the more common impulsive reactions:

Flight

One impulse is to run away from it all. You've seen it in the movies—the violated partner packs up her bags and says, "I'm leaving you. I don't know where I'm going. I may go back to mother's, or I may just go wherever the wind takes me. But one thing's for sure: I'm not going to stick around here and put up with this!"

A betrayed spouse often wants to seek some kind of sanctuary away from her partner in order to deal with her pain. Very few victims of an affair want to let their spouses see the deep hurt and pain they feel. They'll run away to save face and pretend the affair didn't happen.

Running away is fine as long as it's done with some kind of positive end in mind, such as taking time to think things over and decide on a constructive course of action. Done in this way, it provides you a way to regain your composure, give some thought to the whole thing, and try to gather your energies and regroup. If it's merely running out of hurt and fear, without the introspection—and for the purpose of striking back—that can be rather dangerous, because two wrongs don't make a right.

Spending Sprees

Another popular reaction for the betrayed partner is to go out on a buying spree. She'll buy everything in sight and run the credit cards up to the limit, which to her is a way of bilking her spouse and punishing him: "If he thinks he can get away with this, well, he's wrong, because I'm going to make him pay!"

Often a betrayed wife will spend money in an effort to jazz herself up and really look pretty—not for her husband but for the public. It's a way of preparing to flirt and be more visible to other men. Well-off types will go out and get their breasts enlarged or reduced or spend thousands of dollars on all sorts of reconstructive plastic surgery. Some women will want to go back to college; others will demand a new car. They'll tend to center on their own selfish needs. "I may as well get everything I can!" is their motto. It's nothing more than revenge: "I've been good to you; I've tried to please you; I've done everything *possible* to please you. Well, the hell with you now!"

But the spending syndrome backfires: Not only does it create a lot of financial pressure on both partners, it's a foolish thing to do because if you *do* wind up getting divorced, and you live in certain states, that money you've spent either will become part of community debt or will become your sole responsibility. Thus, if a split is inevitable, you may ultimately reduce your own assets by splurging. (Most people don't think about this when they're out there running up the bills!)

Flirting

Flirting is a standard countertactic. It's done to make the unfaithful spouse jealous and to show him or her that "I don't need you. I've got all these other people who want me. And if you don't play your cards right, I may just dump you and go with one of them!"

A betrayed wife will act very seductive with men, even though it may be totally out of character for her. She'll be very "loose" and suggestive in her gestures and movements. When she dances with other men, she'll hold them very close and be very physical and sensual with them. A betrayed husband will play the charmer and flirt with as many women as he can in his wife's presence.

Flirting is a favorite way of striking back; it's easy, it's fairly safe, and it does the job quite well. The reason it's so effective is that it involves much more than hurt. It humiliates the unfaithful partner because it's done in front of friends and others who can see it. Flirting not only sticks the knife in, it twists it too.

Retaliatory Affairs

The logical extension of merely flirting is to have an affair yourself: "If he (she) can do it, I can do it too!" Some betrayed spouses will run out and grab the first person available. But these "knee-jerk" affairs generally turn out to be nothing more than empty sexual flings. In pursuing such an avenue, the betrayed partner is trying to capture what has been lost in the marriage, trying to overcome the emotional castration that has occurred and show that he or she is still a "man" or still a "woman." Thus a retaliatory affair is nothing more than a search for open arms that will give you understanding and compassion. It's a way to find the TLC you feel has been taken away from you. (It's also a way to see what your partner was getting by having an affair. Maybe I've been missing something, many betrayed partners will think.)

But this way of striking back borders on the irrational because it gives the unfaithful partner that much more reason to justify *his* affair: "Hey, great! She's having one now too, so why should I feel guilty?" He'll feel a lot happier now that he doesn't have to carry around any guilt; and that may drive him ever further into his own affair.

"I Want a Divorce!"

The demand for a divorce is probably the most serious retaliatory measure the betrayed partner can take. Many times she'll go to an attorney for advice, in order to protect herself and see where she stands legally. Then she'll go to her spouse and say, "I've seen a lawyer!" It's a not so subtle way of threatening him: "Now I'm going to strike back and make you pay for what you've done to me!" That's like a knife in the heart to him, and he's left there wondering, What do I do now?

But the violated partner's cry for divorce is usually just due to the intensity of the feelings that have come to the surface for her—the sense of betrayal, the emotional rape, the trauma, the disbelief, the anger, hurt, and frustration, and the feeling that everything has been a lie. Oftentimes you'll find that after demanding a divorce, she'll back down on the issue quite rapidly. Even if she's seen an attorney she may not go through with the proceedings.

Of course, the cry for divorce is a flight from dealing with any of the unfulfilled needs that caused the affair. It's a way to avoid taking responsibility and coping with the problem in the marriage. By demanding a divorce, the betrayed partner denies her spouse an opportunity to fight back or do anything to save the relationship: "I don't want anything to do with you anymore! It's over!" Often she doesn't even want to hear the reasons behind the affair—she doesn't want to hear any excuses or rationalizations because her distrust is so strong at that point. The whole trust foundation of the marriage has been shattered, and the belief that everything the couple ever did was a sham prevails: "You just married me for selfish reasons. You used me. I've been a convenience for you. Well, now you can go to hell!"

But in most cases the demand for a divorce is strictly an impulsive reaction, because after so many years in a marriage it's very hard to just put the whole thing on the shelf. How can you take a marriage of ten, fifteen, twenty, twenty-five, or thirty years and just throw it out the window?

THE EFFECTS OF DISCLOSURE ON THE CHILDREN

In the stage before an affair is disclosed, a child's difficulties, though they definitely exist, are subtle and vague, lurking in some "twilight zone" beneath the surface of his consciousness. In the stage following disclosure, these problems come shooting straight up and out into reality—they become very real and tangible and permeate every aspect of the child's daily life. For example, whereas before disclosure a child may misbehave and not know why, after disclosure he'll misbehave purposefully, knowing *exactly* why—and his misbehavior will be much more intense and harmful to himself. Disclosure magnifies all the problems a child has been experiencing up to that point.

It's difficult enough for a husband and wife to have to deal with each other when an affair has been revealed. They must clean up the mess between themselves, as a couple, and they must clean up their own private messes as individuals. Now add to that the element of children, and the mess multiplies. It would be one thing if the partners were healthy and their children were troubled—healthy parents can work wonders with a troubled child. But how can you give your children your utmost attention and your best guidance when you yourself are caught in turmoil?

In addition to experiencing all the problems we saw in Chapter 4—the alienation, the neediness, the social, sexual, and intellectual conflicts—and in a much more magnified way, a child experiences certain dilemmas that are peculiar to the stage following disclosure.

First let's take a look at how the parents themselves interact with their children immediately after an affair has been revealed:

Under the Victim's Wing

One of the first reactions of the betrayed partner following disclosure is to become overly protective of the children in order to save them from the "villain." She'll try to shelter them from the turmoil and conflict they'll sense in the environment. Her every living breath will be devoted to dealing with them and their feelings. She herself will then go through further emotional upheavals on top of the ones she is already experiencing. She'll invest more energy into denying the affair, and she'll feel even more hostility toward her spouse; and her children will tune in to these things and feel fearful of what is happening.

At some point the betrayed partner will generally sit down and try to explain to the children what has happened. They'll often prompt it themselves by asking questions like, "Mommy, where is Daddy? Why isn't he home?" or "Daddy, why did Mommy go away?" Yet there is very little a parent can do to ease the situation for the children, no matter how hard he or she tries, because the conflict has already begun.

The children themselves tend to side with the betrayed partner and nurture her, while at the same time becoming more and more hostile toward the unfaithful partner. What this does is to create a mutual dependency between the betrayed partner and her children. The cheating spouse becomes the outsider and will try to buy back his children's love by getting them gifts, taking them here and there, and doing all kinds of things with them.

Targets of Anger

On a harsher note, sometimes the unfaithful partner will punish the children to release his anger and frustration over his dilemma. Following disclosure both partners are under a great deal of tension. The unfaithful partner especially becomes hostile when he sees his children siding with his spouse. No matter what he does, he feels he is losing his children and cannot bridge the gap between them. Thus he'll strike out irrationally at them, punishing them for the loss of love he feels.

This is one of the factors that many times will cause him to take a closer look at his marriage. Maybe I should reconsider, he'll think. Maybe I should end the affair. I'm losing my children emotionally. They're losing respect for me. They may not even love me anymore. And he'll become very insecure.

Go-betweens

Frequently both partners will use their children as go-betweens by putting each other down through them. For example, the unfaithful partner will make all kinds of excuses to the kids for not getting along with their mother anymore and will slander her to make her look bad in their eyes. It's a way for him to fight back and get the kids caught in the middle, to complicate things. She may paint them a picture of him as a no-good husband and father, a "bum" who runs off with other women and doesn't face his responsibilities at home. Thus the two partners will go back and forth between their children, attacking each other and engaging in all sorts of emotional mudslinging. As a result of being manipulated around in all these different directions, a child will become very confused and will start to develop emotional problems. The trouble is that he must decipher all of the information and double messages he's getting from his parents and figure out which one is telling the truth, which one is honest and authentic. He's torn apart at the seams because he feels an obligation and a desire to love *both* parents; yet every time he tries to seek out the truth he gets two violently opposing viewpoints.

Even though the child may have the betrayed parent at home to comfort him, he'll be torn apart with guilt. It doesn't matter that Daddy had the affair, he'll feel. Daddy's still out there alone now, and he's no longer a part of the family. "When will I see him?" "When will he come home?" "Will he still be my Daddy?" These are all questions a child will ask himself. And all sorts of magnified fears will come about because he'll have no answers to these questions.

Uncertainty

The child's dilemma in this situation can be summed up in one word: uncertainty. At the onset of disclosure there is tremendous uncertainty for everybody, which creates total confusion for the child. With both parents fighting over him and trying to win him over, he's the one who's going to lose. He'll feel abandoned, distrustful, and uncertain that he's loved anymore. He'll feel totally insecure and inadequate because of his fears about what will happen to him. The only thing that will conquer his conflict is certainty.

Until certainty is there for the child, whether the marriage is destined to work or not, he will basically be stuck in a tension-producing, abandonment-oriented frame of mind. He won't know if he's really loved; he'll feel responsible for his parents' conflicts at some level; and either he'll be overprotected or he'll suffer the brunt of the outbursts caused by one or both parents' inability to cope.

Internalization

As long as there is uncertainty for a child in this situation, he will tend to acquire in himself all the negativity and tension he sees in his environment. He'll push everything inward and become very internalized, which will then cause all sorts of emotional problems and fears. He'll feel very vulnerable walking around school, and he won't really know how to relate to his friends when he goes to their homes. He'll feel everyone knows his secret. Often his friends' parents will go out of their way to try to make him feel better. But no matter what anyone does he'll feel uptight and alone.

A child holds in all of his feelings because he is confused. How can he sort out the reality of what's happening to him if both his parents are giving him opposing viewpoints? One parent is trying to protect him, the other trying to win him back—or both are trying to protect him. How does he figure out what's right? And, more importantly, how does he figure out what to do?

His internalization is made worse by the fact that he has no outlet for communication. He won't want to turn to one parent and not the other; yet if he goes to both he'll get two different stories again. This frustrates him, and his frustration will build into anger—anger at either both parents for trapping him in the middle or at the unfaithful partner for being at the bottom of the whole mess. His anger then develops into problems at school and problems with friends. He'll try to reach out for help and affection, even if it means indulging in negative behavior once again. He'll try to get his parents to rescue him, to see if they still love him.

Sexual Conflict

The turmoil of this stage has a strong effect on a child's sexual growth and development. In addition to suffering from the sexual problems cited in Chapter 4, if he is identifying strongly with one parent's role and begins to get angry at that parent, that can impede his sexual development. If he's in a very delicate, impressionable stage in his sexual development and discovers that a parent is having an affair, that can cause him to become angry at all women or all men. Or he could get stuck in his anger and choose to identify with the parent of the opposite sex—which would then totally confuse his sex-role identification.

From all the havoc in his environment a child may wonder, Is this what love really is? And if so, what's the purpose of it? He may feel guilty about a lot of his own sexual strivings because he doesn't have an outlet for talking about them. Or he may feel bad about himself in general and choose to hide his sexual feelings and just put them on the shelf.

Another option is to go to the other extreme. For example, if a young girl is at the age where her sexuality is just starting to blossom, she may seek out some kind of temporary emotional satisfaction and acceptance through promiscuity.

Little Matchmakers

To counter all the uncertainty and alleviate all the anxieties of this stage, a child will often become the mediator and attempt to bring his parents back together again. This generally happens when he sees any heightened tension between the two. (Children respond very strongly to any visible conflict between their parents.) He'll try to get in the middle and make things better: "Mommy, Daddy, why don't you be nice to each other? Why don't you get together?" Or he'll corner them separately: "Daddy, why don't you be nice to Mommy?" and vice versa. He'll try to bond them back together by being the "healer" and the "rescuer," sometimes suggesting common activities: "Why don't we all go to a movie together?" or "Let's all go to Disneyland!"

Yet the matchmaker role is a highly dangerous one for a child to be in, for it's a dead-end street until he feels some certainty about his parents' relationship to each other and to him. Unless his parents attempt to pave the way back to some kind of reunification, his efforts will be doomed to end in utter disappointment and dispair.

Thus we see that unhealthy disclosure of an affair creates turmoil all around. Many people feel that divorce is the quickest, easiest way out of the whole trauma surrounding the incident. Yet don't be deceived. An unnecessary divorce has severe consequences to both partners and their children.

Many marriages end because the spouses are not willing to look at the truth about themselves and each other. I would venture to say that at least 50 percent of those marriages ending in divorce could potentially be saved if both partners were willing to take the time and have the patience necessary to uncover and deal with their hurt and pain. Were they willing to learn to communicate effectively and deal with their feelings and fears, they would open the door to many positive things—and ultimately create from a sense of wreckage a sense of community.

When a marriage ends needlessly in divorce, the couple's children are left in a whirlwind of uncertainty and insecurity. If they remain with the mother—which is generally the tradition—she must become both mother and father to them. She'll have to take on the behaviors of both role models and may even have to become the provider in order to secure more income for her family. All of this can throw a child's role-model identification totally out of whack.

While an unnecessary divorce creates pressure on the parent

who retains physical custody because of the double role he or she must play, it creates pressure on the other parent as well because of the feeling that he or she is missing the chance to watch the child grow and develop every single day.

The children themselves are forced to deal with and adapt to a completely new environment in all ways. They must adjust to having a part-time mother or father. They must adjust to having a parent who functions as *both* mother and father. And they must eventually adjust to the reality that that parent will start dating. At some point the dating parent will want to introduce his or her companion to the children. Each time this happens—and chances are it will happen a number of times before the parent remarries—it will be a traumatic experience for the parent. For the children it will create first suspicion, then high hopes, then ultimately disappointment, in most cases, when the relationship doesn't work out.

What a tragic state for a good family to end up in!

Part Two

RECONSTRUCTIVE DYNAMICS

INTRODUCTION

Reconstructive Dynamics: "reconstructive" in the sense that you are going to reconstruct your marriage and "dynamic" in the sense that you and your partner are going to take a dynamic, or active, role in that reconstruction. The next four chapters will take you through a seven-stage process that will allow you to save your marriage. These stages are: Admission, Ventilation, Identification, Vulnerability, Communion, Acceptance, and Reunion. You may not experience each stage in the order presented; for example, it is entirely possible to experience Vulnerability during the Ventilation stage. This is fine. The act of writing a book dictates that I must organize and structure an emotional process, which is by its very definition somewhat anarchic. Keep this in mind as you progress through Reconstructive Dynamics. Rather than thinking of the various stages as clearly defined steps leading directly to a destination, think of them as broad terrains with no visible borders. All I can say is that you will touch upon them all, and when you arrive at say, Vulnerability, Communion, or Acceptance, you will be aware of it. Along the way I will post "checkpoints," which will enable you to examine how thoroughly you completed the previous stage.

The volcano of emotions you have suppressed for months, perhaps years, has exploded or is about to. In either case serious damage has been done to your marriage. The fact that you are reading this book confirms your willingness to repair the damage. But how? If you are the faithful partner your first impulse was possibly to cry, "divorce!" You have given up that irrational decision. Now what? If you are the unfaithful partner you may have decided to end your extramarital affair. As we have seen, however, the lover fulfilled an important role in your life. How can you give that up? And even if you make the rational decision to do so, how can you guarantee that thoughts of your lover will not insidiously disrupt your relationship with your spouse? Clearly, for both partners, what you must do to save your marriage will not be easy. But it can be done, as you will see.

Reconstructive Dynamics provides a structure within which you and your partner can understand why the affair occurred and how you can overcome it. This process will give you the tools you need to clear yourselves emotionally, to understand each other's needs and to come to terms with what you must do to satisfy those needs—thereby strengthening your marriage and reuniting the two of you into a solid, stable entity. The key to overcoming the trauma of an affair is making your marriage *better* than anything a third party could offer. Believe it or not, many couples succeed in doing this, and they actually feel closer to one another after the Reconstructive Dynamics than they ever had before. So can you.

If you have even the slightest desire to see your marriage survive, you owe it to yourself (and your children, if you have any) to work through Reconstructive Dynamics. It is most effective for those couples who want to stay together and make things work between them; but even if you feel that your relationship cannot work, and you choose to get a divorce, at least you will know, with certainty, that you gave it everything you had. If you do Reconstructive Dynamics the way it should be done, with commitment and intensity, you will have the self-knowledge to make the difficult choice whether to stay with your partner or not. You may very well decide that your spouse will never be able to fulfill your needs; or he/she may conclude that your needs are unreasonable. At least you will be satisfied for having tried; and you will have under your belt a deep, meaningful experience of opening yourself up to communicating with another person. You will also have a sense of completeness with your spouse, which will prevent you from recycling the same old emotional garbage into later relationships. Nothing could be more destructive than carrying anger and resentment into a new relationship. After Reconstructive Dynamics, one way or the other, you will have a sense of completeness and a will to begin your life anew.

Let me give you a brief breakdown of the phases of Reconstructive Dynamics. In the first three stages, Admission, Ventilation, and Identification (Chapters 6 and 7), you bring out the underlying causes of the affair, and you get an intense awareness of your own and your partner's feelings. Admission, Ventilation, and Identification will bring out things about you and your partner that you never came to terms with before. You will discover both good and bad things about yourself and your spouse, things you should have known long ago, things which, because they were suppressed for so long, contributed to the breakdown of your relationship. Once you have confronted them together, you can begin to rebuild.

In Chapter 8, Vulnerability and Communion, you transcend your hurt, guilt, and anger to achieve a clear perspective on your marriage. With a better understanding of yourself and your partner, you can go beyond the initial flood of feelings you experienced after disclosure of the affair and start to integrate the self-knowledge you have gained in the initial stages of Reconstructive Dynamics. The key concept in these stages is self-knowledge. Confronting deeply felt emotions, though sometimes terrifying at first, will teach you valuable things about yourself, which will make you a stronger person.

In Vulnerability and Communion we will discuss what you have been denying yourself by holding back feelings. You will understand that you weren't really the person you thought you were, that you have spent enormous amounts of energy trying to avoid being vulnerable, and that these misplaced efforts have prevented you from blossoming as a person. In Chapter 8 we will show you how important it is to genuinely experience your feelings, no matter what they are. By this point in Reconstructive Dynamics, you have discharged the hurt and anger and achieved a sort of catharsis, which leads to marital bonding. You will actually be able to observe harmony in your relationship. By the time you finish Vulnerability and Communion, you will understand clearly why your relationship eroded to the point it did, and you will be ready to use the valuable communication skills you have acquired to prevent erosion in the future.

In Chapter 9, Acceptance and Reunion, you apply what you have learned in the previous stages to your relationship in order to maintain the harmony you have established. Marriages don't just work all by themselves. They need surveillance and maintenance. We will discuss what it means to be a co-facilitator—how to help each other work through the various cycles of life and adapt to the inevitable changes we all undergo. The key tools in maintaining harmony are: (1) an understanding of the cycles of life; (2) planning the future; (3) negotiation and conflict resolution skills. In Acceptance and Reunion we will show you how to use the communication skills you have perfected in order to prevent emotional garbage from being continually recycled into your lives.

Just one final word before you begin Reconstructive Dynamics. After an affair, couples tend to retreat to emotional sanctuaries. That is, they sometimes get back together without really confronting the issues that caused the affair. They reunite for the sake of the children or because they fear being alone. If you do this you will merely recycle old patterns. Your failure to communicate will leave loose ends lying around that will haunt you. Do you sense that this may be happening to you? If so, you will *never*—and I give you my written guarantee—experience anything akin to marital harmony. In fact, I can almost certainly guarantee that sometime in the near future you will once again live through the emotional trauma of an affair.

A loose end, or incomplete communication with your partner, is merely a refusal to take responsibility. When you refuse to let go of the hurt, anger, resentment, and guilt an affair creates, your spontaneity and your sense of aliveness are stifled. You will stagnate, for it is impossible to grow emotionally when you are caged in by your unexpressed feelings. They control you and make you very unhappy. There is, unfortunately, something very comforting in maintaining old patterns, even destructive ones. Through Reconstructive Dynamics, you and your partner will help one another overcome your fear of confronting the issues between you, and you will come to understand why you resist change and growth in your relationship. By the time you finish Reconstructive Dynamics, you will have done a frightening thing; you will have broken patterns that seemed carved in stone; you will have changed.

Chapter 6

ADMISSION AND VENTILATION

ADMISSION: CLEANSING THE PRESENT

In the Admission stage, the unfaithful partner, quite obviously, admits that he or she had an extramarital affair. At the same time, the faithful partner hears what are probably the most painful words anyone had ever spoken to her (or him). It would be sheer folly to suggest that this can be done without great pain and emotional upheaval. But there is certainly one way that is better than others. In this chapter both the faithful and the unfaithful partner will be given guidelines that not only will facilitate the actual disclosure of the affair but minimize the likelihood that either partner will make any irrational cry for divorce. The goal of this and all stages of Reconstructive Dynamics is not to eliminate pain but to control whatever destructive reactions either partner might have and, ultimately, to keep you and your partner working together to save your marriage.

As the facts of the affair unravel, feelings will come up that will frighten, threaten, and confuse you. Before you get started, I'd like to offer four critical guidelines that will help to avoid the pitfalls the disclosure process places before you.

1. No Dumping.

Dumping, simply put, is blaming your partner: "It's all your fault. Why did you do this to me? I trusted you and you shamelessly betrayed me." Or, "You were totally insensitive to my needs. I had no choice but to go out and have an affair because you were so apathetic and unsupportive."

When we start confronting deep feelings, our first impulse is often to give someone else the blame for *our* problems. It is comforting to be a victim sometimes. It is also very cowardly, an easy solution that clears us of all responsibility. Emotional garbage dumping is a form of scapegoating. It includes all forms of judgment, unconstructive criticism, and accusation. Some very ugly things might come up when you and your partner start communicating again. Allow them to come up. Vent them. But don't spill them all over your partner. Confront your *own* emotional garbage and take responsibility for it!

2. Use "I" Language.

One way to ensure that you take responsibility for your feelings and actions is to use "I" language. When you use "I" language you keep the focus of communication on yourself: "I feel hurt" or "I needed more affection from you." "I" language allows you to take responsibility for what *you* are feeling or what *you* did, without putting blame on the other person. There is far less dumping when "I" language is used. Even if you are talking about the past, you want to keep the focus on *your* feelings: "I felt I wasn't getting enough support," rather than, "You didn't support me." Do you see the difference?

Avoid "you" language: "You made me do this. You weren't giving me what I needed." When you speak this way you put the other person in an active role and make him or her the agent who perpetrated what you perceive as an evil deed. That makes you look blameless, a passive victim. "You" language is nothing but poorly camouflaged dumping.

Also avoid "we" language: "Well, we just weren't getting along. We didn't seem happy together." "We" language takes responsibility for *both* of you. You don't necessarily know what your partner feels or felt. Speaking solely for yourself is essential because it allows focused and unambiguous communication. It prevents imbalances, such as those that occur when you attack the other person or take responsibility for his or her feelings and actions.

Even "it" language can be dangerous. Avoid nebulous statements such as, "It makes me angry." What is "it"? These statements are vague and nondescriptive. They don't tell your partner anything and merely serve to protect you. When we don't want to take responsibility for what we feel, we state things in a convoluted way. Such communication is manipulative and implies the speaker is unwilling to confront his own responsibility.

3. Learn to Listen.

You and your partner must be mutually supportive while expressing feelings. That means that when one person is speaking, the other is listening. Be caring, empathetic, and sensitive. Allow your partner to experience whatever comes up. The best way to sabotage your partner's attempt to vent his feelings is to interject antagonistically in order to prove that you are right and your partner is wrong. This is not a debate, a win or lose situation. On the contrary, you want to support your partner and allow his or her feelings to emerge to the point of completion. That way you both win.

At some point each partner must be the recipient of the other's feelings and also be able to deal with his or her own feelings at the same time. In essence, you have to train yourself to deal with two things at once. You have to put your impulses on hold and listen while, at the same time, you work through your own feelings. If you both vent at the same time, it won't work. Learn to listen.

4. Keep the Lines of Communication Open.

One final but very important tip. At some point during the Admission stage, one or both partners may feel he needs a rest, a certain period of time to gather his thoughts, to cry, or just to be alone. This is fine, even to be encouraged, because a break can provide the distance necessary to view the situation objectively. But be very careful not to let the communication stop there. Don't leave yourselves hanging; this could cause you to fall into a pattern of avoidance. Make sure your "pit stops" are only temporary.

In this first step of Reconstructive Dynamics you are laying the foundation of a new relationship. In Admission, you will be doing things with your partner that you have probably never done before. The ability to communicate is a skill that you may not be very adept at. Here you will be communicating on a level of frankness and candor that will seem frightening at first but which will eventually allow you to overcome your barriers and achieve intimacy and trust. These are the rewards for having had the courage to talk to one another openly. You will get better and better at it as you progress through Reconstructive Dynamics. By the time you finish— actually you will never really finish—you will have the ability to communicate fluidly and naturally.

In Admission your goal is to cleanse the present of all the emotional garbage that has accumulated since the advent of the affair. In the second stage, Ventilation, we will bring to the surface feelings that have lingered for a much longer time, but for the moment we are going to focus on suppressed feelings, which have a more immediate effect on you and your partner. The role each partner must play in order to facilitate the Admission process is quite different, so let's look at them one at a time.

AFFAIR PARTNER

For the unfaithful partner, this is a time to allow yourself to vent your feelings in a constructive atmosphere and to allow yourself to account for your extramarital activities in a positive, nonstressful environment. Certainly, this is going to be a frightful phase, because you will have to reveal everything that has been held inside about the affair—all you have hidden and lied about, all you have covered up for so long. The payoff for being open and honest is a tremendous sense of relief, an unburdening.

You may have another partner to go to who's willing to fulfill all of your needs. You may think he or she will solve all the problems you encountered with your spouse. Yet what if you leave your marriage and then find out it made you happier than you thought it did? And what if your affair loses all its romance and fulfillment once it becomes routine? Sadly, we never know what we have until we lose it. If you've put as many years into your marriage as you have already, why walk away from it without at least giving yourself an opportunity to find out what your marriage has the potential to be?

You want something that is behind a door; that something is love. Have you been tapping too gently at your spouse's door, so gently that he or she couldn't even hear you? Have you been participating in your marriage halfheartedly for reasons that have more to do with you than with your spouse? In Reconstructive Dynamics I am going to encourage you to go all out for a while. You are going to pound on that door with all your heart and give your spouse the opportunity to reply. He or she may not, but this way you will never have to look back in regret and say, "Oh my God, what did I give up when I left my partner?"

The Admission stage, indeed all of Reconstructive Dynamics, constitutes an alternative to an empty "I'm sorry" from the unfaithful partner. You could apologize for the rest of your life, but it wouldn't be satisfying to either you or your spouse.

Reconstructive Dynamics is a process that will allow you to do much more than feel sorry, which is really nothing more than feeling guilty. It will allow you to feel trust, intimacy, and love, which represent an infinitely more meaningful statement to your partner.

The Facts; Nothing But the Facts!

Essentially, the first order of business is to tell your partner how the affair started and how long it has been going on. The more open and honest you can be about these things, the better it's going to be for both of you in the long run. Talk about what you feel led up to the affair, why you felt the need to seek someone outside your marriage. What needs did you feel weren't being satisfied? Tell your partner directly, "I felt as if I couldn't approach you physically, and this created a lot of frustration." Or, "I needed support and encouragement in my new job, and I didn't feel you were giving it." Be candid without being accusatory. You don't have to go into great detail at this stage, as we will be doing in the later stages of Reconstructive Dynamics. But get into your feelings about what you felt you were missing. Why did you need to step outside your marriage? What were you looking for that your spouse couldn't give you?

Second, it's important that you go into some detail about the logistics of the affair. How often did you see the third party? Where did you meet? What did you do together? What were the various aspects of your relationship? Who knows about the affair? Friends? Family? People at work? This may seem like rubbing salt in your partner's wounds. Though it may hurt your spouse to hear these things, the more information you give him or her, the clearer a picture he or she will have of what was missing in your marriage. Also, your partner will not be plagued by nagging questions, such as, Did he take her to *our* favorite restaurant? Was he with her on our wedding anniversary last month? Is *everybody* at work aware that my spouse cheated on me?

Third, it is crucial that you talk about the invisible third party. You don't have to reveal him or her by name or identity, but you want to reveal their personality and characteristics. What was she like physically, sexually, emotionally, intellectually? How did she make you feel? What did she do for you? What was that person able to give you that your spouse could not? Do not allow this to become a comparison. You are not comparing; you are describing objectively in order to achieve understanding.

Normally, the unfaithful partner likes to keep these details hidden from his spouse. He won't want to reveal any of this information because it is "private," or because he feels it will be too painful for his spouse to hear. It reminds him of his guilt as well. But you must realize that if you do not reveal the character of your lover and what this person contributed to your relationship, your spouse will never know what she is up against. There is no way your spouse can compete with an invisible third person. You *must* reveal who that person is in great detail, even though it is upsetting to both you and your spouse. Give your partner a thorough, objective picture of the third party so that she can understand what you got out of having an affair.

Keep in mind that if you do not do this, your partner will always be wondering in the back of her mind, What was she like? What did she give him that I didn't? The more you tell your spouse about the third party, the better your partner can understand what created the affair and what the underlying motives were. Think of this as the first step in getting to the root of the problem. You and your partner do not want to get back together just to avoid divorce. You don't want to apply an emotional Band-Aid to your marriage. You want to dig through the deep and complex feelings you are experiencing and discover the root of your problems. Only then can you

truly heal your relationship with the most therapeutic medicine of all: trust.

The partner who has had the affair must understand that
during the Admission phase his spouse is going to experience a
wide range of conflicting emotions. Even though she may have
already experienced these feelings as a result of an earlier, less
structured disclosure of yours, that does not mean they will
not come up again. Emotions that come up in ways I described
in the chapter on disclosure (anger, impulsivity, hostility, vengeance, and the cry for divorce) often recycle again later on at
some level. She may feel things for you directly or indirectly
and with varying degrees of intensity. It is very likely that at
some point during your Admission your spouse will break
down. She might cry uncontrollably, she might become extremely angry. Allow her to experience her emotions. Do not
fight back. You should understand that expressing anger is just
as much a cleansing process for your spouse as admission is for
you. It is a healthy process in which your partner is unloading
a burden, and you should not view it with a critical or accusatory eye any more than you would want your spouse to view
your admission as such.

You may be scared at the thought of having to admit your
activities to your partner. If so, you have good reason to feel
the way you do. But consider for a moment the consequences
of keeping things from your spouse. Think of the burden you
will carry with you in the future. Unless you have extraordi-
nary powers of denial—which is a problem in itself—keeping
secrets will mar every moment of intimacy you will experience with your partner. You will constantly have nagging
thoughts: This is all a lie. Would she be here with me if she
knew that . . . ? By keeping secrets from your partner, you reinforce the fantasies caused by your unfulfilled needs and risk
locking yourself into a continual pattern of infidelity. True intimacy cannot be achieved until both partners have opened
channels for communication by being completely honest with
each other. Paradoxical though it may seem, by admitting

your activities you open the door to trust. And from trust emerges the capacity to love. Since love is your ultimate goal, this stage should be handled with the utmost seriousness and commitment. In it you lay the foundation for marital harmony.

FAITHFUL PARTNER

If you are the faithful partner, you are reading this book for one of two reasons; either you believe your partner is having an affair and you want to know what to do, or your partner has just told you that he had an affair and you want to know how to handle your anger and hurt. In either case your goal is to save your marriage or at least to give it a chance. In either case you must create an emotional atmosphere in which your partner can vent his feelings in a nonthreatening way. This may sound preposterous. You are feeling deep hurt and possibly violent anger. You feel, as I pointed out earlier, as if you've been emotionally raped. And yet I am now asking you to empathize with your partner, your "assailant." You must, by being empathetic and understanding, create a context in which your partner can express the reasons why he had an affair.

The first thing you must realize is that your partner feels extremely guilty about what he did. The Admission stage will be hurtful for you, but you can be sure it will be excruciating for your partner. He has betrayed you, and he knows it. The breach of trust he has created cuts right to his heart. As painful as it may seem, your job is to listen noncritically, nonjudgmentally, to your partner as he "admits" the circumstances of the affair. If you don't allow yourself to hear the sordid details, if you insist on denying them, you will carry with you the fantasy of the third party, and that will perpetuate the feelings of inadequacy you now feel.

Remember, it takes three to make an affair. You no doubt feel wounded at this point, but your partner experienced a form of emotional injury as well; a deep need of his was not being fulfilled. The immediate goal of the Admission stage is for your partner to admit that he had an affair and to express his reasons for doing so. Your job is to make your partner talk. If you see some hesitancy, you can take an active role by giving him permission to speak freely.

If you are one of those persons Chapter 1 was aimed at—i.e., you suspect your spouse of having an affair but he or she hasn't admitted it yet—then you need to set the stage for an admission. You must sit him or her down and convey the concept expressed by the following hypothetical person in your own situation:

> Dear, I want you to know that I love you and care about you, and whatever happens between us, I really want to work things out with you. I've been noticing that things are not quite right lately, and I don't really know why. I've noticed little things that make me wonder if you are having an affair. Before you get upset, let me say that I may be very, very wrong. If so, then I want to communicate with you and find out what it is that's causing me to feel this way. If I'm right, I want you to know that I can handle this, and I'm willing to deal with it. I'm not going to cry "divorce"!

What should strike you here is the speaker's candor. The essence of what she says is, "There is something wrong, and I feel it might be an affair." I think it's important to articulate your suspicions very frankly. If you're wrong about the affair, that's okay. You certainly weren't wrong about the feeling. There is something wrong in your relationship, one way or the other; your next step is to correct it.

Let's say you were right about the affair. You still have to create a context that will allow your partner to speak freely. We'll let our hypothetical person continue:

> I want you to explain to me the reasons you felt the need to have an affair. I may get emotional, I may get angry, I may

show signs of deep hurt. I have been holding these feelings in for a long time, but I haven't been confronting them, so they may come up, and I might not be able to control them. I ask you to help me do that. I may be critical and judgmental of you—if I am, point it out to me in a gentle way, and I will try to regroup. Let's work this thing out together. Talk to me, tell me what you're feeling. I'm here for you, and I love you, and I want us to be happy.

It would be very difficult for the other partner to be anything less than sincere when given such permission to admit the affair. An accepting, nurturing attitude allows him to open up. On the other hand, if you act belligerently, you will immediately activate defense mechanisms in your partner and cause him to close down. Even in this nurturing, supportive context, however, you are going to feel pain when you hear the details of your spouse's affair. Experience the pain. Tell your partner that it hurts. If you must, tell your partner that you need a moment to get your bearings. The greatest danger at this stage of Reconstructive Dynamics is the temptation to use this as an opportunity for vengeance or punishment. It is very hard for someone who is being open, honest, and vulnerable to accept punishment.

Interpret; Don't React

A word of warning to both partners. You must both understand that whatever comes up between you in verbal form is merely the surface manifestations of a deep, heartfelt emotion. If during your Admission your spouse becomes uncontrollably angry, you might be tempted to say, "Here I am opening up to you, being honest and candid, and you throw it in my face!" Avoid such a reaction. Don't *react;* observe what comes up in your partner and try to *interpret* it. When you are able to observe your partner's feelings without reacting to them, you create an emotional atmosphere in which it is acceptable to experience any feeling that may come up. This is your goal.

While listening to your spouse's admission, you may become infuriated by something he says. You may feel your partner is manipulating you or that he is trying to put the blame on you. Again, it is essential to interpret here, not to react. Try to understand that manipulations and pouring the blame on you are very superficial, often transparent, ways of handling the guilt the unfaithful partner feels. Channel your anger to a positive end; calmly tell your partner, "I feel that you are being manipulative. Try to be more candid and to the point." When you react with an expression of anger, your partner naturally becomes defensive, and you will be further from the truth than ever. The secret is to create a context in which your partner can express his feelings without feeling threatened. Give him permission to tell the truth. Eventually, he will.

The act of admission should be viewed as a very healthy, constructive process. Taking responsibility for his actions allows the unfaithful partner to see things more objectively and will give him insight into the reasons for seeking out a lover. It takes courage to see things as they really are; and it takes integrity. And think of the freedom it will afford both of you in the long run.

The Admission stage is an unraveling of the facts about an affair. In it, the essential thing is to create an environment in which that can happen in the least traumatic and least destructive way possible. This process acts as a catalyst that brings forth a lot of related emotional garbage. You cannot predict what will emerge at this point. But you must be able to deal with just about anything.

This may be the first time in your marriage that you have communicated so openly with one another. You may experience awkwardness, fear, guilt, even persecution. Feelings will be magnified out of proportion, and you will experience uncertainty about yourself and about the future of your relationship. But bear in mind at all times that true intimacy cannot be achieved until both partners have opened the channels of communication by being completely honest with one another. From the openness and honesty emerges trust, and from trust emerges the capacity to love. This is a very important stage of Reconstructive Dynamics—one you will want to go through with the utmost commitment.

CHECKPOINT NUMBER 1

This is the first in a series of checkpoints that will give you the opportunity to examine how successfully you are progressing through Reconstructive Dynamics. Ask yourself now whether or not you have thoroughly cleansed the present of all doubts and uncertainties concerning the affair.

The unfaithful partner must ask himself (or herself), Have I held back something in order to protect myself? Is there something I'm keeping from my spouse that will prevent her from feeling complete about my involvement in the affair?

The faithful partner must interrogate herself (or himself) as well. Is there something about the third party I really want to know but am afraid to inquire about? Is there something that will haunt me later on if I don't confront it now? I knew a man who was obsessed about whether or not his wife had ever slept with her lover in the conjugal bed. It turned out she hadn't, but he let weeks go by before finding the courage to bring up this nagging doubt that tormented him.

I remind you that the purpose of Admission is to cleanse the present, to reveal all secrets concerning the affair. Failure to be honest at this point will compromise the integrity of your experience of Reconstructive Dynamics. Before you go on to Ventilation: Cleansing the Past, be sure that you have tied up all loose ends regarding the affair.

VENTILATION: CLEANSING THE PAST

The Admission stage focused primarily on the unfaithful partner. The goal of Admission was to get him (or her) to reveal the details of the affair. In Ventilation, both partners will do a lot of talking, expressing deep, suppressed feelings that have been stewing for a long, long time. The goal of Ventilation is to release feelings each partner has been holding on to and to do it in a healthy, rational way. Admission was really only a warmup for Ventilation, which you may find to be the most difficult stage of Reconstructive Dynamics. Once the details of the affair have come out, both partners will very likely feel a sense of relief, perhaps even a renewed sense of intimacy, but you are by no means out of the woods yet. You still have to confront all of the incompletions that still exist in your relationship.

Ventilation is a stage of great self-discovery, but the knowledge you will gain about yourself will not come easily. It is extremely difficult to express deep-seated emotions. We have all sorts of reasons for keeping feelings to ourselves, no matter how destructive such behavior can be. In Ventilation you must take a lot of *risks*. No emotional growth takes place in life without taking risks.

Blame

Once the details of the affair are out in the open, complex feelings are going to emerge. The first impulse of both partners may be to blame the other. This is a perfectly normal reaction; it is always nice to believe that it's someone else's fault. But you must recognize that the impulse to blame is nothing more than a refusal to take responsibility. Blame blinds. When you convince yourself that the other is at fault, you lose all motivation to see your own behavior for what it really is. Blame is a defense mechanism we use to protect ourselves. Recognize it as such: an obstacle to self-awareness.

Catharsis

Catharsis is a word, usually associated with Greek tragedy, that literally means "purgation" or "purification." It has puzzled philosophers for centuries that rather than feeling depressed, as one might expect, audiences feel exalted and spiritually renewed when they see tragic representations of suffering and defeat on the stage. Catharsis is the word we use to explain this phenomenon. It is a fact that by bringing feelings to the surface, and thereby affording them expression, we release the tension those feelings created, and we feel better.

Our lives have more in common with Greek theater than you might think. The themes in great literature are always eminently human, and I assure you that the knot of conflicting emotions created by an affair is every bit as real to you as Oedipus's complex was to him.

Ventilation is a form of catharsis. In this state of Reconstructive Dynamics, you want to create a context in which even the most horrifying emotions can be vented. This is an opportunity for self-disclosure, which will free you from emotions that have been locked inside and have been expressing themselves as anger, resentment, guilt, bitterness, and fear.

Submerging the Beach Ball

It is crucial that both partners support one another during the Ventilation stage. Expressing emotions that have been pent up for years can be excruciating, and if you see that your partner is having trouble, you may want to coach him. You will notice that you and your partner will be communicating on a number of different levels. Your goal is to go as deeply as possible. In the hierarchy of levels of expression, blame is the most superficial, and, of course, the easiest to dwell on. Assist your partner in his or her attempt to discover the deepest possible level of expression. Sometimes it takes more than just good intentions to dig to the root of a problem. If you work together, though, you can make it.

Let me give an analogy that illustrates what happens during Ventilation. Imagine that getting your partner to reach the deepest level of feeling is like trying to keep a fully inflated beach ball submerged in water. Your partner's defense mechanisms resist delving deeper and try to bring your communication to a more superficial level, just as the air in a beach ball causes it to rise to the surface. Your job is to keep the ball submerged. If you see that your partner is consciously or unconsciously refusing to delve deeper, you must tell him so. You might say, "I sense that you are being evasive" or, "It seems to me that you are unwilling to go one step further and confront the real issue between us."

As you attempt such gut-to-gut communication with your partner, you will see how the beach ball struggles to reach the surface. When the going gets tough, you may find that either you or your partner change the subject or create distractions in order to relieve the tension. These are defense mechanisms. Going deeper means opening oneself up, which can cause uneasiness. We have been emotionally conditioned to protect ourselves, even from those closest to us, and expressing our deepest needs and our most hidden fears is downright frightening. When confronting a feeling, your mind will be searching for a way out—a phone call must be made, dinner must go in the oven, something good is on TV. Be aware of these contrived distractions. If you feel you can't go on, just say so. Tell your partner, "Please, give me a moment to get a grip on myself." Be honest. It's perfectly all right to stop for a while, as long as you don't allow communication to *remain* incomplete.

Creating a Safe Emotional Atmosphere

When you are in the supportive role, be frank, but give your partner the impression that you want to help him vent his true feelings and that it is okay for him to do so. Creating an emotional atmosphere in which it is "safe" to vent feelings is absolutely essential. The key element in such an atmosphere is *trust*. As we will see later, in Vulnerability and in Communion, expressing one's true feelings, especially hidden ones, is liberating, and it leads to trust and the ability to love.

The consequences of refusing to confront true feelings can be devastating. The following case history provides a case in point. Allan, a construction worker, and his wife Beth had been married seven years when Allan discovered his wife had been having an affair. He was furious, so furious, in fact, that he became violent and beat her. The reasons for the affair were classic. Allan had been unemployed for several months, and his self-esteem was very low; Beth had recently begun a new job, was advancing rapidly, and was feeling very good about herself. This created tension in the relationship, and Beth, unable to find gratification at home, found it with someone at work.

Allan's first reaction was to blame Beth for ruining their marriage. He refused to take any responsibility whatsoever for the affair and immediately filed for divorce. I encountered Allan several years later when he was having difficulties in his second marriage. It took several months of counseling and numerous attempts to probe deeper into what Allan was feeling, but finally he found the courage to express what had really happened with his first wife. Allan admitted that, in fact, his depression during the period of unemployment had made him impotent and that he was convinced that this inability to perform sexually had caused Beth to leave him. Not surprisingly, his impotence had carried over into his second marriage, and, sure enough, that was what had caused his current problems.

Allan's case provides a stark example of how failure to confront emotional issues can wreak havoc in our lives. Had he been willing to confront the role his impotence played in causing Beth to seek out an affair partner, he might have been able to save his first marriage, and he most certainly could have avoided having the problem recycle itself in his second marriage. In any case, he could have spared himself a great deal of emotional trauma.

Vent It!

You can spare yourself a lot of grief and anguish by opening up to your partner and telling it like it is. But what is there to say? If you ask yourself that question, I would suggest that a defense mechanism is at work. Deep down you know there is plenty to say. The faithful partner must, at the very outset, vent his or her anger and hurt. It is essential to verbalize emotions. Say to your partner, "I feel hurt, deeply hurt, by what you have done. I feel rejected. I feel inadequate. I am very angry at you." It may be perfectly obvious to both you and your partner that you are feeling these things—so why say them? Because actually saying "I feel rejected" is not the same as feeling rejected. When you say it, you confront it. You experience your feeling of rejection verbally. I would even encourage you to write down on a piece of paper, "I feel rejected." That way you experience it on still another level, the visual one. Remember, the goal of this stage of Reconstructive Dynamics is to ventilate feelings. The best way I know to do that is simply to state them.

Once you have confronted your immediate feelings about the affair, delve deeper into your most hidden feelings, all those unexpressed emotions that have come up over the years of marriage. Examine the incompleteness between yourself and your spouse. Allow feelings to pour out of you uncensored. If at any point in your relationship you felt unloved, say so. You may at some point in your marriage have felt terribly insecure, or you might have been insanely jealous; or you may have been deeply hurt by something your spouse did but is not aware of. Whatever comes up, *vent it!*

The Ventilation stage is no picnic for the unfaithful partner, by the way. How many times have I seen cases in which people will have an affair, not because of dissatisfaction with their spouse but because they feel deep insecurity about losing their "touch" with the opposite sex? All they needed was a bit of ego-stroking, and the affair merely confirmed that they still had the old charm. If that is the case with you, admit it: "I had an affair because I didn't feel pretty anymore; I felt that no man could be attracted to me." Or, "I had an affair because I felt insecure about my manhood. I needed to prove that I could still 'perform.'" Again, it is essential to verbalize your feelings. It's very hard for a woman to admit that she felt unattractive or for a man to admit that he is insecure, especially about his virility. This stage of Reconstructive Dynamics, however, is about expressing deepset emotions, even troubling ones. You may not even be aware of your motivations for having an affair. If you confront yourself tenaciously and with commitment, Ventilation can be a stage of great self-discovery in which you find out what really makes you tick.

When something significant comes to mind, it may scare you. That tingle in your stomach will tell you not to let go of that feeling, to keep it inside where it belongs. Maybe you didn't tell your wife that the reason you were so unbearable last year was that you were harboring intense frustration and anger toward your boss because he didn't promote you. You deserved the promotion, but the company had passed you over, and you felt like a failure. Perhaps you never told your husband how hurt you were by the way he treated your parents a while back; or maybe you have been feeling inadequate sexually for years but could never bring yourself to discuss it with your husband. It's hard to verbalize these things, especially if you've been protecting them for long periods of time.

But you must. Your goal is catharsis. Verbalize your feelings. Scream if you need to, but let loose your anger, frustration, sadness, and hurt. Tell it like it is to your partner. Tell your spouse about your disappointments, your shattered dreams, and your personal failures. Let it all hang out, as they say. Bring up all the emotional garbage that you have allowed to accumulate. Ventilate until you feel emotionally wasted, completely burnt out. Reach the point of *depletion*.

Of course you have to lay some ground rules for this process. If two people are just engaging in yelling and screaming at each other, nothing will be accomplished. You have to listen to each other. When one person is speaking, the other is absorbing what he or she is saying. You must listen nonjudgmentally, noncritically, perhaps for the first time in your life. Again, this is not a win/lose situation, so it is your job to *interpret*, not to fly off the handle and react. You are trying to save something that is very important: a marriage, a family. Whether you have invested a short time or several years in the marriage, it is worthwhile for you to suspend judgment and listen to your partner—even if it hurts you. Keep in mind that your partner is extremely emotional and that when people are in such a state they say things they don't mean. The goal of ventilation is to let go, and your partner may very well lose control and starting dumping: "You've always been insensitive to my needs." "It's all your fault." "I tried so hard to have a good marriage and you ruined it." And so on. Don't feel persecuted by such remarks. This is a very negative communication, and your spouse should hardly be commended for such dumping, but if it is part of the overall therapeutic process of Ventilation, then you have to accept it. Absorb and interpret. What you are seeing is the dramatic representation of your partner's personal tragedy, of his suffering, and of his defeat. This time, though, when pent-up emotions are vented, when failure is confronted, the drama of your affair can lead to catharsis, not for the audience but for the players themselves. You can rise above your personal tragedy and overcome the trauma created by the affair. The payoff for confronting feeling is a happy ending.

Remember that underneath all the layers of accumulated emotional garbage is what your partner really feels for you. That's what you want to get at. Once you have vented all of the pent-up feelings you've been suppressing, you will experience catharsis, and you will be able to view yourself and your relationship with clarity and objectivity. Beneath all the emotional garbage we harbor dwells the truth, and once you see the truth about yourself you can decide whether there is love between you and your partner, whether there is something to cultivate, something to build from. I strongly suspect that there is.

CHECKPOINT NUMBER 2

The next step of Reconstructive Dynamics is Identification, in which we will discuss the destructive roles people adopt and which can lead to an affair. You will try to identify what risks may have led to an affair in your marriage. But before you can do that, it is critical that all anger, hurt, resentment, and guilt be thoroughly vented.

Both partners must stop here and examine themselves. Is there any residual anger you haven't expressed? Why are you holding it in? Examine your own motivations for keeping something from your partner. Is it really so critical that you guard it? Are you protecting your partner? Or are you protecting yourself? If you hold things in you will feel incomplete, and your feelings will hang over you like wet laundry.

Ventilate! Only by expressing your deepest feelings will you have the self-knowledge and objectivity to understand the behavior patterns that created the need for either you or your spouse to seek out a third party.

Chapter 7

IDENTIFICATION

People spend years trying to discover an "identity." They do this by associating themselves with certain people, philosophies, causes, political beliefs and groups, religions, etc., and by disassociating themselves from others. How seldom, though, is our perception of ourselves congruous with the way others perceive us. The goal of Reconstructive Dynamics is not necessarily to change your identity; but I hope that it will give you a deep insight into yourself, allow you to gain self-awareness, and shake you up a bit. With the help of your partner, you will be able to view your own behavior objectively, almost as if from the outside, and you will discover new and interesting things about yourself.

The goal of Identification is to further your understanding of what caused the affair by examining your own and your partner's pasts. We have already discussed causes at great length in Chapters 2 and 3; however, at this point in Reconstructive Dynamics, now that you have completed two critical stages, you should be able to identify objectively the negative behavior patterns in your own marriage that led to the affair.

So you are going to do some deep probing into your own past. This will not be easy; in fact, at times it will be uncomfortable, and you may feel threatened. You want to get to the truth, though, and the way to do that is to boldly confront your problems. In doing so, you tap into the power you have to overcome them.

Three things to keep in mind as you work through Identification: (1) Don't play amateur detective. There is a tendency to look for "clues" in your spouse's behavior as if under a microscope and say, like Sherlock Holmes unraveling a mystery, "Aha, you did such and such so you must be a Pleaser (or a Distractor, or a Victim)." Such comments are extremely threatening because they put labels on people. Labels are just a little bit too neat, and we like to put them on others but never ourselves. So let's avoid them. (2) Don't accuse a partner, and don't judge him or her. To avoid doing so, you are going to have to examine your own motivations. Ask yourself, Am I anxious to discover faults in my partner's behavior so I won't be held responsible? If in a discussion it should become clear that your spouse's relationship with his (or her) mother created a destructive pattern of behavior, don't say, "You see, it's all because of your mother!" In doing so you disclaim your own responsibility for the erosion of your marriage. (3) Let your partner draw his or her own conclusions. This is a ground rule in Identification. It is okay to point out certain details that will enlighten your spouse as long as they are given in a spirit of support and in good faith, but *do not* put words in your partner's mouth. In Identification you must go through the process of self-discovery. This includes making decisions yourself. If you draw conclusions for your partner, he or she will feel threatened and close down emotionally. You will activate denial mechanisms. If you facilitate your partner's understanding of a problem through positive, supportive intervention, you create a context in which he or she can open up and analyze a behavior pattern objectively.

IMPRINTS

In the first part of Identification, we are going to look at: (1) certain childhood "imprints"—behavior patterns—that usually carry over into adulthood and (2) the way a person's reaction to these imprints can lead to an affair. You may be able to identify with one or many of these imprints. It may not be pleasant to see yourself in any of the people or circumstances we discuss; your objective, nonetheless, is to identify your own particular behavior patterns, even if they are bad ones. When you become aware of them, you have the power to change them.

Unfulfilled Social Needs

Al had been married for twenty years and had three children. A competent, if not savvy, businessman, Al felt very secure and happy in his marriage and was extremely proud of his family. He would often boast that he felt like a king in his castle.

Al, however, had some very strong unfulfilled needs. As a teenager he never dated because of a severe acne problem that had made him painfully shy and awkward around women. He had overcome his shyness but nonetheless had a deep longing as an adult to be attractive and desirable outside his marriage. The king within the castle wanted to be the handsome prince without.

One day on a business trip, Al met Rita, a very attractive, well-built woman who fulfilled this need; she made him feel handsome and graceful, which gave him great self-assurance. This, of course, drastically distorted his self-image, and he actually started to believe he was Prince Charming.

Al continued to see Rita and eventually got divorced in order to marry her. Not surprisingly, the magic wore off quickly, and the need to charm and attract resurfaced as strong as ever. Rita had merely been the missing piece in a puzzle that completed Al's phony self-image. When he realized that he couldn't maintain that image—precisely because it was so false—he became very unhappy and realized that he should never have left his first wife. Al's case is a clear example of how a childhood imprint, if not confronted, can lead to destructive behavior patterns and great personal tragedy.

By the way, I have seen almost exactly the same thing happen with a woman who, in her thirties, found herself very attractive to men after she overcame a lifelong struggle with obesity. Suddenly slender and feeling elegant in her new clothes, she had a series of affairs that threatened her marriage. Again, as with Al, when she found that she could be attractive, an unfulfilled need that had lain dormant for years and years resurfaced.

Weak Communication Skills

Unfortunately, it is often much easier to deny things than it is to talk about them. When parents have poor communication skills it is unlikely that they will be willing to confront the problems (sex, drugs, personal hygiene, career choice, etc.) that come up between themselves and their children. They will gloss over conflict and give their children the message that problems are to be avoided in life rather than worked out. Such denial results in a fear (literally) of feelings. The realm of emotion is perceived as a danger zone.

If your partner comes from a background that made him a weak communicator, you probably have a lot of incompletions between you. Your attempts to get your spouse to "Communicate! Talk to me! Share with me!" will be unsuccessful until after he or she comes to grips with *why* feelings create such a fear. A faithful partner with weak communication skills will usually deny the affair at all cost. In doing so, such a person is acting exactly how he or she was taught to act. An unfaithful partner may have had an affair in response to great frustration caused by pent-up feelings. Affairs are caused by unfulfilled needs. If you can't express needs to your partner, he or she is at a loss to fulfill them.

Expectations in Childhood

Many parents place high, often unreasonable, expectations on their children. They brag about their kids right in front of them: "This is my son Dave. He's going to be a surgeon." There's nothing wrong with having a goal, but if parents place unreasonable expectations on their children they set them up for failure. Such people often become "driven" to succeed and are dissatisfied with the incremental successes they achieve in their lives. They never have a sense of fulfillment or contentment.

Being married to someone like this can be exciting for a while. We are often attracted to people with direction and purpose. But an obsessive drive to succeed in order to meet childhood expectations can be extremely destructive to a relationship. For someone who is speeding down the highway of accomplishment, moments of intimacy are like rest stops—brief and only taken when absolutely necessary.

Dominating Mother

The stereotype of the overbearing, overly protective mother has been depicted ad nauseum through the years in books, plays, and films. It is no less real, however, for having been dwelt upon at such length. I find that one of two things will usually happen to a man as a result of a dominant mother: (1) his anger toward his mother will be transferred to his wife, causing him to view her as the "enemy" or (2) his childhood dependency on his mother will make him totally passive in marriage. His wife will be a surrogate mother, and he will re-create the same relationship of acquiescence and dependency. Both of these behavior patterns are extremely unhealthy, prevent emotional growth for both partners, and create a context in which an affair is likely to occur.

Second Marriages

With the high rate of divorce in this country, the phenomenon of the second (or third or fourth) marriage is becoming quite common. Two problems arise in second marriages that can create great emotional turmoil leading to an affair. Both are compounded by the fact that many people remarry less out of love than from a need for companionship. They are fed up with the singles scene, fed up with coming home alone, so they cling to the security of a marriage, often with partners who are incompatible. I find that there is a high percentage of affairs in second marriages, perhaps due to this.

First of all, when a "first timer" marries someone who has already been married, the former will become disappointed to find that romantic illusions are unfulfilled. It's not so hard to accept this when the stars in your partner's eyes grow dim at the same time yours do; you can talk about it and create new illusions together. But second timers are usually very realistic, if not somewhat jaded, about marriage, and spring brides can become very frustrated by them.

The second problem arises when one or both partners bring children into the second marriage. Sometimes a person can adapt to his spouse's children very easily; often, however, he (or she) will resent the children because they demand so much of his partner's time. It is not uncommon for a child to resent stepparents, not because they are evil as in so many fairy tales but because they don't measure up to "my real daddy" or "my real mommy" or simply because they symbolize the breach between a child's real parents. In any case, a stepparent can very easily marginalize himself from the family unit and become alienated; so alienated, in fact, that he will seek an affair.

DESTRUCTIVE ROLES

In the second half of Identification we are going to discuss a number of destructive roles that I have seen time and time again in my practice over the years. Some of these roles might seem somewhat extreme to you—though they are all based on real people—and you may not be able to identify closely with any *one* of them. But take a close look at your own behavior and see if *patterns* don't emerge that resemble a particular role we discuss.

Again, don't probe your partner's behavior with a fine-tooth comb. Everyone has days when he feels like a Victim. With certain people under certain circumstances, anyone could be an Emotional Seducer; in neither case is one necessarily locked into a destructive role. When reaching what follows, you must review your own behavior and see if *patterns* exist that conform roughly to the roles presented (Victim, Intellectualizer, Martyr, etc.). Do you have a *tendency* to intellectually browbeat people?

The key here is for both partners to look at themselves and the way they interact with one another. Attempt to understand the patterns of behavior you and your partner have woven for yourselves and ask whether or not they created unfulfilled needs that caused the affair. No person will conform precisely to any one of the behavior styles presented. You may have a lot of one in you, none of another. If you identify strongly with a role, confront your destructive behavior pattern, try to find the root of it, and attempt to alter it.

The Pleaser: Geisha Girls and Yes-Men

The Pleaser is a person who will fulfill his or her partner's needs at all levels, to the point of subservience. She caters to her partner's every whim, often at the sacrifice of her own being. When you come home from work she'll take your shoes off, bring you the newspaper, make you a drink. She'll have your bathrobe ready for you when you come out of the shower. If you ask her to, she'll tie your tie for you and dial your phone calls. She finds happiness in providing for her partner, and she draws meaning in life from having someone to nourish and to serve.

That may seem like an ideal situation, appealing to that regal strain in you; but after a while you will almost certainly long for a wife to replace the servant you've been living with. There is no real excitement or challenge in a master/slave relationship. We should be proud of our spouses, and we should be able to feel power in helping them grow and blossom as people.

An excellent example of the male Pleaser was depicted in Flaubert's classic nineteenth-century novel, *Madame Bovary*. Emma Bovary's husband, the self-effacing Charles, a simple-minded country doctor, loved his wife dearly but frankly bored her and sent her into the arms of her seductive lovers, Rudolphe and Léon.

The Pleaser generally has no identity of his own and functions merely as an extension of his partner's ego. By constantly pleasing his partner at the expense of his own needs, he loses his dignity and respect in the eyes of his spouse and those around him.

The Victim

The Victim has found a way to avoid responsibility for just about everything in his life. No matter what happens, he can always convince himself that *"they* did it to me." Nothing scares a Victim more than success. He actually sets himself up for failure precisely because he knows how to handle it; he has become comfortable with that role.

An example of a victim is Helen, whose father was an alcoholic. When she was growing up he abused her verbally— "You're pretty, but dumb"—and she was extremely embarrassed about him. She felt victimized by his attitude toward her and by the fact that fate had dealt her such a mean blow by giving her an alcoholic father, so she spent her entire childhood disliking herself and wallowing in self-pity.

She was, as even her father noticed, quite pretty, had a certain charm about her, and in high school she began to attract some suitors. She responded to their interest by becoming extremely overweight. Years later she recognized this as an emerging pattern of victimization. Since she perceived herself as a victim, she had to create circumstances that would assure she could never come out on the winning end. Getting fat did just that.

People such as Helen get married, of course, and they carry destructive roles into their marriages. The Victim feels extremely ill at ease when he's happy and will go so far as to sabotage a marriage in order to regain the comfort of once again being able to say, "Woe is me." I have seen people who deny sex to their partners for no apparent reason; who become irascible; who taunt and complain and accuse; who literally make life unbearable for their partners and *drive* them into having an affair. Then they can say, "Look what you've done to me now!"

We all do this to a certain extent. Have you ever been late for an appointment and blamed it on traffic when you *knew* in advance there would be lots of cars on the road? Have you ever mailed an important package at the last minute and blamed the post office for nearly ruining your life when the package arrived late? As I said, everyone does little things like this now and then. Be aware of it. Use this awareness to identify more significant areas in your life in which you set yourself up to be a Victim.

The Martyr

The Martyr is much less subtle than his cousin, the Victim. He (or she) openly cries out that he wants to carry the burden of the entire world on his shoulders. He bears the pain of everyone in his family, saying, "I'll take on the problems. I'll gladly worry about them. Lay it on me, I'm strong enough to take it." The Martyr is generally a very internalized person who has difficulty communicating. Pretending to take responsibility for everyone's problems is really a convoluted way of refusing to take responsibility for himself. Upon close analysis, such "heroic" martydom is a very cowardly, devious form of behavior.

Like the Victim, the Martyr is comfortable feeling persecuted and has no desire whatsoever to really confront problems. The Martyr craves empty suffering, not the kind that comes from working through conflict and results in self-awareness but the kind that parasitically feeds a neurotic need to sacrifice oneself. Not surprisingly, today's Martyr becomes tomorrow's Victim. I encountered a man years ago who, when he discovered his wife had cheated on him, actually took all the credit for making her do so. In a very false way, he completely exonerated her and placed all of the blame and guilt on himself. He seemed to feel better for doing so.

The Rescuer

The Rescuer is a person who acts as a savior, constantly throwing life preservers to people in trouble. This is admirable to a degree, but when carried to an extreme, it can create destructive relationships of dependency. When he sees conflict, a Rescuer tends to take charge immediately, solve the problem, and wait for approval. He never allows others the time to resolve problems themselves.

The Rescuer often has a very strong personality and knows it. He is often very intelligent as well. You might recognize him as being the one in school who answered the teacher's questions so quickly that no one else ever got a chance to respond. If the teacher wasn't astute enough to handle him, chances are the Rescuer did almost all the talking in the class. Or you might recognize the Rescuer as the husband who speaks when you address his wife. When you ask her a question—about anything—she immediately looks to him. It is extremely sad to see what can happen when one partner refuses to allow the other to handle conflict and denies that person the opportunity to learn to grow.

A number of things can result from such a relationship. The Rescuer can become horrified at some point in the marriage by the helpless person he has created and feel extremely bored. Or the Rescuer's spouse will realize that he or she is being stifled and take flight. Unless negative behavior patterns such as this are broken—and they can be—they will lock you into destructive roles that will impede emotional growth and prevent self-actualization.

The Belittler

The Belittler makes himself feel big by making others feel small. It is often said that we are our own worst critics. If you are married to a Belittler, however, someone always has the jump on you.

The Belittler's speciality is the bad-faith judgment. If in a discussion with friends he hears you say, "The people in Quebec are extremely hospitable," he will be the first to point out, "I got ripped off when I was there last year in Montreal." Or if you recommend the food at a certain restaurant, he will quickly recall a miserable meal he had there. If you choose to defend the theory of evolution, he will quickly line up all arguments against you, regardless of how he feels about the subject. He splits hairs; he contradicts for the sake of contradicting. You have to weigh your words very carefully around the Belittler because if he spots even the smallest leak in your logic, he will break you open.

I once counseled a man who had had an affair because he became fed up with a wife who constantly judged him. She had made up her mind that he was a weak man and saw everything he did through spectacles tainted by prejudice. Every move he made confirmed her belief; the way he walked, the way he talked, the way he drove the car, the way he acted socially, even the way he ate. As you might expect, she rarely refrained from telling him about it. The man was understandably unwilling to confront his wife with his feelings because even that would only further disparage him in her eyes.

The Belittler is a very insecure person. His belligerent put-down-artist front intimidates people and creates a comfortable distance. If you identify with this character, examine your own past and try to figure out why you need to belittle others. Did you get burned somewhere along the line as result of being vulnerable? Were you brought up to believe you could never do wrong, and do you belittle in order to make others wrong before they can prove you are? Did your childhood instill in you a deep feeling of inadequacy for which you compensate by attacking others?

The Destroyer

The Destroyer is the superlative version of the Belittler. He doesn't just want to reduce people, he wants to annihilate them. If you buy flowers for a Destroyer she'll put them in a vase and go watch television. If you buy a nice dress, get your hair done, or cook his favorite meal, the Destroyer will intentionally act as if he didn't notice. I knew a man who told his son, when the boy proudly brought his fiancée home for the first time, "You could have done worse."

The Destroyer is usually a very sharp person, has a strong personality, and a tremendous ego. He is very charming and an excellent manipulator. A more inept handler of human resources, however, there never was. If you work for him, he'll tell you. "I want this done yesterday"; and when you finish, he'll tell you to do it over an hour ago. Being married to a Destroyer can be devastating to your self-esteem. You tell him you love him and he'll reply, "You're only in this for the money and you know it."

Sounds like an evil person, doesn't he (or she)? But he isn't really. You would probably never recognize him if you met him casually. He has all the marks of a good citizen and a loving family man. In his past you would probably find one of two things: that he was abused physically or emotionally as a child or that he felt abandoned (e.g., lost a parent or was adopted). In both cases such children grow up to be adults whose survival instinct dominates all others. They were vulnerable as children and they got hurt, so they developed a killer instinct that ensures that no one will ever get close enough emotionally to hurt them again. Toppling the barriers Destroyers throw up between themselves and others is extremely difficult. If you see strong tendencies in your behavior to "destroy" others, you have a lot of work to do before you will be able to achieve intimacy.

The Intellectualizer

The Intellectualizer is the cerebral type who is very intelligent, knows it, and uses his intelligence to browbeat people and to keep them at a distance. We've all met him at a party; he's either in some corner holding court or walking around the room tossing about pearls of wisdom as he casually mingles.

The Intellectualizer is eminently logical. He is generally very afraid of feelings, especially feelings that can't be explained rationally. An Intellectualizer, for example, could never admit that he is jealous because jealousy is an embarrassing, irrational emotion. Living with an Intellectualizer is frustrating because he is smart enough to twist and turn facts and circumstances in such a way as to make himself seem right—even if he is dead wrong! Essentially, he uses his intellect to maintain control.

The Intellectualizer chooses to accumulate knowledge in order to defend himself against the world. He wields facts and figures and logical reasoning as he would weapons to keep people out. His insecurity could have been caused by dozens of things. The point is that he chose to develop his mind as opposed to, say, his body as a means to dominate people.

The Romantic

The Romantic is in some ways the Intellectualizer's counter-part. The dichotomy between reason and emotion, between intellect and feeling, between the mind and the heart, has preoccupied philosophers and poets for centuries. Depending on which century you choose to investigate, you will find strong arguments for the superiority of one or the other. Ideally, I think we should probably strive for some kind of balance between reason and emotion. The Intellectualizer and the Romantic represent two extremes to be avoided.

The Romantic looks at the world through rose-colored glasses and wants her marriage to be like something out of a paperback romance. These romances, in case you didn't know, always end with the heroine getting married—they never deal with the marriage itself. The Romantic lives in the past—in those days of vertiginous courtships—not in the dreary present of weekly tennis and Saturday night movies. Everything seems "ordinary" to her, and she is disgusted by the mediocrity of her life. Like Madame Bovary, she is constantly trying to transcend reality rather than live in it.

But isn't it good to maintain romance in a marriage? Of course. But the hard-core romantic destroys all potential to do so. The difference between a healthy and an unhealthy Romantic is simple; the former is happy and the latter is not. The Romantic is never satisfied with the circumstances of her life because they don't correspond to her ideal. She is a victim of reality. She feels no power to change her life, to make the commonplace romantic, which, I believe, is the real key to romance.

Men can be hopeless Romantics as well; they read romances in the bathroom. Male or female, the Romantic is marked by a deep dissatisfaction with life and a longing for the unattainable. This is an extremely destructive, and extremely common, personality type. If your partner has this romantic vision of life, you probably feel inadequate because he or she is not capable of accepting you for what you are. And you've probably thought of finding someone who is.

The Talkaholic

I think it best to brief about this long-winded character. The Talkaholic throws out words as he would darts to keep people away from him (or her). It is impossible to communicate with Talkaholics because they are perfectly content to maintain one-way discourse. (Any attempt to communicate with one will leave you stranded in a cul-de-sac.) A Talkaholic *does not listen;* and, sadly, he is not even aware that he alienates those around him by showering them in a blinding rain of meaningless jibberish.

The best thing you can do with a Talkaholic is to tell him about his problem. But don't just say, "You talk too much." He's been told that a thousand times before. Tell him, if you can get a word in edgewise, "I feel that talking all the time is your way of avoiding intimacy with people. It is a defense mechanism that ensures that no one will ever get close to you." The message may not get through the first time you say it, but keep repeating it; someday it just might.

The Distractor

The Distractor is famous for avoiding conflict, and even intimacy, by skillfully dodging the issue at hand. There is no question that distracting relieves tension. When the going gets tough in a job interview, for example, a telephone interruption, which gives you a chance to gather your thoughts, can seem like divine intervention. When we are confronted by high-pressure salesmen, no pretext is too trivial to get away. With such salesmen, distracting is a permanent solution to your problem; you'll never see the guy again. But in your marriage, establishing a pattern of avoiding conflict can have devastating consequences.

Let's look at some samples of the Distractor's art. Let's say a husband confronts his wife with an issue: "Honey, some things have been on my mind, and I think we have to sit down and talk." The wife, who knows what's in the air, consciously or subconsciously activates a denial mechanism and creates a distraction to avoid confronting the issue: "Oh, you know I was just on my way out the door to buy dinner for tonight." When he confronts her later, the baby will suddenly need changing or the bathroom scrubbing.

Another common tool in this artful dodger's craft is verbal maneuvering. If you get the Distractor to sit down and talk there is no guarantee you will keep him there. While speaking you will use words the Distractor will grab at as if he were chasing butterflies. "Phone! That reminds me that I have to make a call." Or, "Speaking of work, I have to get up early tomorrow morning. Good night." Children and adults who have poor powers of concentration do this all the time. The Distractor is not a child, and he doesn't necessarily have poor powers of concentration. He *doesn't want* to confront the issue you wish to talk about. If you find yourself in a conversation with a Distractor, the thing you wanted to talk about has to be postponed in order to confront the real issue between you: What is it that makes you afraid to talk to me?

As I said, everybody creates distractions now and then in order to avoid ugly scenes or to relieve tension. But if you see in your own behavior a pattern of using distractions to avoid conflict, you may have a problem. Look very hard at your own behavior because Distractors are rarely aware of what they do. Distractors generally come from families with extremely poor communication skills. They learned at a very young age that problems weren't talked about; you just lived with them and hoped they would go away.

The Worrier

This anxiety-ridden personality draws his or her meaning in life from worrying. About what? About anything! If you are married to a Worrier, you are merely a sounding board for your spouse's psyche. We all have fleeting fears that pass through our minds and then disappear. The Worrier isn't willing to let them pass; he articulates every one, no matter how insignificant, no matter how unfounded. In a strange, paradoxical way, the Worrier is comfortable only when he has something troubling on his mind.

The Worrier is unable to live in the present, which occasionally gives us cause to worry but usually does not. The Worrier's mind is always inhabiting some rocky terrain between now and later. Instead of enjoying a good meal, a film, or good company in the here and now, the Worrier is wondering, "Will the business deal go through?" "Is my car safe where it's parked?" "Is the new guy at work after my job?" "Is my son Joey going to get into college?" "What if my dinner guests don't show up?"

A man once came to me complaining that he was unsatisfied with his sex life because every time he would try to make love to his wife, she would start creating anxiety: "Amy hasn't been doing well in school." Or, "Did you hear there have been burglars in the neighborhood?" I asked him if his wife tended to worry excessively at any other times. He replied, "Yes, whenever I try to talk to her about important things." This woman clearly was a compulsive Worrier because it gave her an excuse to avoid intimacy and conflict.

The Worrier has this in common with the Distractor; she throws up a wall of worry between herself and other people; it protects her. Or so she thinks—Worriers are predisposed to stress-related illnesses such as colitis, ulcers, high blood pressure, back problems, psoriasis, and migraines.

The Dramatist

The Dramatist appears to view everyday life as a soap opera. He can raise even the most trivial incident to monumental proportions. If he loses his car keys, the whole family will hear all the plot-enhancing details, with unity of action and dramatic intrigue to boot. When something truly significant happens, the Dramatist is prone to ranting, raving, and other seemingly uncalled-for displays of emotion.

Such theatrics may seem effective to you; but they usually are not. Through the cacophony of the Dramatist's soliloquy, the discerning ear can detect a cry for help. I once encountered a man who had an affair because he could no longer handle the way his wife constantly blew things out of proportion. "She'd be a great writer," he told me. "She can create dramatic tension when brushing her teeth or feeding the cat."

I later talked to his wife. She was willing to confront her theatrics but really wanted to talk about the terrible frustration she felt because her husband, who she thought was much smarter than she was, never listened to her: "He's always either reading a magazine or watching television, and I can't get through to him. I'll ask him to do something, he'll nod yes, and an hour later won't even remember what I had said to him." It's hard to tell in such a situation whether the man tuned his wife out because she had nothing significant to say or whether his unwillingness to listen in the first place caused the neurotic dramatizing to develop.

If you see such behavior in your own relationship, recognize it for what it is: The Dramatist is crying out for attention. The roots of the problem may lie in the relationship itself, as was probably the truth in the case above, or they may lie in childhood. A child who was neglected will often carry into adulthood a deep need to be the center of attention, to be recognized, and, ultimately, to be understood.

The Manipulator a.k.a. The Emotional Seducer

This final character type is a difficult one to discuss because everyone is a Manipulator; anyone who tells you he isn't is either lying or is not very perceptive. The way we dress is manipulative, as is the way we talk, the way we use gestures, and the way we look at people. The businessman's huge desk is a form of manipulation; so is putting potato chips at the end of the soda pop aisle in the supermarket.

After years in a relationship, couples should be able to tell whether each other's behavior is authentic or not, whether they are speaking (or acting) from the heart or the head. However, I have seen couples who communicate so little that even the most transparent forms of manipulation (e.g., bringing flowers to your wife before dropping a bomb on her) seem to go unnoticed.

The Manipulator gets what he wants by being devious and sneaky. The best way to get from A to B is not a straight line but a tortuous, often circuitous trail full of false pretexts, innuendoes, equivocations, and other flimflam. Manipulators squander incredible amounts of psychic energy cooking up schemes. I'm not talking about grand designs here; I'm talking about trivial things such as, "I want to see *Kramer vs. Kramer* tonight, and I know my wife wants to see *Dirty Harry*. How can I get her to see *Kramer vs. Kramer?*" Or, "I don't want to scrub the bathtub; what can I do to make my husband feel indebted to me so that when I ask him to clean it he can't refuse?" The Manipulator is unwilling, or unable, to confront problems directly, to say, "I want to see this film, you want to see that one; let's work out a solution"; or, "I don't feel like scrubbing the bathtub today, could you please do it this time?"

The Emotional Seducer manipulates by delegating sexual favors or by playing on the weakness and reinforcing the strengths of his partner. An Emotional Seducer will use "crocodile tears" if they work. Or she will suddenly begin to pay special attention to the way she dresses or to the food she places on the table. An Emotional Seducer might become more available around the house for handywork, more observant of his wife's charm, or more generous at the beginning of the month. These things are fine when you are motivated by a spirit of love and nurturing. When they are part of an overall strategy of manipulation that serves your own selfish needs, they constitute one of the more destructive behavior patterns that can exist in a relationship.

Everyone who has a mind schemes. The secret to avoiding becoming a Manipulator is to be aware of how your mind works. When you see a scheme hatching, stop it. Ask yourself, Do I really have anything to gain by not confronting my partner with what I want? Nine times out of ten, the answer will be no.

You must have seen yourself in one of many of the characters discussed in this chapter. If you didn't, might I suggest that you go back and read it again, this time with a more critical perspective on yourself.

The crucial thing to understand is that all of the roles presented here prevent you from achieving intimacy with your partner. These behaviors serve to protect the ego of the person who adopts them. It is amazing how long couples can continue their lives parasitically feeding each others' neurotic needs by acting out these roles. Martyrs pair off with Destroyers, and Victims pair off with Rescuers; and life goes on; people survive.

You and your partner hit a brick wall. One of you becomes aware that something was wrong with your relationship and did something about it, by having an affair. Admittedly, it was not the best solution. But it happened, and now you are going to do something about that. In Reconstructive Dynamics you become aware of your own behavior and the consequences of it. Your behavior is a key variable in the equation that is your relationship. If you manipulate, your relationship becomes a manipulative one. If you eliminate that behavior, you give your marriage the chance to become something else, something more positive. You have the power to make your marriage what you want it to be. By identifying the destructive roles that led to the affair, you gain the self-awareness that is essential to overcoming them.

Chapter 8

VULNERABILITY AND COMMUNION

VULNERABILITY: THE POLITICS OF
THE HEART

During the 1976 presidential campaign, Jimmy Carter admitted in an interview with *Playboy* magazine that passing a beautiful woman in the street often kindled the fires of lust in his heart. In his political naiveté, Carter was surprised to see that that particular comment, expressed so candidly and in such good faith, was immediately plastered on the front pages of newspapers and in magazines across the country.

Vulnerable. The word is derived from the Latin "vulnerare," to wound. It is also akin to the Gothic "wilwan," to rob. Vulnerable literally means "able to be wounded or robbed." No wonder people want nothing to do with vulnerability. We are trained, indeed programmed, throughout our lives to protect ourselves from the emotional attacks and rip-offs perpetrated by those around us. "Don't express too much of your feelings," the old adage goes, "because *they* will use it against you." Such ideas are often parental imprints, which we implicitly received as children and which became acceptable, learned behaviors. After we have absorbed such messages thousands of times, we naturally become emotionally belligerent.

Of course, at certain times in our lives we must adopt roles that oblige us to take a warlike stance against the world. Jimmy Carter discovered this the hard way. Like even the most banal cliché, there is a troubling foundation of truth to the "hide your feelings" maxim. If a politician shows the slightest sign of weakness or makes one false move, it can destroy his career. A businessman trying, say, to seal a big contract with a client, must give the impression of absolute integrity, of inhuman competence. This is no time for him to open up and honestly express his self-doubt. You will often hear such people say, "I keep my public and my private lives separate." The public persona offers no opportunity to be human, something everyone needs.

In relationships, we all act, to varying degrees, like politicians. Vulnerability, even with those closest to us, is perceived to be a dangerous and frightening state, so we retire to our emotional fortress and place our feelings under lock and key. We are "protected, defended," but pitifully alone and isolated. It is not surprising that couples fail to express their true feelings to one another and thus force themselves into a position where an affair becomes a likely outlet for unfulfilled needs.

Speaking the Unspeakable

The Vulnerability stage can only occur when anger is fully vented. It is critical that during the Ventilation stage both partners reach a "depletion point," a point at which all the energy used to hide feelings is spent. Nothing must be left to protect. Both partners must be open, revealed.

Clearly an assumption is being made here—that your private and public, or professional, lives are two different things. I am not suggesting that you should go out and reveal yourselves to your colleagues at work, to your clients, patients, students, or whomever you deal with in your job. In your personal relationships, however, I am suggesting that whatever you hide from those you love takes something away from who you are and denies you the freedom to be who you are.

Unexpressed feelings stand in the way of effective communication and are responsible for the accumulation of the emotional garbage I have spoken of earlier in the book. In the Vulnerability stage you must tear down the fences and defenses that "protect" and therefore isolate you from your partner. During the Ventilation stage, when you created a context in which your partner noncritically and nonjudgmentally allowed you to vent your feelings, you essentially relinquished control. You have given yourself permission not to suppress emotions, thus allowing a lot of this emotional garbage to surface. Perhaps for the first time in your marriage you told your partner something that has been bothering you for years. Or perhaps you admitted something about yourself that you had previously thought unspeakable. In doing so you made yourself vulnerable, and it was no doubt a tremendous relief.

Peter and Anna had been married ten years when Anna, frustrated by her inability to communicate with her husband, began seeing another man. When Peter found out, he was crushed. Peter was a very successful architect who came from a wealthy, competitive family. His father was an extremely demanding intellectual who never gave any positive reinforcement to his children. Nothing Peter did in his life was good enough to merit a paternal pat on the back. As is very common in such cases, Peter transferred his hostility for his father to Anna. Any criticism he got from her, even the simplest little thing like telling him he had miscalculated in balancing the checkbook, was taken as an attack. Peter could never, ever, admit he made a mistake. Criticism from Anna meant rejection from his father.

Of course, when Anna found solace with another man, this was the ultimate blow to Peter's ego; it was definitive rejection by his father. Through Reconstructive Dynamics, Peter expressed his feelings of inadequacy and vented his hostility. He allowed himself to be disarmed, to come from the heart rather than from the head, and to reveal his most painful secret. He opened the doors of his emotional fortress. When Anna saw him in this vulnerable state, crying like a baby, she understood the depth of Peter's feelings of inadequacy in relation to his father, and she respected him for having the courage to confront those feelings.

This process of sharing plants a seed that can be cultivated through further communication. Peter realized that he wrongly displaced his feelings for his father onto his wife and that this was the reason she seemed so threatening to him. He had placed himself in a vulnerable, weak, emotional state, a state that had always terrified him, yet Anna was responding favorably to him. The need to protect himself, the need to always be right, no longer seemed important. In opening the doors of his fortress, Peter had let a monster out and had let his wife in.

Anna, in turn, was able to vent her hostility toward Peter for being unyielding and self-righteous for so many years. In doing so, she realized that she had used infidelity as a means to punish her husband. Now that Peter had made himself vulnerable, that need to punish melted away. The ground had been cleared to begin constructing a new relationship.

The Transparent Self

Many people perceive vulnerability as a state in which you are "visible," in which you are a target who can easily be hurt. They think that vulnerability is dangerous or a sign of weakness. In fact, the contrary is true. When you exert tremendous effort covering up your feelings, trying to make yourself opaque, you in fact become quite transparent. People pick up on what you are doing, and they use it to punish, hurt, or abuse you. Your character armor is like a glass shield behind which others see you cowering. They see your fear and weakness in spite of your shield, and they have but one desire—to break it over your head!

In our personal relationships, vulnerability, far from being a state of weakness, is a source of strength. It is a state of oneness with yourself in which you tell the truth. It takes courage to tell the truth about yourself, and your spouse will recognize that, as Anna did with Peter. Vulnerability disarms people. Lies you tell about yourself (and to yourself) can be used as ammunition against you by your partner; the truth cannot. When you tell the truth, no one can play upon your fear, your hurt, or your guilt because you have openly acknowledged them. You have experienced them and in doing so have taken control. This is an essential paradox; in relinquishing control, you instantly regain it. In opening up emotionally, Peter momentarily lost control, but ultimately he overcame his feelings toward his father, and they no longer controlled his life.

When you allow yourself to be open, you gain the control and strength that come with authenticity, truth, and honesty. Being vulnerable allows you to be natural and fluid and to be free of repression, free from rigid, internalized behaviors. With this comes clarity, objectivity, and the power to transcend the dilemma of the affair itself. With the shackle of unexpressed needs undone, you can experience intimacy, which is freedom.

Don't Fence Me Out

A favorite poem of mine is "Mending Wall" by Robert Frost. In his work the poet owns a farm that is separated from a neighboring farm by a wall made of boulders. The poet asks himself why the wall is necessary. The neighbor, however, adheres to his father's saying, "Good fences make good neighbors," and each spring after the wall has been weathered by wind, rain, and sleet, he picks up the fallen boulders and replaces them. The poet can't understand this behavior since he himself grows apple trees and his neighbor grows pines, so no conflict should arise requiring a wall. There is no practical need for it. "Before I built the wall," muses the poet, "I'd ask to know what I was walling in or walling out."

The maxim "Good fences make good neighbors" implies that when interacting with people there is a priority need to protect oneself. The wall in the poem is a symbol of distrust, and this distrust clearly oppresses the poet. He wants communication without walls, a neighborly accord based on trust and acceptance of territorial lines.

What has this to do with relationships? When we become vulnerable, we remove the boulders one by one through open, honest communication, and in doing so we eliminate the symbolic wall of distrust altogether. When the wall is gone, you and your spouse can see one another as you really are. Removing boulders establishes trust and allows you to experience intimacy.

Vulnerability is that wonderful, beautiful ability to be one's natural self, with no impediments, no walls. When you share yourself, you can experience that sublime balance in nature that allows for the most intimate type of closeness available to humankind; it opens the doors for love.

A Word About Exercises

Lack of communication was a key factor in breaking apart your marriage. Open and honest communication is what will put it back together again. In the rest of Reconstructive Dynamics I want to present a number of exercises that will enhance your ability to communicate with your partner. I want you to think of them not as a crutch but as a tool that will aid you for a while until you develop skills that will make open communication easier in the future.

You might also think of these exercises as a catalyst that sets the communication process in motion and permits it to develop autonomously. You have made a commitment to yourself and your partner to make an effort to purge yourself of the emotional garbage you have created over the years. The only way to bring it out is through communication. But communication is risky, and we are not always willing to take risks. These exercises allow you to do so in a structured, safe environment.

You and your partner are a team with a common goal—to save your marriage. You are not a limited partnership; you can't make a token investment in the business of your marriage and then expect it to flourish while you get tan in the Bahamas. A marriage is a cohesive, organic unit that demands total commitment. On the path to marital happiness one partner carries the flashlight, the other carries the map. You have to work together to reach your destination.

In the exercises that follow, you will see how important it is to work as a team to solve your problems. I encourage you to approach these exercises with tenacity and vigor and with a deep, firm commitment to cutting through the barriers that block communication between you and your partner. You must coach one another, support one another, understand one another. I should warn you that at first these exercises may seem somewhat awkward. You're used to carrying both the flashlight and the map yourself, whereas now you must make a conscious effort to cooperate with someone else. Once you get accustomed to being open and vulnerable with your partner, I assure you the awkwardness will disappear and genuine communication will seem natural and effortless. These exercises are a sort of training that will make you a skilled communicator.

Want Ads: Wanting is Needing

This exercise will greatly facilitate communication in your marriage. In a subtle, unthreatening way, you and your partner will be able to express deep and crucial needs that have not been fulfilled.

This exercise is very simple, and it can be a lot of fun. Write on a 5 × 7 index card a "want ad," just like one you might see in the classifieds. In this want ad tell your partner what you would like from him or her. For example: "Wanted, husband who will be available for romantic dinner this weekend." Or, "Wanted, wife who will support me emotionally during high-pressure period at the office." Or, "Husband who will give more *quality* time to his family." Or, "Wanted, wife who will give me a kiss every night after work and who will hold me."

Use these want ads to express very fundamental needs, such as help cleaning up around the house, or secret, hidden needs, such as the need for more physical affection. In any case, be creative, open, and honest.

This is an excellent exercise in being vulnerable. It is harder than you might think to express what you want to your partner. In telling what you want, you are, in fact, admitting what you need. When you ask for a supportive partner during a difficult time, you are really saying that you *need* help, that you choose not to cope by yourself. It takes courage to do that; and it takes trust.

After you've written up a card, place it somewhere in the house where your spouse will be sure to see it—on the driver's seat of the car, on the coffee jar, or in the medicine cabinet, for example. When you receive one, keep it. Hold on to all the cards until the end of the week, then go over them with your partner and check to see which needs were fulfilled and which were not.

I should caution you against performing this exercise apathetically or with anything less than unquestionable sincerity. Nothing must be contrived in your communications to your partner. Nor should any request be unreasonable. If your partner should begin compromising the integrity of the exercise by making insincere demands, it is your duty to remind him or her that such behavior reflects an unwillingness to be vulnerable and therefore prevents you from attaining your goal of intimacy.

The want-ads exercise creates a structure within which you

can express your needs to your partner. It also gives you an opportunity to observe to what extent you are responsible in fulfilling your partner's needs. If at the end of the week you tally up the cards and find that many of your partner's needs are unfulfilled, you will be confronted with that in black and white. Ask yourself why. Were you too busy? Or were you apathetic? Were you unwilling to fulfill the need? Or were you incapable of it? So often in life we are able to gloss over such questions. In the want-ads exercise you must not. Answer them, and see what they tell you about yourself.

You may find that your partner is responding to certain want ads in a perfunctory way, that he or she is merely "going through the motions." Perhaps your next ad might say: "Wanted, partner who will *really* be with me this weekend in heart, mind, and soul."

Be careful not to let this exercise turn into a test. If you find yourself writing want ads that are designed to see how far your partner will go, to figure out what he will or will not do to prove he loves you, catch yourself before you are disappointed. By the same token, if you begin receiving requests you find unreasonable or testing, feel strong enough to say no. There is a fine line to be drawn here, and it is up to you and your partner to *negotiate* limits. The key to preventing this exercise from degenerating into a test lies in requesting only genuine, sincere needs. These are almost never unreasonable.

One very important point to mention about this and all the exercises. After several weeks or months you will begin to see patterns of behavior woven into your conjugal cloth. Most people never really observe themselves long enough to see threads of behavior emerge. The want-ads exercise forces you to do so, and it will teach you interesting things about yourself. This, and all the other exercises in the book, are geared to helping you gain self-awareness. You may discover, for example, that when confronted with a request to spend more time with your children, you create household tasks that exempt you from this duty. You might observe that each time your spouse proposes some activity that you could engage in together, some latent illness, pain, or injury is reactivated. Or it could become apparent that each time you and your spouse sit down and attempt genuine communication, you begin creating petty distractions; pictures suddenly need adjusting, the stain in the carpet begins to glare at you, that phone call to such and such just can't wait, or the mail might have arrived. People do these things! Use the want ads and all other exercises as a means of discovering the patterns in your relationship that prevent communication. Then, of course, attempt to alter them.

Understanding Closet Demons

Let's look at the example of Rick and Jill, a young couple who began experiencing difficulties early in their marriage. Rick was a mellow, rather laid-back sort of fellow who worked construction. Jill was a much more ambitious individual and driven in her career goals. Their relationship developed into a typical Destroyer/Victim pattern. Jill got fed up with Rick's passivity and sought out a strong, dominating man.

Rick and Jill, however, managed to save their marriage. When they finally got down to communicating with one another, they discovered the root of their problem. Jill's father died when she was very young, and she had grown up with no male figure in the household. In ventilating her feelings to Rick, she expressed this need she had never come to grips with. It was very difficult for Jill to do this because for her the states of emotionality and vulnerability were associated with the feeling of abandonment she had lived with as a child. Her father, by not being there, had exposed her to the world unprotected, and Jill responded to this terrible fear of being wounded by becoming a Destroyer: Destroy them before they can destroy you! Through Reconstructive Dynamics she realized that the reason she hounded and persecuted Rick was that she subconsciously wanted to punish him for not being the strong father figure she needed. Of course their relationship totally lacked intimacy because Jill could not allow anyone, not even her husband, to get close to her. She had taken on the dominant male role in the relationship in order to ensure that she would never be vulnerable. For Jill, vulnerability was synonymous with abandonment. Fortunately, Rick was strong enough to accept his own responsibility for allowing himself to be victimized. It was devastating to hear Jill had cheated on him, but he was willing to help her overcome her feeling of abandonment. Jill, by allowing herself to be vulnerable, opened the door and confronted a closet demon that had been running her life. In opening herself up, she let another person get close to her for the first time, and she experienced a sense of power where she had expected weakness and fear. In becoming aware of her problem, Jill took a courageous first step in overcoming it. She recognized that though Rick was not a paternal disciplinarian, he had other good qualities and was in many ways very masculine. Ventilating feelings led to a new sense of trust and a feeling of intimacy that Rick and Jill had never experienced before; their relationship was on new ground and could flourish.

Behind the Mask

In the Vulnerability stage, with anger fully vented and with burdensome internalized feelings released, you and your partner will be able to look at each other with more clarity and objectivity, without utilizing the past as a weapon in the present. Your communication will be entirely "here and now." There will be no dumping, no accusation. The ability to be vulnerable is the ultimate form of power, for it allows you to express your pure essence, with no veneer or facade between you and your spouse. In giving up the excess baggage you've carried around, you return to a state of naturalness, one that allows your relationship to achieve harmony and authentic communication.

The essence of being vulnerable lies in that natural, spontaneous feeling you experience when you are able to interact with your partner on a level of honesty, with no masks. Not that there isn't some residue from all the past hurts; there is. But by allowing yourself to be vulnerable, you can dilute that residue, and past hurts will no longer control your lives. You can lay the foundation for a new relationship. "True love," a Zen koan* says, "is giving a person the space to be what he or she is or is not." It is giving him or her the freedom to be "self" with no conditions attached. This is the essence of true, unconditional love: the ability to be oneself and to give another that same freedom. Of course, there has to be trust in that freedom. It doesn't mean that the marriage is over and you can do anything you please. We are speaking of liberty within the boundaries of your relationship, within the confines of your marital contract.

Assets and Liabilities

In this exercise, which I call the "truth process," you and your partner will tell what you think of each other. To start off, designate a Partner A and a Partner B. Partner B will take a pen and paper and draw a line down the center of the page forming two columns, to be labeled "assets" and "liabilities." Partner A will then tell Partner B, using only one word at a time, what he *likes* about her. He might say "caring" or "intelligent," "sensitive," "sociable," etc. Partner B will list in the asset column each word Partner A says.

Then Partner A will tell Partner B what he *doesn't like* about her. This, of course, is more difficult, probably much more so than you might imagine. When you tell someone what you don't like about him or her, you are often revealing something about yourself, which can be threatening. But I want to insist that Partner A be open and honest and that Part-

---

*A koan is a nonsensical statement that forces the individual to confront the reality of his own existence. Within the texture of the koan experience, the individual reaches a "core experience" with self. The awareness from the koan experience stimulates strong motivation for change.

ner B make an effort to absorb nonjudgmentally what Partner A says. He might say "moody," "insecure," "picky," "browbeating," "castrating," etc. Partner B will record each of these responses in the liabilities column. When Partner A has stopped speaking, the roles are reversed.

Why the one-word responses? There is something honest about a single word written in black on a white background. When you see the word "moody" written on the page, you can't really argue with it. If someone tells you in a snide tone of voice, "You're so goddamn moody!" your mind will pick up the snide tone, and you will feel hostility toward the speaker; or your mind will focus on the intensifier "goddamn," and you will be telling yourself, "I'm not *that* moody!" In either case, the impact of the message is mitigated. "Moody," all by itself in unpretentious black and white, says it all.

Quite clearly there is a danger in this process. If you feel that you are dumping on your partner, stop. This is no time to wound your partner with vicious attacks on his or her character. Partner A must speak from the heart, not the head. If he is speaking with deep sincerity and understanding, it should be as difficult for Partner A to say "castrating" as it is for Partner B to hear it. Remember, there is a behavior in your relationship that keeps it from blossoming, and you must change it *together.* After all, you both created it.

Dialoguing

A variation on the "truth process" is an exercise called Dialoguing, in which you and your partner will have a conversation using only one word at a time. Dialoguing is in some ways similar to Assets and Liabilities, but this time you will not write anything, and you are free of a structure; you can take your conversation in any direction you choose. A conversation might look something like this:

HUSBAND: Problem
WIFE: Nights

HUSBAND:	Work
WIFE:	Lonely
HUSBAND:	Money
WIFE:	Love
HUSBAND:	Payments
WIFE:	Children
HUSBAND:	Career
WIFE:	Family
HUSBAND:	Time
WIFE:	Weekends
HUSBAND:	Relaxation
WIFE:	Family
HUSBAND:	Golf
WIFE:	Family
HUSBAND:	Family

This dialogue could go on and on. Notice the density of the conversation, as well as its focused movement. The wife is lonely because husband works nights. From there comes implication that the husband has placed career ahead of family. And from there the realization that even when he has time, the husband prefers to play golf rather than "relax" with his wife and children. As with Assets and Liabilities, using one-word responses avoids all sorts of pitfalls. Communication is much more direct, perhaps even more natural, when we use poignant one-word responses that cannot be flavored by any syntactic seasoning. Practice the above dialogue with your spouse, using the intonation and emphasis you deem appropriate when articulating each word. This should give you a feel for how this exercise works. Now try one of your own.

In the Vulnerability stage, the first steps toward closeness are taken and the seeds of intimacy can begin to grow. Now that you have bared your souls to one another, the truth will have been revealed to you, and from there emotional bonding can occur. This bonding is based on trust. Trust is the cement that holds a relationship together, and it can only come from the willingness to be open, honest, and "real."

Being vulnerable allows both partners to achieve authentic communication from the heart, not the head. It allows you to experience clarity, objectivity, strength, and power; and with all these feelings will come the ability to transcend the dilemma of the affair and go beyond it to understanding and Communion.

CHECKPOINT NUMBER 3

I hope that by now you have allowed yourself to experience the beauty and power of being vulnerable. It may have been years since you felt so vital, so natural, so "real."

But let's take a moment and examine ourselves before we go on. Have you really allowed yourself to be vulnerable? Is there still an obscure need you feel that separates you from your spouse? Or have you left a few boulders intact, just in case? If so, you are denying yourself the opportunity to experience vulnerability, to tap into your "essence," which can only be revealed when all of the lies you have told about yourself are discarded. You've gone this far, now it's time to go all the way. Let your partner see inside of you; allow him or her to trust you. If you conceal at this point, you are merely deferring disappointment to a later date. Remember, you are trying to create from wreckage and disorder a new state of community and balance. The problem in your marriage is that there has been a breach of trust. The breach, or break, can only be repaired through honesty, openness, and the willingness to be vulnerable.

COMMUNION: MUTUAL PARTICIPATION

You have now shared yourself from the position of total vulnerability. In doing so you have created a sense of togetherness, a bond with your partner. Besides him or her, there may not be another person in the entire world who has seen the "real you," so to speak. The real you is what you have been protecting for so long; it is your essence, that which lies behind your "act," behind a wall of boulders you've erected to keep people out, behind the lies you tell about yourself. When you and your partner abandon all this, you create a sense of oneness; you can experience Communion.

Communion literally means "mutual participation." We have seen in Identification that the roles couples allow themselves to assume prevent any attempt to participate mutually or on an equal footing in their marriage. The notion of equality is essential in this stage of Reconstructive Dynamics. There can be no Communion until both partners have unconditional regard for another, until they deeply respect one another as equals.

A meaningful relationship results from the ability to share joys, sorrows, good times, bad times, children, and friends. The Martyr who says, "Lay it all on me!" is, in a false way, assuming total responsibility for a problem that is not all his own. He seeks not Communion but disjointedness. He is comfortable in a destructive role that makes him something more or less than equal. The Intellectualizer, that insecure cerebral type who belittles her partner by intellectually browbeating him, creates not only intellectual but emotional distance. Mutual participation in a relationship, or Communion, is impossible when partners are locked into rigid, mutually exclusive roles, especially when one implies superiority over the other. The Intellectualizer may very well be smarter than her spouse, but she should recognize that he has good qualities of his own; she and her spouse are *different* but equal.

No Saints/No Sinners

Bill, an advertising executive, had always played the puppet in his relationship with his wife, Kathy, a devious manipulator. Bill was the kind of person who rolled with the punches and much preferred yielding in a confrontation to causing a stir. Kathy, however, had strong opinions about how to do everything from mowing the lawn to trussing the turkey. Her ideas were etched in stone, and she would stop at nothing to get her way. Bill was a pushover; if he wanted to spend the holidays in Seattle and Kathy preferred the East Coast, she would decline to have sex with him until he gave in, which he always would. Or she would curry favor with him, offering to bake his favorite cake if only he would take care of the kids while she went to the beauty parlor.

After several years of this, Bill, feeling henpecked and emasculated, had an affair. He and Kathy did get back together, though. Now you might think that the marriage was saved because Kathy pleaded forgiveness from Bill for manipulating and persecuting him for so many years. She did do this, but that's not what brought them back together again. What saved the marriage was Bill's courage in accepting responsibility for having *permitted* Kathy to manipulate him. Kathy's manipulative behavior was wrong, and it caused great problems in the relationship. But Bill's failure to confront negative behavior allowed it to continue to the point of being destructive. Rolling with the punches is all right to a certain point, but in Bill's case it sent him reeling into the arms of another woman and nearly cost him his marriage.

I can't insist enough on the fact that it takes two to create a destructive relationship. The Pleaser's spouse is as guilty as the Pleaser. The husband of the intellectual browbeater is as guilty as she is. The manipulated share responsibility with their manipulators. Destructive behavior feeds off itself and will poison a relationship, so we must actively seek to *alter* patterns that lock us into destructive roles.

In Identification you and your partner isolated the cause of your marital breakdown. In the Communion stage it is very important that both of you accept responsibility for your part in creating the affair. The case in which someone is viciously victimized by an unfaithful spouse is extremely rare. The faithful partner, in almost all of the cases I have seen, contributed to his or her spouse's infidelity, either by accepting destructive behavior or by not responding to basic needs.

Active Listening/Speaking From the Hip

By the time you reach this stage in Reconstructive Dynamics, you and your partner are no doubt much more skillful communicators than before. But your decision to open up to your partner has probably brought forth a lot of emotional garbage that you have been carrying around for years, and communication will get very strained at times. There are always ways, however, to avoid the pitfalls that openness, honesty, and frankness place before you.

One way is to be an active listener. I cannot stress enough the importance of being able to listen nonjudgmentally. This is not a time for manipulation or dumping; it is a time for cooperation and support. Let your partner speak. Just sit and absorb noncritically. If your partner gets stuck it's okay to help him along, but do not interject so that *you* can make a point.

Don't worry about long silences; they often precede meaningful disclosures. If you simply allow your partner to speak, and if you listen in a spirit of cooperation rather than constantly trying to defend your point of view or get a word in edgewise, I can guarantee that amazing things will come up. This may be difficult for you to do. You always may have been the vocal component of your relationship, a much better talker, a more succinct communicator. But if you just sit back and listen, you will discover new things about your spouse.

For the partner who is speaking, it is essential that you speak only for yourself. Again, I want to insist that you use "I" language. "I failed to understand your feelings when you had an abortion a few years ago." Or, "I knew you were feeling inadequate when you were unemployed last year, but instead of being supportive, I persecuted you." Whatever you do, don't dump on your partner. Constructive criticism is okay. If you're not satisfied with lovemaking in your relationship, don't say, "You don't turn me on." That is a punishing remark that suggests your spouse is incapable of satisfying you. Instead say, "I would like a little more foreplay." Or, "I wish intercourse could last a little longer." These requests give your spouse an opportunity to choose to fulfill your needs. They give your partner power.

Also, avoid sermonizing or lecturing. Speak straight from the hip. Don't ramble on or get carried away on tangents and digressions that justify your behavior. Get to the point! Respect the fact that your partner is listening nonjudgmentally to you and that this may not be easy. And remember that your partner will be honest with you only to the degree that you are honest in return.

"We're In This Together"

So in the Communion stage you must verbalize to your partner what responsibility you accept for creating the affair. And let me repeat that you *both* created it! This is not an opportunity to dump on your partner. Forget his or her responsibility for the moment. Just look at yourself, at your own behavior during the marriage up to now, and articulate to your spouse the way in which you think *you* are responsible for the affair.

Make this a structured exercise if you like. Sit down in a quiet place where you won't be interrupted and allow one another to speak uninterrupted for ten minutes. For the person who will be listening, if at any point you perceive that your partner is dumping on you or blaming you, stop him (or her) and simply say, "I feel as if you are dumping on me." This is an essential ground rule in all communication from now on in your marriage. Feel free to interrupt, but be sure to use "I" language and never prod or in any way antagonize your partner. He's doing his best. If he starts dumping, think of it as a slip; your job is to get him back on the track.

I repeat that your goal at this point is for you to express

where in your marriage you accept responsibility for neglecting your partner's needs. Probe your memory and find times when you were aware of a need your partner had but you did not respond to it. Was there ever a time when you knew your partner needed to be stroked for something she did, but you consciously held back? Think of times when you flirted a bit at a party to make your spouse jealous. Think of a time when instead of buoying your partner up in a time of stress or vulnerability, you shot him or her down. Was there ever a time when you manipulated your partner and made him do something that benefited you but was clearly not right for him? Think of all the times you were less than the spouse you promised to be when you said "I do" so many years ago.

In the previous stages of Reconstructive Dynamics you have exposed yourself to your partner emotionally. Now you have accepted responsibility for your actions. The roles you have played in your relationship—the ones that have prevented communication, closeness, and intimacy—have been revealed and cast aside. What remains is You and Your Partner, and from here you can go on to *reconstruct* your marriage.

P.S.: Write Back Soon

Here is another exercise that will provide you with a structured context in which to communicate with your spouse. In this one you and your partner will compose a letter to one another in which you will express "Why I'm afraid to communicate feelings to you." Both you and your partner should take about fifteen minutes to write the letter, then exchange copies. After you have read the letters you will each take time to respond individually to the content. For example, you might say, "I feel that you are absolutely right to say that I create distractions every time you try to communicate with me." Or, "I feel extremely hurt that you didn't trust me enough to tell me about your fears before." The key here is for the speaking partner to use "I feel" statements and for the other partner to listen noncritically. Of course, it's perfectly okay to say, "I feel you've been too harsh." Avoid at all cost any judgments you may be tempted to make. Whatever you do, don't say, "You're wrong!" There is no such thing as a wrong feeling. If your spouse told you in the letter that you seem cold and unapproachable, it is because he felt that way. Instead of trying to invalidate that feeling, try to find out what caused it.

Letter writing is an extremely valuable exercise for many reasons. When we speak, we are experts at playing all sorts of games. When we write, however, our message is more straightforward, uncluttered by body language, gestures, eye contact, and tone of voice. This exercise can give the less powerful personality, or the less articulate person, in a relationship a chance to express him or herself more clearly. In this sense it is an equalizer. Also, when you get it in writing, so to speak, you are confronted very directly with your partner's message ("Every time I try to communicate with you, you create an upset stomach or a headache."), and you will find that in future communication this deactivates denial mechanisms.

I recommend that once a week you take the time to write your partner a letter. You can choose any subject you like. "Why I'm afraid to communicate feelings to you" is a difficult one to write, so the following week you might try "Why I want to go on living with you." Here are a few more:

> "What goals do I have in our marriage?"
> "The areas I felt hurt, anger, frustration in our marriage."
> "How do I avoid intimacy with you?"
> "In what ways can we constructively deal with our feelings of disappointment?"
> "What are the most important emotional ingredients for trust in our relationship?"
> "What do we have going for us in this relationship?"
> "The most unfulfilled needs I feel in our relationship are as follows:"

"How I perceive you getting in the way of your own happiness."

"What do I consider to be your major assets?"

You can continue this list yourself. As with all the exercises you'll be doing in this book, do the writing only for as long as you feel it is necessary. Your goal is to transcend the need for structured communication. Eventually you will learn to communicate spontaneously, effortlessly, and naturally.

Freedom In Marital Bonding

Back to our Zen koan: "True love is giving a person the space to be what he or she is or is not." The key to the Communion stage is sharing the feeling of freedom that results from having opened oneself up emotionally. Paradoxically, in reestablishing harmony in your marital relationship (which is admittedly somewhat confining), you will experience a sense of freedom. Gone is the tremendous burden of guilt on the unfaithful partner. Gone is the anxiety of having to cover one's tracks constantly. The faithful partner no longer has to live with denial mechanisms, feelings of guilt, inadequacy, and anger. When you and your partner open up to one another and reveal your innermost feelings, you experience together a sort of catharsis, a releasing of pressure. In doing so, you sow the seeds of intimacy.

When I speak of freedom in a relationship, I am not talking about the so-called open marriage, in which couples are free to have sex with third parties. Freedom within a structure can often be much more liberating than total freedom, which most people do not really want. I am talking about freedom within the confines of marriage. I am talking about the freedom a husband can give to a wife (or a wife to a husband) when he allows her to be herself, to communicate her true feelings, and to express her genuine needs. The Communion of the two souls is freedom.

Often what led to the affair in the first place is a feeling of emotional confinement. The thesis of this book is that affairs are the result of *unfulfilled needs*. Nine times out of ten, an unfulfilled need is an unexpressed need. Take, for example, the case of Richard and Claire. Richard was brought up in a rather wealthy white Anglo-Saxon Protestant family on the East Coast. His father was a driving, ambitious businessman, a product of the Protestant work ethic who was as inept at handling the emotional needs of his family as he was successful in business. Richard's mother was deeply religious, and there was little, if any, touching in the family; they never talked about sex or, for that matter, any problem that had to do with feelings.

Richard grew up unable to express emotions yet craving physical contact. Claire, though a loving wife and supportive partner in many ways, seemed quite content with a minimum of kissing, hugging, and holding hands. Instead of expressing his feelings to Claire, Richard allowed himself to become frustrated because his wife rarely initiated physical contact. As a result, he began recoiling from her, suppressing his need to be touched, thus creating resentment, anger, and all sorts of complications in the relationship. Because of his inability to express this simple need—which Claire *was* capable of fulfilling—Richard threw up a fence between himself and his wife and ended up seeking out a woman who was as starved for physical affection as he was. Claire never knew what was bothering her husband.

When the affair was revealed, Richard, after much agonizing, finally communicated his need for affection. Claire was at least as surprised as she was hurt, and when she saw how difficult it was for her husband to tell the truth, and when she understood how tormented he had been, her anger at having been betrayed gave way to compassion. Richard, by allowing himself to be vulnerable, gave his marriage a new direction and created the possibility of a nurturing relationship rather than an antagonistic one. Claire, moved by Richard's feelings, was able to take a fresh look at her own attitude toward physicalness. The whole experience was one of great self-discovery for both Claire and Richard. They ended up negotiating a sort of contract whereby Claire would try to be more affectionate and Richard would unblock his feelings. Needless to say, once the initial hurt and anger had dissipated, they were much closer after the affair than they had been before.

This is what I mean by Communion. It is an emotional bonding between two individuals who have opened their souls, who have become vulnerable, and who have come to trust one another completely. When you allow your partner to "be who he or she is or is not," your partner will allow you "to be who you are or are not." You will experience incredible freedom from this unconditional acceptance of you as a person. You will know what it is like to love and be loved.

Unshackling Your Spouse

But what about later on? What will happen weeks or months later when the initial euphoria of this union of souls wears off? Can't giving so much freedom be dangerous? What if your partner decides that he or she is ready to experiment with other people! It is very unlikely that this will happen if indeed you give your partner all the freedom he or she needs. Nothing makes a person desire freedom more than confinement. If you put a choke chain on someone, he will run from you the first chance he gets.

Let me give an example to show how destructive such confinement can be. After several happy years of marriage, Dick began to suspect that his pretty wife Janet was searching for extramarital fulfillment. He would watch her like a hawk at parties when she talked to friends and acquaintances. In the street he would notice if Janet looked at a man passing by. She, of course, began to pick up on this. Although she had no reason to feel guilty, Janet actually started acting as if she were. She noticed that she felt uncomfortable conversing with men at work; she found herself being aloof even with neighbors so as not to arouse suspicion; and if she answered a phone call at the house from a man, she would tell Dick it was a woman. Eventually, Janet began to resent her husband's unfounded suspicions as well as the negative effect it had upon her, so she actually went out and had an affair. Dick became the victim of a self-fulfilling prophecy.

Many of the destructive role models we discussed in Chapter 7 are destructive precisely because they limit the freedom of one or both partners. The Pleaser, for example, in subserviently catering to her partner's every need, crowds him and ultimately alienates him. The Rescuer denies his spouse the feeling of autonomy and the ability to work out problems herself. She becomes helpless, like an animal trapped in a pit, and must always wait for her Rescuer to throw her a rope.

Ask yourself whether you play such games of entrapment. You must at this stage be willing to give your partner freedom, no matter how difficult or scary it may seem. This is especially hard for the faithful partner who has been burned once, so to speak, and is in no mood to play with fire. You must, however, give your partner options and choices. I realize that this can be terrifying. Your partner may choose not to stay with you or may be tempted to stray again. But look at it this way. Denying your partner freedom will *never* get you the result you desire. If your partner stays with you it will be because you are loving and nurturing and allow him or her to be a whole person. If you insist on confining your partner, your strategy will almost certainly backfire. He or she will resent you and choose to take flight.

Gender Exchange

Experiencing another person's reality can be very enlightening. In this exercise, try exchanging roles with your spouse for a day or perhaps for an entire weekend. Even if the roles you presently play are not destructive, the fact that one of you is a man and the other a woman dictates a certain rigidity, which can result in mechanical behavior. For example, the man always repairs things in the house, always mows the lawn, and always cleans the garage. And the woman always cooks, always does the shopping, and always responds first when the baby cries.

I know a couple who have a very synchronous relationship; they each have certain tasks they perform faithfully, and their home is always shipshape. But they have little appreciation of the other's role: consequently they both believe they do 51 percent of the work around the house.

Gender exchange can be extremely valuable. A wife might discover that fixing the plumbing is more difficult than it looks or that more things can go wrong installing storm windows than she expected. A husband might discover that spending eight hours a day with the children is even more stressful than a day at the office or that there is more to keeping a house clean than just dusting a few tables. He might even discover that he feels uncomfortable playing the role of househusband—in spite of the fact that the role is clearly temporary.

Joint Plan

In this exercise you and your spouse will jointly plan some activity. The purpose here is to get you to work together on a physical activity that has strong emotional implications. Let's say, for example, that you are hoping to spend a month at a seaside resort. First, sit down and prepare a plan; delegate responsibilities to each partner, preferably assigning a given task to the person who normally would not do it. If your husband always makes reservations for airline tickets, hotels, and such, *you* should do it this time. If your wife always prepares food for the road, calls friends and business associates to tell them you'll be gone, and shuts down the house before leaving, this time *you* should take care of these things.

Also, you must plan *together* the activities of the trip. No one will just be going along for the ride this time. Make a list of things you would like to do, and ask your partner to do the same. (Once again, it is important to use "I" language here; don't write, "We ought to go deep-sea fishing." Instead write, "I think we should go deep-sea fishing." Or, "I would like to go deep-sea fishing.") See where your interests intersect and where they don't. Negotiate; give one another feedback; make some decisions together. The goal of the joint plan is to assure that both partners take responsibility for whatever happens on the trip. If it fails—and it might—you both did your part, and there will be no hard feelings. If it's a success, you have the satisfaction of having worked together on a project that made you both happy. You will feel like a team.

There are many tasks in a marriage that can be performed together. It is unfortunate that so many households implement a factorylike division of labor, which, in the interests of efficiency, has partners constantly performing parallel duties. Institute as many "joint plans" as you can. Invite some friends over and cook a meal together. Of course, your spouse might make a much better béarnaise sauce than you, but you can chop up the vegetables, sauté the meat, or make the salad. The idea is to at least be in the same room talking to one another, and performing a task together. And when the guests say "That was delicious!" it will be a compliment you can both enjoy.

Of course, you can't do everything together. Each person in a relationship needs room to move, needs time to be alone. But I assure you that if you are able to work jointly in some areas of your marriage, if you are able to experience the gratification which comes with cooperative teamwork, the time you do spend alone will be much more satisfying.

Restating Your Marriage Vows: Rewriting the Script

There is a beautiful passage in Maya Angelou's autobiography, *I Know Why the Caged Bird Sings*, in which Angelou recounts how she, as a child, first understood her identity as a black poet. The revelation occurred one day when she was singing the "Negro National Anthem" and for the first time actually *heard* the words. "Every child I knew had learned that song with ABC's and along with 'Jesus Loves Me This I Know!'" writes Angelou. "But I personally had never heard it before. Never heard the words, despite the thousands of times I had sung them. Never thought they had anything to do with me."

At this point I am going to ask you to restate your marriage vows to your partner. Think back to the first time you recited them. Did you really *hear* what you and your partner said? Did you really grasp that the words "love, honor, and cherish" and the expression "till death do us part" had anything to do with you? This time you are going to write your own marriage vows. This time you will not state them merely as a perfunctory ritual for the benefit of friends and relatives. You are personally going to compose, from the heart and not the head, a new set of guidelines that you will negotiate with your partner. You are going to redefine your relationship. You are going to create a new marriage.

Why is this marriage contract necessary? You and your partner have both experienced a great emotional pain in the recent past. Something went wrong in your marriage, and now you are going to correct it. Think of your marriage as a screenplay. The first years (however many that may be for you) were merely a rough draft, an experimental period during which you made a lot of mistakes. The protagonists, you and your spouse, were right, if somewhat undeveloped, and the basic plot was sound but in need of tightening. The affair was a digression from the story line, and the affair partner a character who simply didn't fit. As any good writer will tell you, in such a case you must be willing to discard what doesn't work and start over with fresh paper and fresh mind.

At this stage of Reconstructive Dynamics, you are both ready for your second draft. Sit down with your partner and rewrite your marital vows. Tailor them to your particular relationship. Make them what *you* want them to be. Let me suggest a format for drawing up your new vows. I recommend that you merely draft a number of "I" statements such as these:

> I realize that fairy-tale romance doesn't really exist and that "happily ever after" demands a lot of work.
>
> I understand that if I am not happy with myself, I will never be able to make you happy.
>
> I realize that communication is the most important aspect of any relationship, and I promise to share my deepest secrets with you.
>
> I promise that I will confront problems as they come up, not wait and hope they will go away.
>
> I understand that marriage is a commitment and that it is in some ways confining; I *choose* to accept that confinement in the firm belief that it will help me to grow as a person.
>
> I understand that there will be joy in our relationship and that there will be pain and sorrow as well.
>
> I will not try to change you so that you better fulfill my needs. If I want to see change, I will fulfill your needs and see what happens.
>
> I will keep my mind and body healthy, and I will expect you to do the same.
>
> I believe that self-knowledge is the most powerful tool a person can have, and I expect you to help me know myself better, even if it means criticizing me.
>
> I will give you unconditional respect as a human being at all times and I expect the same in return.

I promise that I will never be too busy to sit and watch the sunset with you.

Of course, you must tailor this contract to fit the circumstances of your own marriage. If you and your spouse have been unable to listen to one another, if your mutual defensiveness has blocked communication in the past, then you might want to write one like this:

Instead of merely taking stock of my own ammunition when you speak, I will listen to what you have to say. The goal of my communication with you will never be to make you wrong.

I encourage you to put your own personal stamp on your new marriage contract. Perhaps you're a poet:

Each day with you I will make
As fresh as the rains of Spring,
As warm as the breezes of Summer,
As lovely as the colors of Autumn,
As passionate as the fury of Winter

These are just a few ideas: I hope you will think of many more. By all means be creative. Have your new vows typed up or printed, with graphics if you can and frame them somewhere in the house where you will both see them often. Think of these vows as a symbolic rebirth. Your marriage, for all practical purposes, begins when you sign this new contract. It represents a symbolic erasing of the pain and disruption that plagued your "first" marriage. It establishes that newness, that vitality, and that vigor that accompany the setting of fresh goals in life. It creates a bond between you. It is Communion.

CHECKPOINT NUMBER 4

You have now rewritten your marriage vows. Are you satisfied with all of your stipulations? Is there any clause you don't think you can fulfill, which will come back and haunt you later on, thus creating a sense of incompletion? Do you think your partner is capable of fulfilling his or her end of the bargain? If not, make whatever changes are necessary.

I hope that the exercises have been fruitful for you and your partner. Have you been performing them with integrity, allowing yourself to be open, honest, and vulnerable? Has some residual anger been activated through these exercises? If so, now is the time to deal with it. By openly communicating with your partner you can cleanse yourself of this remaining emotional garbage.

It is essential that emotional garbage be purged at this point. The next stage of Reconstructive Dynamics is Acceptance. Your partner wants to accept you for what you are, not for what you pretend to be. If something makes you angry, hurt, resentful, or afraid, that is a part of "you." It is extremely important to pull out any vestigial demon that may be lying dormant in the closet, so to speak. If you don't do it now, it will come up later; I guarantee it. And it will be much more difficult to deal with it then. It could even sabotage much of what you have worked so hard to achieve thus far through Reconstructive Dynamics—which is a lot.

Chapter 9

ACCEPTANCE AND REUNION

ACCEPTANCE

A friend of mine once said to me, "You know, I think marriage is an impossible institution. I can't get used to the notion that in committing myself to one woman, I am denying myself the opportunity to experience many more times in my life the giddy sensation of falling in love, that feeling that there's no tomorrow because you're so incredibly alive today." There's only one response to that statement: It is entirely possible to fall in love with the same person over and over again. And luckily so, because otherwise marriage really would be the ordeal many people think it is.

The Second Honeymoon

In the Acceptance stage, you share a renewed sense of intimacy and trust, precisely what it takes to fall in love again with your partner. You experience something akin to a second honeymoon. Your relationship is new and vital, and the energy level of both you and your partner is very high. You experience the spontaneity you felt as a newlywed, that elusive spark of love you thought you'd never feel again, with your spouse—perhaps even the giddy feeling my friend seems to live for. You may realize that for the first time in years you do not take your partner for granted.

At this time you should feel better about your partner and about yourself than you ever have before. The future should look exciting to you and promise to bear beautiful fruits of joint efforts. You've been through a lot together thus far—through tremendous emotional stress, through deep hurt, through the often excruciating process of venting feelings and becoming vulnerable—and have finally reached the point of reestablishing trust and love. These are the things in life that draw human beings close to one another. By not merely crying "divorce" when the affair was disclosed, you and your partner chose to stay with one another, to work out problems together, and to take measures necessary to ensure that your marriage will survive. You chose to reconstruct—and this verb implies time, patience, and hard work—your relationship.

You come into this, your "second time around," if you will, having learned valuable lessons that only experience can teach. You have gone through a process of self-discovery that made you aware of your own and your partner's needs. And you are developing communication skills that ensure feelings will be "expressed" rather than "suppressed." When you have the power to express yourself, you feel more alive. All aspects of your life will be revitalized.

Forgive and Accept

When I speak of Acceptance, I am referring to acceptance of the affair *and* acceptance of your partner for who he or she really is. By this stage of Reconstructive Dynamics you should both have accepted that an affair has been added to the list of things you have experienced as husband and wife. You cannot deny that it happened, but by accepting it, you can minimize its effect on your present relationship. The purpose of the previous stages of Reconstructive Dynamics was to eliminate the residual negative feelings that can continue to poison a relationship if they aren't confronted. By now all anger and hurt associated with the affair have been vented; and more importantly, both partners have taken responsibility for their part in creating the affair. Only now are you free to move on with your lives.

Perhaps the best way to manifest your mutual acceptance of the affair is to actually forgive one another. Sit down and say the words—"Do you forgive me?" "Yes, I forgive you." Don't make it sound like a religious confession, which it is not. It's just a way of openly acknowledging that you made mistakes and that you can accept your partner with his or her faults.

Even more essential at this stage is for each partner to accept the other for who he or she is. In the Vulnerability stage you both opened up entirely and revealed your inner secrets, including your most hidden needs. That may have been extraordinarily difficult for you. Often your faults are derived from earlier childhood experiences we cannot erase. Furthermore, some faults are downright bothersome and may be offensive to people. But there is really no point in trying to hide them. Your partner has accepted you with all your weaknesses and limitations, and if you acknowledge them, he or she will no longer blame you.

This is an essential point that has been made before but is worth repeating. When you acknowledge your faults, you create context in which people can accept you for who you are. They have no desire to attack you because you no longer seem threatening to them. I read recently: "If you try to make an impression, that is precisely the impression you will make." If you are sensitive about your nose, say, and you pretend that you aren't, people will most likely guess that you are pretending not to be sensitive about your nose. You can't fool your spouse about issues so heartfelt, and if you try to, he or she may very well intentionally push buttons that will activate your defense mechanisms. But if you acknowledge your feelings, that desire to attack disappears. Let your partner accept you for who you are.

And, of course, accept your partner for whoever he or she is. Ask yourself, Can I accept the direction my partner might choose to take with his or her life? If you can't, attempt to find out why. It is essential that you transcend your own considerations and give your partner freedom at this point. If you don't do this now, you will compromise the final stage of Reconstructive Dynamics, Reunion. As you will see, "co-facilitating" and "negotiating" must be done in a spirit of total acceptance.

Looking Out For the Next Curve

Very often at this stage of your new relationship things are going so well that you can't imagine anything disrupting the harmony of your marriage. You feel cleansed and clear, and you are enjoying trust with your partner. All residue from the affair seems to have been eliminated. Then, bingo! Some situational conflict will emerge, like a snake in the grass, which will bring it back. It's very easy to let this happen. During Reconstructive Dynamics you went through an intellectual and emotional cleansing of your relationship. You focused a great deal of psychic energy on yourself and on your partner. For a given period of time, your relationship was the central focus of your existence. Once you get it back in line, everyday life begins creating situations that upset the harmony you worked so hard to establish. Life suddenly starts throwing you curveballs.

It is essential that you be able to distinguish between normal, everyday stress and stress that is recycled from the conflict of the affair. It is not difficult to confuse the two. When things are going well, we tend to forget that stress and conflict are a part of life and that we will never be immune to them. So when things come up, you may think they are related to the affair when in fact they are not. On the other hand, you may find that you are suppressing a feeling of incompleteness concerning the affair, that you are walking around with a cosmetic smile and a false air of reassurance that hide your pain and anger. Use your new sense of awareness to discover the truth about yourself. No one else can.

The Respect Factor

An affair inevitably results in a loss of respect. The faithful partner feels betrayed, emotionally raped, and expresses utter contempt for her assailant at first. The unfaithful partner has lost respect for his partner as well. He may have gone out and had an affair because he felt let down by his partner, because he was disappointed that he or she could not fulfill basic needs. Reestablishing respect in such a situation takes time and patience.

Your respect for your partner has gradually grown as you moved through Reconstructive Dynamics. You respect your partner for his or her willingness to struggle with you to save your marriage. You respect him or her also for being willing, and for having the courage, to become vulnerable and to open up. You have learned things about yourself, gained a new self-awareness, and you appreciate your partner for helping you attain it.

You have just gone through a tremendous healing process together. You have both suffered emotional injury, taken the therapeutic steps necessary to treat the wound, and are walking hand in hand on the road to recovery. You deeply respect one another for having the strength—and it takes a lot of it—to persevere. Intimacy, trust, and respect for your partner are by-products of this process.

You probably learned new things about your partner as well. Very often people who seem fragile respond to difficult situations with uncommon strength and grace. Perhaps you now are aware of how powerful your partner really is. Perhaps you always assumed that your spouse was an intellectual lightweight, but during the turmoil of the affair, he or she offered penetrating insights about you, about people in general, about life. Perhaps he or she led you to a new definition of "intellect." I don't know what will come up between you, but very likely the holocaust of the affair will bring forth hidden qualities that will strengthen your respect for one another.

One of the reasons an affair may have taken place is that your marriage had aged, had lost its vitality. You became bored with your partner or he or she became bored with you; you took each other for granted. The only thing keeping you together may have been the children or the fear of being alone. In Reconstructive Dynamics you arrest that aging process; you stop the atrophy in your relationship. You do this, as you have no doubt seen, through hard work and painful soul-searching. In the Vulnerability stage you opened yourself up and took a good hard look at what was inside. What you found was "you." When we get in touch with what has been hiding behind the emotional barriers we create, we experience an incredible sense of freedom.

You should discover that your entire outlook on life is different. All of the deception, hurt, and anger from the affair are gone. The need to cover up one's tracks, as well as one's emotions, no longer exists. All the energy you expended on these things can be directed to developing yourself and your relationship. You have become vulnerable and discovered that it is okay not to be the emotional equivalent of Mount Rushmore all the time. This gives you the freedom to be who and what you really are and to accept yourself. You will be able to express your needs and wants without feeling intimidated and with no fear of persecution. You will feel real and alive. You will grow.

The Emotional Helping Hand

By this point in Reconstructive Dynamics you and your partner should be very supportive of one another. You have weathered a storm together, so to speak, and overcoming hardship has created a bond between you. You probably noticed that before disclosure of the affair you constantly criticized one another. The tension between you sought outlets in petty demonstrations of hostility. At gatherings you might have intentionally challenged or contradicted your partner in front of friends; or you might have jumped at an opportunity to humiliate your partner by poking at a tender spot she has. This type of behavior is a very common symptom of residual anger. When the anger disappears, so does the negative behavior. Watch yourself closely; if you feel the urge to attack now and then, if you find that you aren't always supportive, try to figure out what it means. Of course, there will always be moments of tension in even the best marriage, but keep your finger on the pulse of your relationship and be aware of any residual anger or resentment that might still be poisoning interactions with your spouse.

There is nothing so beautiful as a couple who support one another. When you marry you choose to spend your whole life with one person, to eat your meals together, to sleep in the same bed, to spend Sunday afternoons together, to take vacations together; in sum, to play the game of life as a team. Yet so few couples develop a sense of teamwork, the sense that if one half of the team isn't functioning well, then the marital machine temporarily breaks down, and it is the duty of both partners to get it working again. You do this by supporting your partner physically, emotionally, and spiritually.

Setting the Scales Straight

One point I want to make very clear is that your goal is not to have a relationship in which each partner always contributes 50 percent. We do not live in a perfectly equilibrated world.

There is no reason why if one partner feels emotionally weak because of stress or illness, the other can't pick up the slack. You have no doubt noticed how emotional rhythms can work. When we see someone suddenly become successful, we immediately feel inadequate. When we see people who are mentally or physically handicapped, we suddenly feel "okay." When a friend or relative comes to us for support in handling the death of a loved one, we immediately feel that selfless power of contributing to someone who needs us. We often get this feeling when someone we love is ill or in a state of emotional weakness, and we jump at the opportunity to nurture. Why? Because life has created a context in which we can contribute more than the normal 50 percent without risk. We perceive an imbalance and feel a sense of power in setting the scales straight again.

In a relationship, both partners are going to experience ups and downs, periods of great energy and creativity followed by periods of indolence and low motivation. As a couple you must attempt to maintain a sense of balance. Support each other; give 80 percent to your relationship sometimes, if that's what it takes. Next week you might only be able to give 10 percent, and your partner will have to balance things out. That's fine. You can probably think of many examples of when you did this in the past without even realizing it. Be aware of such things. Understand the power you have to restore balance in your relationship.

Take a moment and think about the power you have gained through self-awareness thus far in Reconstructive Dynamics. Now is the time to use that power. You have seen your partner as he or she really is, with all his or her weaknesses, and you have accepted that person. Now tap into the power and love you feel and *make* your spouse all he or she can be—try to make your team the strongest around. If you see someone evolve for the better because of you, think of how powerful you will feel and think of how much better your marriage will be.

Healthy Awareness

Now that you have gone through the trying process of self-revelation together, both you and your partner will be much more aware of your own feelings, of each other's feelings, and of the rhythmic ups and downs you experience together as a unit. This new awareness of yourself, of your partner, and of what your marriage means, places your finger on the pulse of your relationship. More than ever before, you will detect the slightest irregularity that occurs.

Let me offer a physiological analogy to explain what I mean. If a nonsmoker inhales a single puff off a nonfilter cigarette, his lungs will immediately react to the shock and respond with a cough. A pack-a-day smoker's lungs, on the other hand, feel absolutely nothing when assailed daily by the smoke of twenty cigarettes. They have become desensitized to the toxic effects of nicotine and God knows how many other poisons. A smoker's body no longer tells him, "Hey, I don't like that stuff you're putting in me."

By eliminating the emotional garbage that clogged the channels of communication with your partner, you cleansed your relationship in a sense. When you and your partner were inhabited by toxic suppressed anger or resentment, you were not in touch with your own feelings, with your partner's feelings, or with the subtle rhythms of your relationship. This emotional garbage, along with denial mechanisms, desensitized you and created a context in which something so tumultuous as an affair could take place with one partner not even knowing it. I am suggesting that now, after you have cleansed your relationship, this is impossible. You and your partner have reached a state of emotional balance and awareness. Even the slightest change will be perceived immediately, and any poison you throw at one another will draw an immediate response.

A New Response To Old Problems

And there will be poison. It would be foolish to tell you that no conflict will ever again inhabit your marriage. Life is by definition a series of conflicts and problems to be overcome. The emotional garbage I so often speak of is an inevitable by-product of being human. The way to prevent emotional garbage from accumulating and constipating you in your interactions with others is to develop the means to eliminate it. You do this by cultivating good communication skills that allow you to open up and release emotional waste. The ability to communicate effectively is the most valuable tool there is to deal with emotional garbage and to cope with the problems that come up in your marriage.

Later in this chapter we will discuss many of the areas in which problems could possibly arise in your marriage. No one will be exempted from conflict; but if you successfully follow the stages of Reconstructive Dynamics, you will better be able to handle it. The rigid roles you used to be locked into made your relationship brittle, with surface strength fortified by denial but subject to cracking under pressure. Now, your relationship is more elastic; the strength you gain from intimacy and trust has made you and your partner resilient, able to absorb the shocks you will encounter in life.

At this stage in Reconstructive Dynamics you feel at ease with your partner, for you have created a space in which you can both move comfortably, with confidence and freedom. You have a foundation of love, warmth, empathy, sensitivity, and supportiveness in your relationship now. When you deal with a problem, your point of departure is one of acceptance and love, not one of anger and hostility. This, of course, makes all the difference. With this fresh outlook, you can begin to really look at your partner's needs—and, of course, fulfill them.

New Music in the House

The affair and the turmoil it creates affect the children much the same way they do you and your partner. Children often feel victimized by marital discord. They feel anger and hostility, which leads them to take sides with one of their parents, usually the faithful partner. If the unfaithful partner leaves the house, children feel abandoned, and they may even feel responsible for their parents' breakup.

The healing process you and your partner go through in Reconstructive Dynamics will affect your children as well. Children are very observant, even—perhaps I should say especially—very young ones. No matter how hard you tried to hide the tension between you and your spouse during the affair, you can be sure that they picked it up. Good feelings send out vibrations the same way bad feelings do. When you and your partner express love for one another, this reassures your children in the same way as discord confused them. Demonstrate your love for one another in front of them. Hold one another; kiss one another; sit together when you watch television. These tokens of affection will not go unnoticed.

Your children will sense the harmony that exists between their parents now, and they will begin to respond in no time. When the strain between you and your partner became unbearable during the affair, and the children saw that you might break up, imagine what that did to their neat little world. Mommy and Daddy represent the cornerstone in the structure of a child's universe. When he sees a crack forming in that cornerstone, it causes great insecurity, which manifests itself in a number of ways: bedwetting, nightmares, hostile and strange behavior, severe introspection, and so on. A child wants to be secure and certain of the future; he wants things to be predictable. The schism between Mommy and Daddy destroys the most certain thing in his life, the family unit. When he sees the breach has been repaired, he may be suspicious at first, but he will come around quickly. Play a tune that makes your children feel secure; they will follow you as they would the Pied Piper. Their world will be predictable and balanced again, and they will begin to take part in the new feelings of joy, intimacy, and love.

Naturally, when you and your partner see your children responding so favorably to your reunion, this will tighten the bond between you. You will understand the tremendous power you have over your children's psyches, and the positive feelings you generate will reinforce your commitment to one another.

By this point in Reconstructive Dynamics, your relationship has been transformed. Supportiveness has replaced the antagonism that neediness and dependency created. When you accept your partner for who he or she is, you eliminate the destructive behaviors we have discussed thus far in the book. The early steps of Reconstructive Dynamics gave you a new sense of awareness, both of yourself and of your partner. You have learned valuable things about your own motivations and expectations vis-à-vis your partner. This awareness should have allowed you to achieve that crucial balance between needs and wants that lead to marital harmony. Perhaps most importantly, you and your partner have made a choice; you have decided that your relationship must survive rather than your preconceptions and prejudices. You've decided to get on with your lives in a spirit of cooperation—togetherness. You are ready for Reunion.

REUNION: MAKING THE REST OF YOUR LIFE THE BEST OF YOUR LIFE

You have now reached Reunion, the final stage of Reconstructive Dynamics. You and your partner have come a long way since the tumultuous disclosure of the affair. You might have thought at that time that saving your marriage was impossible; that the breach separating you could never be repaired; that your only option was to find another partner and start a new relationship. In a sense, that is what you and your spouse have done; and you did it without ever leaving the house.

The stormy seas that swept up your marital boat and sent it crashing against the rocks have calmed; you have taken the wrecked shell of your former relationship and given it a complete overhaul. Your marriage has reached a point of peacefulness, harmony, and stability. You and your partner are comfortable with yourselves, and you radiate the joy and confidence that go hand in hand with the setting of fresh goals in life.

This chapter is about maintaining the stability you now enjoy. In Reunion you will continue to apply what you have learned in order to clear the way for the future of your relationship. It is not easy to maintain stability; it takes constant surveillance and hard work. You must work together and help each other avoid the snags that could cause your marriage to run aground again.

Co-Facilitators

Co-facilitating is a key concept in Reunion. Everybody has mood cycles and varying rhythms of behavior. We all respond differently to the stresses of everyday life. As individuals we experience these things, and as couples we will too, obviously. On a bad day, for example, you might experience a regression, a recycling of some emotional garbage left over from the affair. This is perfectly normal and should be expected. But, as I said before, now you have tools to deal with it. By communicating openly and encouraging your partner to do the same by co-facilitating, you can ease life's stresses.

How does one co-facilitate? You should be able to answer this question yourself by now because you have been doing it throughout Reconstructive Dynamics. First, co-facilitating means making it easier for one another to be open and honest;

also, it means catching your partner when you see him or her indulging in negative behavior. But now that you are balanced and in tune with one another, contrived behavior that lacks authenticity and naturalness will be very obvious.

When you observe contrived behavior, you can be sure that there is some incompleteness between you and your partner. Ask him or her, "Do you feel any anger or pain in regard to me?" Or, "Do you feel that you can trust me at this particular point?" You have been educated throughout Reconstructive Dynamics to be aware of your partner's emotional makeup or his or her chemistry. You should now possess the antidote to treat the poison of pent-up feelings.

Perhaps the partner who did not have the affair experiences moments of doubt about his or her spouse's current fidelity, and this translates into vaguely hostile behavior—smoldering antagonism. If your partner acts this way it is up to you to facilitate the surfacing of the emotion. You might say, "When I'm away from the house, do you wonder if I will do it again? Is there a danger left over? Are there certain gestures or expressions I use or other things I do that reactivate the negative thoughts associated with the affair? If so, I will try to change them."

By co-facilitating I also mean being willing to give 70, 80, even 90 percent sometimes in order to support your partner. When you do this, of course, you make sacrifices; it might mean conceding something to your partner that normally you would staunchly defend; it might mean giving up a golf or tennis game to be with your partner in a time of need. This might sound restricting. Just remember that it can also mean asking your partner to do the same for you.

Of course, there is a line to be drawn somewhere. At what point does one partner in a relationship become parasitic? You'll have to judge that for yourselves. But I believe that if you are aware of your own and your partner's needs, and if you are both honest enough to confront the other when destructive patterns emerge, you will avoid this dilemma.

Obviously, co-facilitating implies a deep commitment to cut through barriers and get at the essence of the problem. Sometimes it will be uncomfortable. You may—as was the case above—have to make painful references to the affair itself long after the fact. But I'm sure you understand how important it is not to have any loose ends in your relationship. As a co-facilitator you must see to it that both you and your partner are complete with one another. Unexpressed anger is incomplete; expressed anger is complete. The former will linger, whereas the latter will go away.

Again, there is no such thing as a wrong feeling. Anger, hurt, and resentment are never "wrong." As a co-facilitator you must create an emotional climate in which feelings can be expressed. Allow your partner to open up. Do whatever it takes to let your partner express his or her anger, disappointment, hurt, and resentment, if that's what's there. If you don't, it will be deferred to a later date and will disrupt the sense of community you have achieved.

We have seen how pent-up feelings can poison a relationship and generate very negative behavior. If you see that your partner is depressed, you now have the ability to recognize that some negative feeling has been internalized and should be ventilated. When negative behavior emerges, it is your duty to share your awareness of the problem with your partner. In a very understanding and sensitive way, you must point out what is incomplete and together with your partner go back to the stage of Reconstructive Dynamics that allows you to deal with it.

Adapting to Change

People change. If you were the same person at age forty that you were at age twenty, you would be a sad case indeed. Every experience we have in life has a particular effect on us and alters the way we perceive reality. At some point in your marriage, you are going to stop and say, "Wait a minute, this isn't the person I walked down the aisle with." Of course, he or she has the same features, the same gestures, the same voice, but things such as habits, tastes, and attitudes can change drastically over the years. Naturally, it is unlikely that you and your partner will follow the same evolution. Indeed, it would be unfortunate if you did.

So how do you handle such changes? Many people respond by grabbing each other by the throat and insisting that the other undo the change he or she has undergone. Such a destructive approach usually leads to separation and divorce. I suggest working out a system of compromise that will allow you to adapt to your partner's changing emotional needs. In the early stages of Reconstructive Dynamics you have already entered the first few commands into this new piece of emotional software you will have at your disposal. In this section of Reunion we are going to complete it.

Negotiation is too much of an intuitive art to permit my setting down any rules to follow. But I can suggest that you be willing to accept whatever is best for your relationship. There are three possible outcomes to a successful negotiation: you will abandon your position because it is not good for the relationship; your partner will abandon his or her position because it is not good for the relationship; or you will decide that both of your positions are tenable and you will compromise.

Consider "Us" Not "Me"

Negotiation must always be done from the position of "us." You and your partner must both have the future of your relationship in mind when you negotiate, not your own particular considerations. Let me offer a case history to demonstrate a negotiation that was conducted with a "me" consideration rather than an "us" consideration.

Bill and Melanie had been married for ten years when Bill, having reached a midlife virility crisis, felt the need to experiment sexually with a young woman. Bill and Melanie worked out their problems, however, and got back together. Melanie had been talking for years about returning to college, and after the affair had been resolved, she felt it was time to go ahead and complete her degree in economics. Bill argued strongly against her doing so, insisting that it would take a lot of time, that she had no financial needs, and that it would get her involved with a whole new set of people, possibly compromising the closeness they had established in the relationship. In sum, Bill argued that Melanie's going back to college was bad for their marriage, or bad for "us."

Fortunately, Melanie didn't immediately concede. She patiently talked with Bill and asked very pointed, focused questions: "How do you feel about the university?" "How do you feel about me eventually having marketable skills that could allow me to pursue a career?" "How do you feel about me having a B.A. or an M.A. after my name?" After a lot of soul-searching, Bill admitted that he felt threatened by the thought that Melanie could become self-sufficient, that she could fend for herself in the world. Getting a degree was just the first stop in Melanie's departure from his sphere of influence. If she had her own job and career, she certainly wouldn't need him. In other words, deep down Bill felt very insecure and couldn't believe that Melanie would still love him if she weren't materially dependent on him. Therefore, in negotiating whether or not Melanie should go back to school, the fundamental issue for him was fear of letting his wife grow and become a free, independent person. This is clearly a "me" consideration.

Challenge? or Expectation?

In the Acceptance stage, we discussed how important it is to accept your partner for whoever he or she is. A poor self-image is usually tied directly to the feeling that one is "unacceptable" as he or she is, and this feeling can create havoc in someone's life. A couple I knew a few years ago provided a case in point. David, a doctor, had established a very good practice, which he loved, and by age forty-two was happily married with two children. He was, by any standards, very successful. Then suddenly one day he came home and announced to his wife Michelle that he had decided to become a surgeon, which meant three grueling years of residency and internship. Michelle, who had supported David through medical school fifteen years before and had been through the loneliness and strain of being a medical student's wife, was less than thrilled at the thought of sleeping alone three nights a week again and having to cook meals for a sleep-deprived automaton. They sat down at the negotiating table. David said that he was unhappy with the lack of excitement in his present practice and insisted that he needed a challenge. Michelle responded that she felt that specializing would totally disrupt their lives, that they had already been through a lot of hard times knowing better days were ahead; now that they had arrived, she was satisfied to merely enjoy them. David, though understanding Michelle's fears perfectly, could not ignore his need for a challenge. They seemed to be at an impasse.

After much discussion, however, it came out that David's need for a challenge was really nothing more than an inability to accept himself for who he was. He had convinced himself, even though he loved what he did, that being a mere practitioner made him somehow unworthy and being a surgeon would give him prestige and raise his self-esteem. Michelle, however, was able to make David aware of his true motivation and to demonstrate to him that she loved him just as he was. With her help, David was able to work things out within himself, and he managed to give up his impulsive desire to be a surgeon. And luckily so, because given the circumstances, going ahead with his original plan would probably have wrecked the marriage.

This doesn't mean that altering one's plans in middle age is always a bad idea. Had David truly been miserable in his job, and had his dissatisfaction spilled over into his home life, it might well have been worth the sacrifice to go ahead and specialize. But after giving it some thought, Michelle and David were able to identify David's decision clearly as a "me consideration" rather than an "us consideration." In your own marriage you and your partner must examine your own motivations thoroughly. Only then can you negotiate effectively.

As I mentioned before, negotiating is an intuitive art. It is up to you to discern your own limits. It's also up to you to realize when you are being taken advantage of or manipulated. If you feel this, tell your partner. Again, use "I" language ("I feel you're manipulating me" rather than "You're manipulating me."). Feel free to be in opposition to your partner. Disagreeing with someone does not mean you don't accept him. It's perfectly understandable that you and your partner disagree on a wide variety of subjects. If you didn't, your relationship would be extremely boring. Say what you feel, keeping in mind that a negotiation with your partner is not a win/lose situation.

Planning the Good Years to Come

Any good executive will tell you that there is nothing quite like setting goals and objectives for getting things done. Your marriage, of course, is not a business; but I believe that establishing goals can give you not only direction but a sense of unity and meaning. When you have a goal, you are conscious of the need to move toward something; this prevents stagnation. It doesn't really matter what the goal is. You and your partner might set out to become the President and First Lady, or you might simply wish to save money together to buy a new refrigerator.

I want to make clear the distinction between goals and expectations. A goal is something you and your partner set and try to attain together. An expectation is a one-way street. It comes across as a demand, whether explicit or implicit, that one partner makes upon another, or upon himself, and the burden of fulfilling that demand rests upon only one person. Expectations are, not surprisingly, often unreasonable. High expectations equal high risk of failure.

A self-imposed expectation is outer-directed, the result of a desire to be recognized by others or the need to prove oneself. We often are driven to fulfill expectations, and we end up swallowing life whole rather than sitting back and enjoying it. David, the general practitioner who felt he had to be a surgeon, was very likely responding to an expectation placed upon him by his parents or peers. Had he fulfilled that expectation, he would almost certainly have been dissatisfied, wondering, Is that all there is?

A goal is set to satisfy one's own needs. A goal is flexible; it can change and it need not be achieved within any strict time frame. In your relationship you should have mutual and individual goals. For example, you might set a goal to buy a house within two years and make sacrifices together to achieve that. I encourage you, however, to maintain this cooperative spirit in helping your partner fulfill his or her individual goals as well. If your husband decides to quit smoking cigarettes, you can support him in many ways to help him reach his goal. Or if your wife wishes to open a small business, your knowledge and support could help her succeed. You'll get genuine satisfaction from doing that. It is extremely important that both you and your partner have direction. By supporting your partner to reach his or her goal, you are fulfilling that person, and that gives you a feeling of power and movement.

Seasons of Change

In the rest of this chapter we will discuss a number of areas in which conflict is likely to arise in your marriage. It takes more than good intentions to keep a marriage functioning smoothly. It takes hard work, and it takes a high level of awareness. Without awareness and understanding, you face unarmed life's slings and arrows.

Think of your life as a series of seasonal changes. You will experience in the future a number of phases, some as predictable as colors of autumn, others as unforeseeable as a summer squall. Perhaps the most important thing to remember is that, like the seasons, these phases are temporary, and with time you can work through them. Everyone will confront some, if not all, of the conflict areas in questions. Use the tools you have acquired thus far in Reconstructive Dynamics to deal with the problems as they come up.

Career Change

In the United States people now change jobs about once every three years. It is unlikely that you and your partner will work in the same place for the rest of your lives. Few things are as important to our state of mind as our work. You spend the greater part of your waking day at work, and the feelings generated by your job are inevitably carried over into your family life. New direction in one's career, for better or for worse, can be very disrupting in a marriage.

Success can be just as devastating. An extreme example was portrayed in the film *Valley of the Dolls*. The protagonist is a struggling performer who marries her agent, a timid, low-key, rather homely fellow, the very antithesis of Hollywood glitter. He supports her through some rough years until finally she makes it big, at which time she begins to frequent the movie jet set. Her husband, who had helped her succeed, doesn't fit in. Of course, she leaves him for some flashy guy. Hollywood would have it no other way.

But in real life this sort of thing happens all the time. A couple will marry while in college, when they seem to have a lot in common and share similar values. One partner will become very successful in his career and enter a new social realm with different values. It's very difficult to separate the work milieu from one's personal life. If you land a job as an executive in a big company, you will dress in a certain way, speak in a certain way, dine with the bigshot clients and colleagues, and your children will attend different schools and frequent different friends. You will have moved up a rung on the social ladder. You will have a new class identity and a self-image to match. If your partner is unable to move comfortably in your new circle of peers, if he or she is unwilling or unable to adopt new values, there will be a great deal of strain in your relationship. It is extremely frustrating for someone to see his spouse resisting his career growth. We want to share our successes; if our spouse cannot do so, we will find someone who can.

Sex Cycles

Quite obviously, the sex-cycle drive of either you or your partner is likely to change at some time in your marriage. Few things are as misunderstood as sexuality; keeping two people's level of sexual desire perfectly tuned to one another is impossible. As you age, your cycles of sexual desire are likely to become even more complex and mercurial. A woman during menopause will often experience a lower sex drive but a greater need for physical contact. After menopause, a woman enjoys a new sense of freedom, and she may have a strong sexual desire coupled with a great need to be recognized for her femininity.

A man might at some point see his sexual drive increase in response to anxiety about losing his ability to perform sexually. As with women, there are very complex and unpredictable physical and emotional factors that can influence sexual behavior.

The key to avoiding problems in this area is to interpret, not to react. If your sex drive decreases, or if you sense that your partner's has decreased, don't ask, What's wrong with me? That is reaction. Be aware that at certain times things such as this come up and that they are not permanent. Interpret your partner's behavior and try to understand it. Your partner needs reassurance from you, not hostility or guilt. Act as a co-facilitator. Allow your spouse to experience whatever feelings come up. This is especially important in the area of sexuality, as you will see when we discuss it in detail in Chapter 10.

Menopause: Biology Strikes

In our society, many women have been bred to do essentially one thing: bear and raise children. Sometimes in their midforties most women's biological clock strikes, and they can no longer become pregnant. This physiological change can have deep psychological consequences. Suddenly a woman's very purpose in life, her raison d'être, is negated. In our culture the shock is doubled by the fact that at about the same time children are beginning to leave home to go to college or get married. Not only has a woman's body denied her the freedom to fulfill her child-bearing role, the circumstances of her life suddenly deny her the right to be a nurturing, maternal figure for her children. She feels, quite understandably, unneeded. The enormous responsibility she had borne for years and years is suddenly lifted, leaving her depressed, moody, and confused about her purpose in life.

All she has left is her husband. Often, men will respond to their wives' problems by saying, "Oh, it's all in your head." Or, "Go get some medicine from the doctor." A convenient solution to a complex problem. But it isn't really a solution at all. At this point in her life a woman needs signs from her partner that she is loved and needed. She needs to be nurtured.

It is not uncommon for a husband to actually feel threatened by the changes he sees in his wife. Along with the host of conflicting emotions a woman feels comes behavior that will seem incomprehensible at times. She will feel depressed for no apparent reason, burst into tears without warning, lose interest in things that normally excite her. Understandably a man might feel he's responsible for his wife's depression and create feelings of inadequacy—precisely, of course, what she doesn't need.

What she does need is support. She needs a co-facilitator, someone to be with her during a difficult period. Very often women have a great need for physical contact—not sex, just touching, caressing, hugging. You as a co-facilitator might make a special effort to see that your wife feels needed and to assure her that she is still sexually attractive. You must make conscious efforts to validate her, to let her know you are looking forward to spending the rest of your life with her. Make some long-term plan or set some goals. Make an effort to involve her in activities such as sports, hiking, boating, etc. You might just bring her flowers now and then. Anything that will fill the great void that has been created in her life.

Midlife Crisis: Don't Look Back in Anger

You have no doubt heard the term "male menopause" used from time to time. Some dislike the term because men experience no observable physiological (i.e., hormonal) changes as women do. But most men unquestionably go through a sort of crisis sometimes in their forties or fifties. A man's career, which has been the focus of his psychic energy for years, is now quite stable, and he is financially secure. That drive to "make it," which gave meaning to his life up to now, evaporates because he has indeed "made it." Often he will notice that his sex drive isn't what it once was; he questions his own virility, and it scares him. He becomes intensely aware of his own mortality and starts counting the years, wondering whether enough time remains to do all the things he wants to do. This malaise very often translates itself into a spirit of wanderlust, the desire to escape the confined life he leads, or into a need to experiment with other women in order to prove he is still attractive.

Few men actually pack their bags and go sailing around the world. Somewhat more have an affair with a younger woman. Most, I would guess, never do or say anything about their feelings. It is difficult to say to your wife, "Honey, I feel that I need to leave you and the kids for a couple of years so I can experience all things I should have done twenty years ago." Or, "Honey, I'm experiencing a virility crisis, and I need to spend some time with younger women." Consequently, most men say nothing at all. They keep their feelings to themselves, feel intensely guilty about them, and let them smolder for a few years until they pass.

This may sound fine and dandy; such a man may seem a model of self-control. But if you've got this far in the book, you should understand what suppressed feelings such as these result in. There may never be a volcanic explosion, but pent-up frustration will cause tremors of discontent in your relationship. A man suffering from such a midlife crisis will vent his antagonism toward his wife and children in petty ways he won't understand. He loves his family deeply, but they are his ball and chain; they keep him tied down.

A very interesting case came to my attention not long ago. Frank was a successful businessman who had launched his career immediately after college and gotten married in his early twenties. He worked very hard for twenty-five years and finally had the time to enjoy the fruits of his efforts. However, he began creating extreme problems with his family. He became irascible, subject to unexplained outbursts, and would make condescending, snide remarks to his wife and children.

Frank's negativity was the result of a deep feeling of regret for not having lived life more fully when he was younger. Reflecting upon what he'd done thus far in his life, Frank confronted the "I could've, I should've, I would've, but I didn't" syndrome. He began to regret having married so young rather than traveling and living a more free-spirited youth. His frustration spilled over onto his wife and his two sons, who, to complicate matters, were doing exactly what Frank had wished he had done. In their early twenties, neither had chosen a career yet; they were quite openly experimenting with women, something Frank hadn't had much time to do, and they had traveled the four corners of the globe—on his money yet! Frank became extremely jealous of his sons. He urged them ad nauseam to get jobs, to settle down. When their friends would land a good career position, he would never miss an opportunity to dwell on it. His resentment, of course, created an enormous rift between himself and his sons. He saw in them the very mirror of his own frustration and inadequacy. They were free; he was bound—and he was going to get them for it. Of course, George was utterly unaware of what he was doing. It seemed to him that he was merely being a good father, encouraging his sons to be successful. If George had confronted his true feelings, if he had openly vented the shapeless feeling of discontent that had so unexpectedly come over him, he would have recognized that his sons were doing just what he wanted them to do; indeed just what he had set them up to do.

If you should see such behavior in your marriage, it is crucial to understand that it is a very common reaction to the anxiety one feels in middle age. As a co-facilitator, it is your task to make your partner aware of the consequences of his negative behavior. Encourage him to vent his feelings.

Both menopause and midlife crisis will create problems; be ready for them! Facilitate for your spouse. Allow him or her to experience feelings as they come up. They will come up, and there is no point in denying them. All the seasonal crises in your relationship should be discussed openly. Keep them in perspective. Try to control them through awareness rather than allowing them to control you.

Retirement: A New Sense of Purpose

Some people slip into retirement gracefully, ready and willing to accept the peace, quiet, and freedom they are finally able to enjoy after years of hard work. Others will not be so lucky. They have difficulty in adapting to the radically different emotional and psychological climate they now inhabit.

A man working every day for forty years will often find it extremely difficult to fill the hours of the day once he's retired. He may feel worthless and bored. The structure of his working life validated his existence by keeping him busy and by allowing him to be productive. Now he can think of nothing better to do than watch television.

A woman, on the other hand, doesn't necessarily see a radical shift in the way she spends her time. But now all of a sudden she has a husband on her hands twenty-four hours a day. Women can develop a strong sense of territory. The house during the day is their space, and now it has been invaded. I knew a man who at age sixty-five decided he wanted to start making bread. Unfortunately, he could only practice his new craft in his wife's kitchen. After only a few days she could take it no longer and expelled him from her temple.

We are talking about suddenly breaking patterns of behavior that have been formed over not just years but decades. The structure in which both partners have moved comfortably has been reshaped, and they become utterly disoriented.

One couple I encountered, Bert and Joan, had a fairly typical experience trying to adjust to retirement. Bert had been a machinist and worked ten hours on weekdays and eight hours on Saturdays for forty years. His schedule hadn't permitted him to develop hobbies and interests not related to his work. During the first few months of his retirement he was absolutely despondent. He felt useless, confused about his purpose in life, and angry at himself for not enjoying the freedom he'd longed for for years. His new-found freedom was a burden, and he felt as if he were crawling on bruised knees to his grave.

Bert's depression took its toll on Joan. Over the years she had developed a healthy social life, which she continued to lead. She had friends, interests, hobbies, and responsibilities. Bert became a burden to her. He resented the fact that her life was so balanced while his was floundering. Eventually they were tearing one another apart, and a happy marriage was turning into a nightmare.

Bert slowly began to come around, though, and Joan was responsible for much of it. She became so fed up with him sitting around the house moping that she coached him into getting involved in activities. They joined a bowling league together.

There they met new people. Bert became friendly with a fellow who did woodworking as a hobby, started making furniture himself, and was soon fascinated by it! It was especially gratifying because he was able to develop similar skills to those he'd perfected for forty years as a machinist.

When retirement begins, couples very often find themselves face to face with one another on a daily basis for the first time in years. This can be terrifying. With children in the house, there is always a third party on whom to focus attention when things get uncomfortable. A third party can act as a smokescreen that hides one partner from the other. When that third party disappears, communication seems somehow incomplete; or perhaps it would be more appropriate to say that for once the incompleteness is apparent. It can no longer be camouflaged by directing one's attention elsewhere when a problem comes up. A couple must look at themselves in a new way, suddenly vulnerable. They are obliged to confront the truth about themselves. They might be horrified to find they have nothing to say to one another. They have been communicating for years, not *with* each other but *through* one or several intermediaries.

How can you avoid the pitfalls of retirement? The best way is to prepare for them. Cultivate hobbies to keep you busy: gardening, woodworking, writing, arts and crafts. Become involved in organizations that can use your skills, so that you feel needed. As a couple, makes plans for yourselves well in advance. Sit down and decide whether you are going to travel, continue your education, buy a new house. Make individual plans and joint plans. Problems will arise, but confront them in a spirit of co-facilitation.

The ABC's of Conflict Negotiation

Here is an exercise that will help you handle conflict in the areas just discussed or in any situation that might come up. The goal of this exercise is to get to the essence of a problem.

Finding this essence is not unlike peeling away the layers of skin on an onion. Don't cut right to the center; instead, move slowly, one step at a time.

Write at the top of a blackboard or large piece of paper, the problem you and your partner face. Let's say, for example, that Charles is having trouble accepting the fact that his wife Sally has chosen to pursue a career. The essential thing to get down on paper right away is, "Charles is unhappy" or perhaps, "Charles is uneasy." Now I am going to demonstrate what I call "A, B, C, D therapy."* "A" stands for "activation" or cause. "B" stands for "belief." "C" stands for "consequence." "D" stands for "direction" or new course of action.

Start with "A." What activated Charles's problem? Quite clearly Sally's decision to pursue her career. Now, "B." What is Charles's belief about this? Charles believes that Sally will make new friends, develop a stronger self-image, become financially independent, and ultimately lose touch with him. He feels threatened by his wife's decision. "C," the consequences? As a result of his insecurity, Charles has been boasting a lot and at the same time belittling Sally. This negative behavior has caused the initial tension to grow out of control. I want you to actually write this out. I want you to experience your conflict visually. When you get done with "C," stop and look at what you've written. Sit back and absorb it. Try to understand the dimensions of the problem.

Finally, move to "D" and write down the new direction you and your spouse intend to follow in your relationship. To do this, you will have to negotiate. Sally and Charles would have to sit down and discuss each other's feelings. Hopefully, Charles would overcome his fears, and Sally could pursue her career with his blessing. In such a case, for "D" they might write, "Charles will support Sally in her career" and "Sally will help Charles overcome his feelings of inadequacy."

I like A, B, C, D therapy very much because it allows you to

---

*Adapted from a model devised by Albert Ellis.

actually *see* the anatomy of a problem. This exercise can be quite difficult to do with integrity because it demands a lot of thought. But I think you will find the results both interesting and rewarding. Try it.

CONCLUSION

You have now completed Reconstructive Dynamics. Perhaps before you go on you should sit down with your spouse and think about what you have learned about each other and about yourselves. Try to recall where you were before you started and where you are now. What benefits have you reaped from being honest with your partner, from expressing your feelings, from being vulnerable, from accepting each other, and from agreeing to support one another in the future?

I sincerely hope that Reconstructive Dynamics has been a cleansing process for you and your partner. I hope that ventilating your feelings has taught you that being open and honest with those you love draws you much closer to them and makes you feel new and alive. And finally, I hope that you have developed a fresh perspective on what it means to "communicate" and have acquired the skills to do so effectively.

One final comment before you go on. Reconstructive Dynamics is an ongoing process—you never really *finish* it. For example, the tools you used to communicate in Reconstructive Dynamics will serve you for the rest of your life. By opening up and revealing who you really are, you have allowed yourself to break out of destructive roles, or life scripts, that prevented you from growing as a person. Now that you are unstuck, so to speak, you can evolve—you can change! Reconstructive Dynamics is a continuous process of keeping yourself and your partner from falling into destructive patterns of behavior. When two people are committed to helping one another grow emotionally, they feel alive and excited about life—and, of course, their marriage can really work, not just survive.

Part Three

REVITALIZING THE MARITAL AND FAMILY BOND

Chapter 10

REAPPROACHING
PHYSICALNESS AND SEXUALITY

A political science professor of mine years ago opened the quarter by telling his audience of nearly one thousand freshman that at any given moment 80 percent of the class would be thinking about sex. "Chances are I will be too," he added.

Sex. That little three-letter word is more emotionally charged than any other in our language. People die every day in lover's quarrels or over trifles. Advertisers exploit sex to sell anything from automobiles to whiskey to dandruff shampoo. The mere word "sex" in a newspaper or magazine headline can assure a constant draw of customers at the street-corner kiosk. Why all this hubbub about sex? Certainly words such as "murder," "injustice," "inflation," and "plutonium" deserve more attention, don't they?

Maybe so, but they don't get it. Sexuality is the most complex, sensitive, misunderstood and—alas—interesting aspect of our personalities. Sexuality is mysterious; it defies reason. We try to understand it, but strangely enough, we don't really want to solve the mystery, because that would take the romance out of our lives.

Nevertheless we have to deal with our sexuality, that most private, vulnerable, and frightening part of what we call "self." When trying to reconstruct a marriage after an affair, the most difficult piece to fit back into place is the sexual one. I've seen many couples who get their marriage functioning smoothly everywhere but in the bedroom, and it prevents them from being truly happy. Sexual intercourse is the ultimate form of intimacy, so it is in the area of sexuality that a couple really test their ability to experience the emotional bonding that a marriage is all about. When a couple fail to reestablish a healthy sex life after an affair, the other aspects of their relationship will suffer because of it.

An extramarital affair is a breach of contract. One partner has broken the marriage vows he or she spoke on the day of the wedding. In Communion (Chapter 8) you rewrote your marriage vows and made a new commitment to your partner. In Reapproaching Physicalness and Sexuality you and your partner have to deal with another breach of contract, this time an unwritten one. When two people establish physical intimacy with one another they make an unspoken agreement not to share their bodies with anyone else. Those who advocate unbridled sexual expression within a marriage or without often ignore the strong implications the sex act has for human beings. For both men and women it is an intensely private part of a relationship. When two people experience true intimacy, or love, sex is not merely a carnal bond but a sacred emotional pact. It is no coincidence that we refer to an affair as a breach of "faith"—we speak of *faith*ful and un*faith*ful partners—a profane betrayal that results in deep hurt and passionate anger. This chapter is about the consequences of this broken pact and the ways a couple can handle them.

A MAN AND A WOMAN

Let's take a moment to examine the concepts of masculinity and femininity. They are both attitudes, or states of mind, that have been inculcated in us since early childhood by our parents and reinforced by such things as fairy tales, the school system, and the media. Some people struggle against, and a few even transcend, the culturally established male and female roles, but most of us accept them without much resistance.

How do you explain masculinity? First it is important to understand that a man's sexuality is an essential part of his being, when one feels "masculine" he senses the unity between his sexuality and his being. To put it less esoterically, he feels complete, or whole, especially when he sees that his masculinity attracts women. Of course, there are different definitions and varying degrees of masculinity; for example, you have the macho toughness of a disheveled Charles Bronson, the gentle cuteness of a well-groomed Tom Selleck, and the artistic charm of a rather homely Alan Alda. All know they are masculine, though for different reasons.

And femininity? A woman can appear feminine for as wide a range of reasons as a man can appear masculine. Femininity is exuded by the way a woman walks, by the curves of her body, by the look in her eye, by her smell. Women do all sorts of things to enhance these tokens of their femininity, such as wearing high heels, revealing clothes, makeup, and perfume. When a woman senses that men find her feminine, she feels powerful. I once met a very beautiful and very feminine Turkish woman who was wearing a lovely dress with no stockings on an icy cold day. I asked her if she wasn't uncomfortable. "No," she replied. "When a woman feels pretty in a dress, her legs don't feel cold."

Many say that having a child is the ultimate fulfillment for a woman. This purely biological function and the mysterious bond that is created between mother and newborn child are affirmations of a woman's femininity. Only a *woman* can have a child. Femininity is the union of a woman's sexuality and her being.

When a person first understands that he or she is loved by someone of the opposite sex, we could say that person experiences the unity of sexuality and being. What happens when a person realizes that his or her partner has had an affair? The unity between sexuality and being is broken; the terrible feelings of fear, hurt, and confusion are the result of this disunity. A woman feels violated; we often refer to what she feels as "emotional rape," an appropriate sexual image. A man feels "emasculated" (literally "made unmasculine"), sexually inadequate, even "castrated." The image of "castration" is very interesting. When we say someone feels "castrated," we are figuratively, if somewhat grotesquely, implying that his genitals have been removed. Again, disunity of sexuality and being.

After an affair, a couple who wish to stay together must reestablish intimacy on all levels, including the sexual one. Even after Reconstructive Dynamics, even after the wounds of the affair have been patched up and anger and resentment have been vented, remnants are going to surface—especially in the most delicate area of human existence, sexuality. It is hard enough to have a good sex life in a smoothly functioning marriage; after an affair it can be downright difficult. One or perhaps both partners will likely experience some form of sexual-identity crisis. You must work to overcome it. A man who doubts his masculinity, or a woman who doubts her femininity, will bring all sorts of complications into a couple's sex life. Sexual insecurity leads to repressed sexual fears and rigid, unspontaneous sex. In the worst of cases it can lead to impotence and frigidity.

You can imagine how the unwillingness to confront sexual fears can cause problems that will spill over into all aspects of a relationship. A person who is sexually insecure wears his frustration like a fig leaf, and it can wreak havoc in the work environment and the family as well as in the actual relationship.

THE TRIANGLE

An affair superimposes a complex triangle on a couple relationship. Each partner must deal not only with his or her spouse but with the invisible third party whose presence is strongly felt emotionally if not physically. Both partners tend to be very self-conscious, and sex can be very mechanical, lacking in spontaneity.

I think it is important to discuss the problems facing the male faithful partner and the female faithful partner separately. First, the male. In the past a man whose wife cheated on him was labeled a "cuckold," and he usually wore that shameful social tag to his grave. In certain countries even today, not even in jest do you dare call someone by that name. Fortunately, in the United States the word "cuckold" is one we vaguely remember from Shakespeare, and most people probably don't even know what it means. The sooner it disappears from the language the better. But the concept still lingers. In the past twenty years the feminist movement has changed sexual attitudes to some extent, yet we still live in a society that accepts male infidelity more readily than female infidelity. Consequently, the social stigma on a man whose wife cheats on him is greater than it is on a woman who has been betrayed.

So when a man reestablishes intimacy with a woman who has cheated on him, he has to deal with deeply ingrained cultural imprints that surface when an affair takes place. He feels that his wife has been "soiled." He feels "betrayed" and may elevate that betrayal to mythical, sometimes biblical proportions. After the disclosure of the affair, he may have gone through the stages of righteousness, in which he falsely perceived himself as the very image of virtue, and vindication, in which he called for vengeance and retribution. Those stages pass, but traces of anger and hurt will be recycled later on.

And most likely, they'll be recycled in the bedroom. A man can *talk* about his virility all he pleases; he can give off signals that entice and seduce women; he can make himself the talk of the town. But when you really get down to it, the only thing that matters to a man is what he actually *does* in the bedroom. I have know a lot of men who have difficulty rehabilitating their sex lives after an affair because they try too hard. They almost always think that the reason their wives cheated on them was because they were inadequate sexually. A man's immediate reaction to an affair is to look down at his penis and say, "you failed." When he starts having sex again with his wife, there is tremendous pressure to make up for that failure. Sex becomes for him exactly what it should never be: a performance.

Women I've talked to often tell me that their husbands will pester them after sex with questions like: "Did you have an orgasm?" "Did I wait too long?" "Was I premature?" "Was I good?" Such men see sex as a theatrical production; they want to be applauded afterward and asked back for an encore. This attitude, however, creates unnecessary pressure and prevents both partners from experiencing what sex *can* be. It very often leads to "stage fright," translated here as impotence, or exaggerated sexual exhibitions that seem rehearsed and ridiculous. In a performance there are always expectations and judgments, and there is a barrier between actor and audience. You don't want that kind of a relationship. You want to perform together in order to mutually experience pleasure and achieve a feeling of oneness. When you finish having sex you should never say to your partner, "You were great," but *"We* are great."

A woman whose husband has had an affair probably will not suffer so badly from the social stigma of an affair, although I have seen cases where women do. The greatest obstacle facing a woman in reestablishing physicalness and sexuality with her husband is the feeling of emotional rape we discussed earlier. This is especially true if the affair had been going on for a long time before she found out about it. She will feel disgust for the man who violated her, who lied to her, and who betrayed her.

A woman will question her sexuality after an affair. The fact that her husband sought out another woman reminds her that she is no longer as young as she was and that she may not be as attractive. As with men, most women will immediately think the affair was caused by unfulfilled sexual needs (although this is usually not the case), and they will have doubts about their femininity. It is very common for women to diet and pay great attention to their appearance after an affair in order to make themselves feel more feminine again.

FAKING IT, NOT REALLY MAKING IT

To really feel complete, however, to reunify her sexuality and her being, a woman must feel that she can satisfy her husband sexually. Unfortunately, she will often try too hard to fulfill her partner and convince him that she can be just as good or better than his lover was. In doing so, many women lose sight of the fact that they are supposed to enjoy sex themselves. They will be "faking it and not really making it." Motivated by a blind desire to please (not unlike the Pleaser we discussed in Chapter 7), they will sacrifice themselves for fear of disappointing their partners. If you should find yourself doing this, recognize that it is dishonest, and that while pretending may seem to keep things running smoothly, it is a device you use to avoid being vulnerable. When you refuse to be vulnerable, you deny both yourself and your partner the experience of true intimacy.

Understandably, a woman who has been betrayed will be uneasy in the bedroom for a while. As feelings of hurt and anger are recycled, she will very likely feel cautious and unspontaneous. Let's face it, making love places you in a very vulnerable situation, and you have to have absolute trust in your partner to really enjoy it. Very often women tell me that they think they trust their husbands, but when it comes to making love with them, all of the fear and insecurity suddenly resurfaces, and they begin to have doubts. They begin to wonder, Does he really want to be with me, or is he thinking about her? Or, Is he just acting as if he enjoys this in order to please me?

If you are constantly doubting your spouse's sincerity or comparing yourself to the invisible third party, it will poison your sex life and prevent you from achieving your goal of renewed intimacy. I encourage you to confront your insecurities; express them to your partner. Tell him, "Dear, I constantly compare myself to what I imagine your lover to be, and it's getting in the way of my trusting you." If you have the courage to confront your feelings this way, you give your partner the chance to help you overcome them. When you work together to overcome fears, you *create* good feelings, which replace the bad, and you can then experience intimacy.

LOVE AND INFATUATION

Most affairs are inspired not by love but by infatuation. The word "infatuation" literally means "to make foolish," which is precisely how many unfaithful partners feel when the initial euphoria of an affair wears off, and it usually dies quite quickly. When a couple reapproaches physicalness and sexuality, it is extremely important for both partners, but especially the faithful partner, to understand that no foundation of "love" was established in the extramarital relationship.

What is the difference between love and infatuation? Infatuation is a temporary, ephemeral feeling of sexual attraction for another person. Infatuation can never be sustained; it necessarily turns into something else. Occasionally it may develop into love, but nine times out of ten it becomes indifference. The bond established in a relationship based on infatuation is purely physical and affords only very superficial gratification. I call it "gland to gland" intimacy.

There is nothing necessarily wrong with gland-to-gland sex. If that's what both partners are looking for, fine; but it's important to recognize that it has nothing to do with love. Love is a permanent feeling rooted in our very souls. In a week you could easily forget someone you were infatuated with. If you ever truly loved someone, and that includes experiencing total vulnerability and trust, you know that person will stay in your heart forever, regardless of whether or not you remain physically together. When you love someone, sex is heart to heart, never gland to gland. The *quality* of the experience of sex in a relationship based on love is entirely different.

In reapproaching physicalness and sexuality after an affair, this is perhaps the most important thing to keep in mind. The affair was *not* based on love; your marriage is. You and your partner have been through a lot of good and bad times over the years, and your experiences have created a strong bond between you. That doesn't mean you won't have problems; in fact, two people who truly love one another are much more likely to have problems than two people who are merely infatuated. Many of the affairs I have seen amount to little more than a quick thrill, after which the unfaithful partner feels rather silly for having yielded to a physical urge that gave him only very brief and superficial satisfaction.

In Chapter 6 I insisted that the unfaithful partner express precisely what he (or she) got out of the affair. It is extremely important to really probe your psyche and figure out what the payoff was for risking the breakup of your marriage. You may have had a very deep unfulfilled need, but you may also have been responding to a superficial desire to feel attractive to the opposite sex. Describe your feelings to your partner: "I had an affair because I felt insecure about my sexuality. I allowed myself to become infatuated with someone because I thought that would solve my problem. It didn't, and now I feel pretty foolish."

It is important that both partners understand this distinction. The affair was based on infatuation whereas your marriage is based on love, and it's worth saving if only for that. I'm convinced that if you've come this far in the book, you believe this too.

THE UNFAITHFUL PARTNER

The unfaithful partner's greatest obstacle to reestablishing intimacy is the memory of his or her lover. If you have been having sex with someone else for some time and you suddenly stop, you may have difficulty readjusting to your partner, especially if your lover was very attractive physically. A lot of people tell me that when they are making love to their partners after an affair, they have trouble getting excited without fantasizing about the former lover. This is a serious problem because the faithful partner will usually know that her (or his) spouse is emotionally absent and will feel deeply hurt. When making love, you give off all sorts of nonverbal messages that tell your partner where your mind is really at. If you close your eyes, drift off to some hotel room, and have an orgasm with the image of your former lover, your spouse will sense that—and will no doubt resent you for it.

Sex under these circumstances is mechanical, rigid, and unsatisfying. Instead of bringing a couple closer together, such mutual masturbation merely draws attention to the pathetic gap between "what is" and "what could be," and both partners end up erecting barriers to protect themselves from the flood of bad feelings they have created. If both partners are not psychologically in the same room together, sex is a perfunctory act, more a duty than a delight, and while it may provide you a superficial appearance of marital harmony, it ultimately deprives you of true intimacy.

When you live with a person for many years, you get to know his or her habits very well. In no aspect of your relationship is this more true than in your sex life. One of the reasons sex can become monotonous is that couples establish certain sexual habits together, and they very rarely deviate from them. Even the slightest variation will raise eyebrows. Naturally, after an affair, the unfaithful partner will have created a new sexual relationship and will have acquired some new, however subtly different, sexual habits. When reestablishing intimacy in his marriage, the unfaithful partner is usually very sensitive about hurting his spouse's feelings. If he learned something new and exciting during the affair about sex or his own sexuality, he will want to share that with his spouse but will often be afraid to do so. For example, I knew a woman who took a liking to oral sex during her affair and was frustrated because she was afraid to try it with her husband. She felt he would assume she learned it with her lover and want nothing to do with it. I also knew of a man who had had a problem with premature ejaculation with his wife but who had overcome it completely with his lover. Of course his wife noticed that he had great control all of a sudden, and even though it stood to improve their sex life, it created tension. The man's wife felt inadequate for not having been able to help her husband before.

OVERCOMING THE BEDROOM BLUES

To overcome the bedroom blues you have to use many of the skills you developed in Reconstructive Dynamics. If you are having problems reestablishing physicalness with your partner, you need them now more than ever. If you see that your partner has a barrier that prevents intimacy, you have to help him or her overcome it. You can do this by communicating, by co-facilitating, by supporting and nurturing your partner. If you sense a barrier within yourself, communicate it to your partner and allow him or her to help you. Sometimes it takes great patience, but with time you can make it.

Paul was a physician who traveled a lot, often several times per month. His wife, Johanna, though she loved her husband, had a series of brief affairs over a period of two years. Finally she admitted her activities to Paul, who was furious and left her. Two months later, though, he decided to come back and give it another try. Paul and Johanna were quite successful in rebuilding their marriage, except in the bedroom. Though Paul vented his hurt and anger to Johanna, the specter of her lovers seemed to fill the room, and he couldn't perform sexually; he was impotent. You can imagine how devastating it was for Paul to accept impotency after the emasculating effect disclosure of the affair had already had on him.

Johanna, however, was very patient, and she eventually helped Paul overcome his problem. She convinced him that her affairs meant nothing to her, that they were merely physical relationships that fulfilled none of her deepest needs and made no lasting impression on her. Most importantly, she fed Paul's self-esteem, nurturing him *outside* the bedroom, making him feel important and needed. One of the reasons Johanna had had affairs was that she needed a great deal of physical contact—touching, caressing, hugging—which she felt she wasn't getting from Paul. Through Reconstructive Dynamics she candidly voiced her own needs, thus placing herself in a vulnerable position and allowing Paul to fulfill those needs. By making herself vulnerable she removed the threat Paul consciously or unconsciously perceived in her and gave her husband a sense of power and validity.

If a man should sense that his wife is trying a little too hard to please and is not truly getting satisfaction from sex, he has to confront that. He must ask himself, What can I do to get my wife to enjoy sex herself and overcome her "fear" of not pleasing me? One answer might be to convince his wife that the real excitement in sex is making one's partner happy. He might tell her that it really turns him on to see her have an orgasm, for example, or that he gets great pleasure from caressing her body and just looking at her. This takes pressure off his partner, and she will eventually understand that she can please him by merely *being there*, without making the forced and awkward efforts she'd been making before.

If you should find yourself fantasizing about your former lover, or if you should sense that your partner is doing so, you *must* confront that. Don't just expect it to go away; it won't. Tell your partner: "Honey, I'm fantasizing about my former lover, and it's getting in the way of enjoying sex with you. How can you help? What can we do together to solve the problem?" Or, "Honey, I feel as if we're not really making love to one another. I get the impression that your mind is elsewhere. I want you right here with me. What can we do to overcome that?" Simple as they may look on paper, these words are very difficult to say. It takes incredible courage to confront issues having to do with our sexuality. Take the risk. You have nothing to lose but the fear and anxiety that stand between you and your partner.

It is crucial that neither partner impose expectations on the other. Expectations are very threatening, and they put great pressure on people: "I expect you to get an erection." "I expect you to have an orgasm." You may not actually be saying these things to your partner, but if you act disappointed when they don't occur, you are sending that message. When you expect your partner to do something, you absolve yourself of all responsibility to achieve whatever you may expect your partner to accomplish.

The "orgasm expectation" is one of the most common and most perverse of all. Orgasm is often the equivalent of applause in a sexual "performance." It is sometimes perceived as recognition that one has done his or her job well. But sex is *not* a performance, and you should not expect an orgasm every time, either of yourself or your partner. Think of orgasm as a by-product of sex, not its essence. The essence of sex is mutual pleasure and a feeling of oneness that you cultivate over an extended period of time. Orgasms are great, but they last only a few seconds; besides, it is during orgasm that you feel most self-centered, the least in touch with what your partner is experiencing.

The "erection expectation" is more complex. If your partner is experiencing temporary or chronic impotence, it is up to you to tell him that you want to help him overcome it. Instead of imposing unilateral expectations, set mutual goals. Volunteer your time and effort to solving the problem. Be supportive and nurturing. Share the responsibility for success and failure. When you do that, regardless of the outcome, you create a sense of common purpose and renewed intimacy.

The problem the unfaithful partner confronts when he wants to try new things with his spouse is a very tricky one. The best advice I can give is to suggest that you buy sexual literature and learn new things together. Your goal is to achieve a sense of renewal in your sex life, so it makes sense to try new things. If you get your ideas from a book, you eliminate the awkwardness that can arise when the faithful partner assumes that some new idea or technique came from the third party.

After an affair we tend to think that the major issue is overcoming the hurt and pain the faithful partner feels as the result of her (or his) betrayal. But there is another, equally important, thing that has to be worked out. I remind you once again of the thesis of this book: affairs occur as a result of unfulfilled needs. When a couple get back together, the faithful partner must not get so preoccupied with her own hurt that she ignores the fact that the spouse's needs may still be unfulfilled.

Mike and Carla had been married for four years when Mike, immediately after changing jobs, was laid off. Carla had a good job herself, and during a six-month period of unemployment, an extremely frustrated Mike had an affair with a woman for whom he felt only a physical attraction. His self-esteem had plummeted, and he felt inferior to his wife, who was advancing rapidly in her career and seemed to be insensitive to his needs. Mike felt stripped of his masculinity; he had an affair to reclaim it.

When the affair was disclosed, Carla was extremely hurt but didn't want to get a divorce. Mike did, however. He was so humiliated that he couldn't even face his wife. His affair was no casual outlet to have a good time as some affairs seem to be. It was a betrayal that symbolized his own failure as a man and generated intense feelings of self-hatred. Clearly, in Mike and Carla's case, the burden of reestablishing intimacy fell on Carla. It was up to her to be understanding and supportive of Mike and to help him regain his self-esteem.

GETTING THE UPTIGHTNESS OUT OF YOUR SEX LIFE: PUTTING THE ROMANCE BACK IN

If we all had a minute of true intimacy for every paperback romance published each month, we would all be perfectly satisfied. The fact is that many people aren't, which may explain why romances sell so well. Every relationship has romance at first; both partners feel a sense of excitement, a freshness, a newness that makes them feel totally alive. Sex is vital, spontaneous, and fun. But after a while, the novelty disappears, giving way to apathy and boredom; sex becomes stale, mechanical, and routine, lacking in vigor and interest. Does this have to happen? The dwindling of the glow of romantic love seems to be an unyielding law of nature. But there is something you can do to fight back. Most people don't realize that when love is new, romance happens all by itself, whereas after years together, it is necessary to *create* it. Most people don't realize the power they have to make their sex life dynamic and vital by approaching it with a new attitude. The enemies of romance are inhibitions, rigidity, routines, mechanistic behavior, a thought-out approach to sex, and strong emphasis on sexual technique. In the pages that follow we are going to take a look at some ways to overcome fears related to sexuality and to eliminate the monotony of uninspired sex.

This is especially important after an affair, when you and your partner want so badly to redefine your relationship in order to erase the pain you've been through and to avoid having to go through it again.

Examine for a moment your attitudes toward sex. Are you rigid? Apathetic? Fearful? Uptight? Overly aggressive? Submissive? Do you have preconceptions about sex? Do you have limits? Are you concerned with technique? After the trauma of an affair, when you are clearly in a transition stage, this is a very good time to examine your beliefs about sex. Was your sex life repetitious and mechanical before the affair? If so, it may have been because of the way you approached sex. Many of us get caught in life-script roles, and as a consequence our attitudes become automatic. Often a man and a woman in a relationship will assume things about each other sexually, and their preconceived notions about what they can and cannot do lead to routines. This not only makes sex boring, but it can prevent both partners from fulfilling each other's needs.

I once did a group experiment that I found very revealing. I gathered several couples together and asked individuals to come up with a different and unusual way to stimulate their partner; something truly creative and erotic, untraditional, yet not kinky. One woman deliberated for several minutes and finally said in disbelief, "Wow! You know I really can't think of anything!" Her lover, a little less resourceful by his own admission, thought hard and soon gave up as well. "Gee," he said, "you've got me on that one." The others' responses were similar; heads were shaking, shoulders shrugging, foreheads frowning.

These were normal, everyday people, and it's not that they lacked creativity; it's just that they—like most of us—have never allowed themselves to experience the power they have to make sex new and exciting. We all have within us the potential to put romance back into sex, but for some reason or another we get blocked. I hope in the rest of this chapter to put a flea in your ear and get you thinking new thoughts about sex.

That's an important first step in bringing romance back into your marriage.

CONFRONTING INHIBITIONS

In order for both partners to reestablish physical intimacy, they must both reclaim confidence in their own sexuality. You do this by taking responsibility for your own fears. Admit to your spouse that you feel inadequate sexually in some way. You may really be inadequate, or you may not be. But if you hold it in, you will feel threatened and will create barriers to intimacy between you and your partner. We've stressed a lot thus far in the book that in reconstructing a marriage you and your spouse must work as a team. Co-facilitate! When you confront feelings of sexual inadequacy or sexual inhibition, observe them together, and then try to overcome them as a team. If you are struggling to hide from your inhibitions or your inadequacies, chances are you are sabotaging your own masculinity or femininity. When you expend so much energy covering up, you become rigid and uptight; you lose the spontaneity that is what masculinity and femininity should really be about. At one point in the movie *Klute*, Jane Fonda remarks that inhibitions are great because they are so much fun to overcome. I concur. Inhibitions and feelings of inadequacy are often very silly and unfounded, and if you set yourselves the challenge of overcoming them, you usually can.

FOREPLAY

I have seen many a couple who think of foreplay as three strokes of the breast and a kiss on the neck. I usually tell them that foreplay should begin not thirty seconds before penetration but several hours before. Touching is an extraordinarily effective form of communication, yet so many couples forget it even exists after a few years of marriage. Stop and think for a moment how many people you know have the freedom to touch at will in anything other than a ritual way (a handshake, for example). Not very many, I'll bet. Perhaps only one, your spouse. Use this great tool you possess. You can say so much with it.

Foreplay can begin at breakfast when you run your finger through your husband's hair while he drinks his coffee. It can continue with a kiss after lunch and a fleeting caress at dusk while your partner reads her book; after dinner a hug and a nibble on the ear; a shoulder message while watching TV.

Foreplay need not be explicitly sexual; it can be a series of sensual gestures with which you acknowledge your partner. It can include various forms of seduction, such as wearing nice clothes, jewelry, or perfume. It can even be a flirtatious gaze or a smile. In any case, foreplay creates a sense of oneness and an emotional bond. It is a nonverbal form of communication that demonstrates to your partner that you are willing to recognize him or her as an entire person, not just a sexual object. Extended foreplay reinforces the sense of renewal you and your partner feel when reconstructing your marriage.

I like to think of foreplay as a combination of physicalness and playfulness. By "physicalness" I mean touching, caressing, stroking, massaging, and other sensual gestures. By "playfulness" I refer to bringing out the child in us all. Allow yourself to experience the childlike spontaneity, imagination, and inventiveness that are just waiting to come out. Let yourself go sexually. Confront all those adult inhibitions that make you less alive; observe them and overcome them. Try to experience that giddy feeling of romantic intoxication you felt the first time you fell in love. Everyone has experienced that feeling at one time or another, and it is always accessible, if you are willing to recall it.

EMOTIONAL APHRODISIACS

You will never get that feeling back, though, if you refuse to take risks. Falling in love the first time was a risk, and so is falling in love all over again. Try new things with your partner, things you may never have dreamed of doing. You must take chances. Making love with the same person over and over again for years gets very boring. The only way to avoid atrophy in your sexual relationship is to ensure that your attitude toward sexuality evolves. If you never take chances and try new things, your attitudes will be anchored in the mud of old prejudices, your sexual consciousness will remain low, and you will not enjoy sex. When you experiment, you learn new things about yourself; you change. And when you do that, you bring a new person to each act of lovemaking. If your spouse never knows what to expect from you, sex never becomes routine, and your entire relationship will maintain its vitality.

Experiment? Try new things? But what? I recommend what I call "emotional aphrodisiacs," not physical aphrodisiacs, which chemically stimulate the sex drive, but emotional ones that create romance and the desire for closeness and intimacy. Be playful: have a pillow fight, pinch or tickle one another, chase each other around the house naked, take a bath together and wash one another. Be daring; make sensual phone calls to your partner during the day, taunt one another teasingly with four-letter words, write messages on one another with body paints, try new positions and new techniques, make love at different times of the day, make love in strange new places. Be creative and imaginative: wear sexy lingerie or other clothing, read *Lady Chatterley's Lover* together in bed, undress for one another to risqué music, tell one another sexy stories, eat dinner naked in bed, massage one another with flavored oils. And by all means, be romantic: watch a love story on television together, listen to romantic music while you make love by candlelight, kiss one another passionately, tell your partner that you love and appreciate him or her, walk through the park hand in hand. Sound corny? Perhaps. But I would guess that some of your fondest memories are of doing just these things years ago. Recreate romance in your marriage; don't be content to experience romance vicariously through the movie screen, novels, or soap operas.

Sex is entirely between the ears. You can make it whatever you please. If you choose to, you can create romance and put warmth, tenderness, and intimacy back into your marriage. You may feel awkward doing new things at first, but after a while you won't; it's as simple as that. Don't be afraid to be silly. In the bedroom, ignore that inhibited adult voice that suppresses the child in you and wants sex to be dignified. The alternative to letting yourself be playful, creative, and child-like, is dull, cheerless, geriatric sex. Do you want that?

BON APPETIT

All innuendos aside, sex should be like a gourmet meal. You whet your appetite for several hours before, you slowly sip your apertif, then you savor each course as it comes before the main dish arrives. Humans are the only creatures on this planet who genuinely relish their sexual nourishment, and there must be some reason for it. So make sex the gourmet meal that it is; prepare for it with care and love; and don't just gobble it up like barnyard fowl eating scratch feed.

If the preceding paragraph seems a bit flippant to you, I assure you it is meant to be. I hope that its playful tone will rub off on you and encourage you to be playful and spontaneous as well. Of course, you can't have gourmet sex every night, so don't put pressure on yourselves to do so. But spice up your sex life whenever you can. Together, you and your partner can revive the feelings of newness and intimacy by allowing yourselves to be vulnerable and take chances.

AFTERPLAY

The pace of afterplay is different from foreplay, but you can do many of the same things. Afterplay is a time of gentle stroking and caressing and, of course, talking. One usually feels extremely relaxed after making love, and such a mood is ideal for discussing some of the issues that concern you. Talk about your sexual preferences, discuss the fears you have concerning your sexuality, express what you felt while having sex and what you'd like to feel next time.

After making love you should experience a feeling of closeness, a sense of oneness. If you and your partner are truly making "love" and not merely copulating, you shouldn't have to worry about one or both partners rolling over and falling asleep. Ceasing to be intimate immediately after orgasm is like writing a letter and neglecting to sign your name. You don't want anonymous sex with your partner. You want to really be there in the room afterward, and you want to sign your name to the love act you just completed. Did you ever notice that when reading letters you love to get a P.S. at the end, that little something the writer wanted to add? Write a postscript to lovemaking by caressing, stroking, or just talking to your partner. That validates her (or him), acknowledges her as a person and not just a body, and reinforces the bond between you.

What follows is a series of suggestions and exercises that will help you and your partner overcome the uptightness that inevitably affects your sex life after an affair. Some of the exercises you will remember from earlier in the book, others are new. Do them in the same spirit of playfulness, yet with integrity. They should be fun, but you should nonetheless take them seriously and recognize them as a valuable means of freeing yourself up, and regaining spontaneity and fluidity in your sex life.

SEXUAL ASSETS AND LIABILITIES

In our society, sexual inhibitions are such that many people I've counseled have gone years without ever communicating with their partners about sexual wants and needs. I once talked to a woman who was very frustrated because her husband didn't stroke her breasts as much as she would have liked him to. "Why not?" I asked her. "I don't know," she replied. "Did you ever tell him you liked it?" She squirmed a bit in her chair and muttered almost inaudibly, "No."

This exercise allows you to articulate your sexual wants and needs to your partner. It is structured exactly like Assets and Liabilities in Chapter 8. Designate a Partner A and a Partner B, take a pen and paper with columns marked Sexual Assets and Sexual Liabilities, and, using one word at a time, describe your partner's strengths and weaknesses. In the Strengths column you might say "enthusiastic," "vulnerable," "sharing," "adventuresome," "uninhibited," "passionate," or "gentle." For weaknesses you might say "rigid," "conventional," "hurried," "distant," "uninterested," "unadventuresome," "guarded," "cautious," and so on.

Keep in mind that the purpose of this exercise is to give your partner an awareness of his or her own sexuality and of your needs. When you say that your partner is "unadventurous," you are really saying, "I want to explore new things," and your partner should perceive it as a suggestion rather than a label. Always do this exercise in a spirit of support. Talking about sexual liabilities (and we all have them) can be threatening, especially if your partner feels incapable of eliminating them. Obviously, you wouldn't make any reference to a physical quality (i.e., genital size, breast size, obesity) that your partner may be sensitive about. Use your own common sense, be honest and candid; I think you will discover things about yourself and your partner that will open up new sexual horizons.

SEXUAL WANT ADS

Don't confuse these with the suggestive, often bawdy, personals you see in a lot of underground newspapers and magazines. Sexual want ads are just between you and your partner. This exercise is structured exactly like the one in Chapter 8. But this time the ads all have to do with sexual matters. For example: "Wanted: Evening with sensual delights." "Wanted:

Woman who will seduce me." "Wanted: Man who will be passionate." "Wanted: Woman who will be aggressive in bed." "Wanted: Man who's grown up but still a little boy to seduce me tonight." "Wanted: Man who loves to engage in extended foreplay." "Wanted: Woman who will talk to me after we have sex."

Just as in the previous want-ads exercise, when you tell your partner what you want, you are really telling him or her what you *need*. The want-ads exercise is not just a silly game. It is a game, and it should be fun, but your goal in this and all exercises is to express yourself to your partner. When you place an ad for a man who will engage in foreplay, you are telling your husband that you need more of that in your sex life. It takes courage to say what you want, because in doing so you *admit* what you need.

Sexual want ads can really help you get unstuck. If your spouse asks you to do something you feel uncomfortable about, examine your feelings and try to determine why you feel uncomfortable. You may decide that your feeling is entirely justified; however, you may also discover that it is caused by a preconceived notion that needlessly inhibits you sexually and that you would love to break away from.

SEXUAL STROKING

In this exercise you answer the question, What do I like most about your body? We all have doubts about our bodies, especially as we get older, and we often wonder if we are still attractive sexually. A woman might feel self-conscious about her sagging breasts or the fact that her buttocks aren't as firm as before. Men can be very uptight about baldness, poor muscle tone, and thickness around the waist.

You can do this exercise in a structured way (i.e., with a tape recorder), or you can make a point of commenting on your partner's body either casually during the day or while making love. Say things such as "I like your breasts" or "I love your penis" or "Your legs really turn me on" or "I really dig your hairy chest." You might feel awkward saying these things; that will pass, I'm sure, when you see that your partner responds favorably. Whatever you do, don't lie. Focus on your partner's strong points and really make him or her feel good about them. If a man is bald but knows that his hairy chest is sexually appealing, he can forget about his head for a while. A woman with small breasts will obviously feel less self-conscious if she is reminded often that her behind is sexy or that her face is pretty. It is very important to do things like this when recreating intimacy with your partner after an affair. Very often the faithful partner will imagine that some bodily defect was responsible for the affair and needs more than just a token denial to be convinced that it isn't true.

The point of this exercise is for you to get a sense of the power you have to raise your partner's self-esteem. The reason sex can become boring and routine after many years of marriage is often not so much because a person thinks his (or her) partner is unstimulating but because he doesn't feel attractive himself. Make your partner feel sexy by giving her acknowledgment for what is appealing about her. A person who feels sexy will *be* sexy and will have much better sex with you— guaranteed!

SEXUAL CORRESPONDENCE

Here is another letter-writing exercise. In this one you will write for ten or fifteen minutes on a subject related to your sex life, such as, "My greatest fears with regard to my sexuality are ..." "What I need from you sexually is ..." Once you and your partner have finished writing, exchange letters and respond to each other with "I feel" statements. For example: "I feel you exaggerate your concern that being slightly overweight makes you less attractive sexually." Or, "I feel good that you finally communicated your needs to me because I really think I can fulfill them now that I'm aware they exist."

Here's a list of some more possible topics:

> Sexually speaking, I like your body because . . .
> Sexually, my greatest joys are . . .
> The things about you that really turn me on are . . .
> Some things I wish you would do more of in bed are . . .
> I feel that your greatest fears sexually are . . .
> Our sex life could be better if we . . .
> When I think of you sexually I feel . . .
> The ways I think you best express yourself sexually are . . .
> My fears and concerns regarding your sexuality are . . .
> Things I enjoy sexually that you do not are . . .

Be creative and make up your own topics. As in all the other exercises you have done thus far in the book, be careful not to let yourself become judgmental. The purpose of these exercises is to get you to communicate your sexual needs to one another in a safe, structured environment. It is not an opportunity to wound or dump on your partner.

Be a good facilitator at all times. If you suspect that your partner is not being honest, tell him so: "I feel that you haven't really expressed all your fears to me. It's okay to do so. If you have a problem it's my problem too, and I want to help you overcome it." This is good, supportive communication.

SHARING FANTASIES

A lot of books have come out in the past few years talking about sexual fantasies. People are generally less inhibited about them than they were before, but sharing them is nonetheless awkward for most. But I encourage you to do so. Fantasies are very private, and when you share something so personal you reinforce the intimate bond between you and your partner.

I think it is easier to express fantasies in a structured exercise. Perhaps you could use the want-ads exercise to request fulfillment of a fantasy. Or you could express a fantasy in sexual correspondence (either written or spoken into a tape recorder). For example:

> My primary fantasy is . . .
> The most frightening fantasy I have is . . .
> Your role in my fantasies is . . .

You may have to really think hard to actually describe your sexual fantasies. If you can't recall them, allow your mind to fantasize the next time you have sex, and afterward describe to your partner what came up. And, of course, encourage your partner to do the same.

GENDER EXCHANGE

Earlier we described an exercise in which you and your partner were to change roles for a day or two. The purpose of that exercise was to give you an awareness of your spouse's daily routine and thereby strengthen the bond between you. This time, switch roles when making love. If you always saw yourself as the aggressive male dominator in the bedroom, try being the submissive type for a change; or act like a helpless romantic heroine from a cheap novel; see what it feels like. I encourage women to be extremely aggressive during this exercise. Seduce your spouse, not with feminine charm as you normally would but with overbearing, virile directness. Imitate the brash fellow who tried to pick you up in a bar one time or the obnoxious wolf-whistler who bothered you in the street.

You might actually try to do an imitation of each other. If your husband has certain gestures or caresses that he always does the same way, try to duplicate them. Or if your wife is generally passive at first but becomes more and more aggressive as lovemaking continues, try to imitate this pattern. I think you will find this exercise amusing and, I might add, quite revealing.

OFF BROADWAY

Normally, I would say that sex should never be rehearsed, but in this exercise we can bend that rule a little. Sit down with your partner and write a short play together with dialogue, action, and even a bit of dramatic intrigue:

> Agent 001 picks the lock on the hotel room door and slips stealthily in. On the bed is a beautiful Russian double agent named Tanya. She is clad only in a bra and panties, and her ample breasts gently rise and fall as she breathes softly in her sleep. The room is unlit, but light from the street below streams through the blinds and casts dark shadows.
>
> The shadow of 001 falls on Tanya's abdomen. She lies before him, vulnerable, unaware, helpless. She appears angelic, with her subtle curves and her skin as soft and white as the Siberian snows. "I've come here strictly on business," murmurs 001 as he reaches down and strokes Tanya's inviting breast. She stirs and moans softly. He begins to unbutton his shirt . . .

Well, you know the rest. Write your own sexual play. Be creative. Be funny. Be sexy. You don't have to rehearse this play, nor do you have to follow the script just as you wrote it. Once you get started you can improvise, create subplots and new characters and a different ending. I find that adopting a persona and acting out a sexual script can be extremely valuable in overcoming inhibitions. I hope you will too.

In this chapter I have given you a lot of ideas that I hope will loosen you up and enable you to reestablish the physical intimacy you once knew. But you have to take the baton from here. Whether or not your sex life remains healthy and exciting depends on the amount of energy you are willing to put into it. Perhaps the most important thing to understand in reapproaching physicalness and sexuality after an affair is that sex takes place between the ears, not in the genitals. You and your partner can make your sex life interesting and rewarding if you choose to. The exercises I suggested in this chapter serve to help you communicate with your partner, and they provide you with some new ideas that will get you "unstuck" for a while. Eventually, though, you will have to use your own imagination to ensure that your sex life remains vital. Don't let merely copulating become a substitute for intimacy. After an affair, that can be very dangerous. Tap into the power you have to put romance back into your marriage and make your sex life exciting and interesting. You *can* do it, especially if you work together.

Chapter 11

OTHER PEOPLE— HOW TO HANDLE THE CHILDREN, THE "OTHER WOMAN/OTHER MAN," FRIENDS, RELATIVES, AND OTHERS WHO KNOW

HOW TO HANDLE THE CHILDREN

Statistics show that affairs don't usually occur at the beginning of a marriage but about three to five years into it. It follows, then, that most people who have affairs have children. A child is a couple's most prized possession, and the last thing they would want to do is hurt him. Unfortunately, parents often damage their children emotionally without realizing it. Few situations in a marriage have as much potential to harm a child's psyche as an affair, so in its aftermath you must handle your children with the utmost integrity.

Children detect negative feelings in the house whether you explicitly express them or not. Even if you and your partner were very careful never to fight in front of them, your children nonetheless felt the tension between you. If you think the trauma of the affair has passed without your children noticing it, I suspect you are wrong. The affair had an impact on them, and the way you handle them after the storm will determine how it will affect them for the rest of their lives.

You may be very tempted to just let things slide. Your marriage is working again, the hurt and anger you felt during the affair have been vented, the house seems to be gay and cheerful once more; so why bring up the trauma of the affair all over again with the children? Because your child may have internalized feelings, and his emotional development may have been affected. He experienced hurt, fear, guilt, and anger at his own level—that of a child—and he, just like you, needs to get it out of his system. This chapter is about helping your children resolve the conflict caused by the affair.

Children of various ages react to the affair differently, and parents should approach them in different ways. I will discuss individually four specific age groups in this first section, elaborating on the problems children in each age group face and offering suggestions about how parents can deal with them. Before I do that though, let me bring up some points that apply to parents of children of all ages.

Sit Down and Talk

The alternative to "letting things slide" and hoping no damage has been done, is allowing your child to confront his feelings exactly the way you did in Reconstructive Dynamics. You and your partner, as a couple, must create a context in which your child feels safe and can vent his feelings. Set aside a time when you can sit down and talk to your child. Choose a time when you will not be interrupted by telephones, doorbells or impromptu visits. If you have several children, it is important to approach each one individually, even if two of them should fall in the same age group. All children have a particular "emotional profile," which means that they will react to situations in different ways. Some children, for example, open up very readily, whereas others tend to internalize feelings. Clearly, you would approach the first differently from the second. Also, your children are likely to be very confused, even frightened, when you speak to them, and it is much easier to deal with them one at a time.

Approach Each Child as a Couple

When speaking to a child about a family problem, it is essential that both partners be there. The child must recognize that his parents are a unified element and that they are working together. The turmoil of an affair, especially if it resulted in one partner's temporary absence, can be frightening for a child. Psychologically, it is extremely important to show your children that you are now back together again and that you plan to stay that way.

When explaining things to your children, be very careful not to give off any signals that conflict still exists. Neither partner, for example, should give the impression that he is dominating the other or in any way twisting the facts to his advantage. Children have incredible power over their parents. We saw earlier how during the turmoil of the affair both partners will curry favor with their children in order to win them over. Even at this stage one of you could slip and say something that would offend the other. Imagine what effect that would have on the child. Think over what you have to say *before* you actually sit down and talk. Remember, the message you wish to convey is that you and your partner love one another very much, that you love your children, and that bad times are behind you. See to it that your child gets that message loud and clear.

Children Who Take Sides

It can be very painful to a parent when children take sides as a result of a family conflict. When an affair occurs, children will almost always take sides with the faithful partner. In attempting to communicate after Reconstructive Dynamics, the unfaithful partner may be the object of his child's anger and frustration. Even when the child knows nothing of the affair, he will usually sense that one of his parents is responsible for the turmoil in the family and will express his anger toward that parent, either explicitly or implicitly. If you sense that your child is angry at you, recognize that feeling for what it is: internalized frustration and fear. Instead of reacting to that anger by feeling rejected, interpret your child's behavior. Empathize with him; try to understand what it means for a child to see his parents breaking up. Encourage your child to vent his feelings just as you did in Reconstructive Dynamics, so that he too can bring internalized feelings to the surface. If he is allowed to vent his anger, it will pass, and if you create a context of love and support, you will very likely be much closer to him after the affair than before. If feelings of hurt, anger, frustration, and guilt are internalized and never vented, children may carry those feelings into adulthood and develop destructive behavior patterns.

The Organic Family

Earlier in the book we talked about how important it is for you and your partner to demonstrate your affection for one another in front of your children. It is especially important when you approach your child to let him know that he is speaking to two people who love one another very much and want to share their love with him. Without making it seem contrived or phony, show your child that you care very much for your partner by holding hands, hugging, kissing, and touching. This not only reinforces the bonding between you as a couple but creates a safe, loving environment in the home and encourages your child to open up and express himself. It gives the child the sense that he is no longer part of a broken home but of a unified family, which is exactly what he wants and needs.

A family is an organic unit, a combination of several parts that make up a whole. To remain healthy, a balance must be maintained among those various parts. In any organic unit, an imbalance that occurs in one part is felt by the others. For example, if a problem develops in the kidneys, symptoms of that problem can show up in several areas of the body. By now you should understand that the key to restoring emotional stability, or "balance," to your children lies in the way you and your partner feel and act toward one another. You're the most important parts of the organic family unit. Children respond favorably to the authentic love and affection they see between their mother and father; they want to take part too. By the same token, if they sense tension between their parents, they will internalize fear, frustration, and anger, and they will withdraw. It is up to you as a parent to create the balance necessary to function as a healthy family.

Explain the Emotional Conflict

Sit down your child and explain to him, in terms he can understand, why there was conflict in the family. Do not mention the affair (except in certain cases with children over eighteen) or anything about a third party. It won't do your child any good to know that, and it may even make things worse. But your child knows that *something* was wrong, and he will not be complete until he is satisfied that the problem has been solved. Explain to him what you learned about yourself in Reconstructive Dynamics. Explain the unfulfilled needs that caused you to be unhappy and caused conflict with your partner. Your child may not understand exactly what you mean, but he will understand that his parents had a problem, were willing to confront it, and now seem to be over it. That's all he really wants to know. That will make him feel secure.

Now let's take a look at the individual age groups. Keep in mind these groupings are artificial and that some twelve-year-olds are more emotionally mature than some fifteen-year-olds. When deciding which group your child falls into and how you wish to approach him, take into account your own knowledge of his emotional profile.

One Through Six

I'm certain that even a six-month-old baby can sense that something is wrong between his parents. Quite obviously, though, you can't explain to him that the tension was caused by problems related to your domineering father. All you can do with children under the age of three is convey a sense of nurturing and bonding that will make him feel loved and protected. A child of, say, four, however, can speak and understand. He knows what a problem is, having been read stories about ogres and trolls and wicked stepmothers, and he may even have had a few personal conflicts himself with big kids in the neighborhood. With a child between four and six, you have to explain in very simple terms what happened between you and your partner. You might say: "Mommy and Daddy were having some problems. There were some things we didn't understand, and there were some bad feelings, but now things are better and everything is going to be fine for you and your brothers and sisters." Keep it very short and basic. Just get the essential message across that there were problems and now they are gone.

Sometimes it takes a little more imagination than that. If, for example, there was a lot of screaming and yelling during the crisis, your child may need some explanations for why you and your partner seemed to be hurting each other. Small children can relate to fairy tales, fables and parables better than concrete explanations, so you might try out an allegory or metaphor on them: "The reason Mommy and Daddy were yelling at each other was because there was something bad in us, like poison, and we had to get it out. When we got the poison out, it was all gone, and now everything is okay." (Perhaps you could remind your child that when Snow White coughed up the poison apple, she was all better again.) Try to find a movie, a story, or a cartoon character your child can relate to, and structure your explanation around that. This gives your child something external to relate to and will help him to understand. It doesn't matter how you do it, but with a young child it is essential to get the message across that bad feelings are gone and good ones have replaced them. Convince your children that the story of their family life will have a happy ending.

Seven Through Eleven
A child in this age group understands pretty well what is going on in his environment and how it relates to him. He has heard about things such as divorce, affairs, and child custody on television, and he is able to make the possible connection between these things and himself. Unlike his four-year-old brother who when he hears his parents fighting understands only that something is wrong, an eight- or nine-year-old can actually understand the content of an argument. He is also intellectually developed enough to take that content and draw conclusions.

Again, *do not* tell the child about the affair. Just give a good, clear description of what caused the tension and anger between you and your partner. Explain to your child what an unfulfilled need is: "Everybody needs certain things in life; you, for example, need a house, a bike, a baseball glove, and all sorts of things. If you don't have something you need, you get upset, right? Well, that's what happened with Mommy and me. But now we have what we need and everything is okay."

The point here is that with an older child you need not use metaphor and allegory; you can give him a relatively straightforward, concrete explanation. One way to get your point across is to compare your marital problems with your child's sibling or peer rivalries: "You know how you and Joey get mad at each other every now and then? Well, Daddy and I get mad at each other too, but that doesn't mean we don't love each other. You still like Joey a lot, don't you, even though he called you a bad name once? Well, Daddy and I love each other, too."

With a more mature child in this age group, you might even explain the nature of your unfulfilled needs. A man I counseled, who had actually left the house for several months during an affair, explained to his nine-year-old daughter that when he was a boy his father didn't give him much freedom, so the reason he left home was that he needed to be free for a while. He insisted that that need was no longer important, that he was very glad to be back, and that he loved his daughter very much. She responded beautifully to that.

You *must* give a child in this age group a reason that explains the emotional turmoil you put him through. Keep in mind that you have tremendous power over your child's psyche and that he wants to believe whatever you tell him. Even if he doesn't understand exactly why adults worry about such silly things as unfulfilled needs, he will be satisfied with just about any plausible explanation. And perhaps most importantly, he will know that *he* wasn't responsible for the turmoil himself.

Twelve Through Seventeen

This is perhaps the most delicate and difficult age group to deal with. Children at puberty are beginning to emerge socially and to blossom sexually, and they tend to identify with their mother or father as role models. Finding out that one of their parents had an affair can be devastating to a teenager's self-image; so, once again, unless it is absolutely clear to your child that you had an affair, do not tell him. The damage you risk inflicting is far greater than anything you stand to gain.

Children in this age group are "young adults," and they can no longer be treated like little kids. Now that they have command of the language, they can read books and magazines that deal with grown-up problems, and they are beginning to understand the subtitles of the adult world. Therefore, talking to them on a childish level would seem condescending. So you have to abandon the parent/child relationship and communicate with your teenager as an adult, which gives him a sense of responsibility and integrity. I recommend giving your young adult a very detailed explanation of the problems between you and your spouse. Explain all of your unfulfilled needs, trying to relate them to adolescent experience. A fifteen-year-old may very well understand what it means to be rejected by someone of the opposite sex. If you discovered in Reconstructive Dynamics that fear of rejection led you to seek out an affair partner who made you feel secure, explain to your teenager that you had this fear and that it caused problems between you and your spouse. Don't mention the affair! Just make it clear that beforehand your spouse was not fulfilling your need for security but that now she (or he) is and the problem is resolved.

Teenagers have an enormous capacity for internalizing feelings. They feel extremely awkward with their bodies growing so quickly, their sexuality developing, and their minds trying to make the transition from childhood to adulthood. Even when there is no blatant imbalance in their everyday lives, teenagers suffer from terrible self-image problems. You can certainly understand how traumatic it can be for a teenager to deal with his parents' marital crisis. It is crucial that you be supportive. Allow your child to express his feelings openly. If he seems internalized, provide him with a context in which he can express whatever feelings may come up—including passionate anger directed toward you! Young adults can be extremely self-righteous and judgmental, and when they sense that one of their parents is hurting the other (e.g., unfaithful partner hurting faithful partner), they become very protective of the hurt partner and belligerent toward her (or his) assailant. I have a friend whose father had an affair and left home when she was seventeen, and since that time she has not spoken a word to him. I find it sad that she has carried this unexpressed anger around with her for all of these years.

I remind you once again to interpret your teenager's feelings and not to react to them. Let him express his hostility, and then calmly explain to him that his feelings are perfectly understandable but that you want to make amends. A teenager is capable of understanding the full range of your feelings, so don't hesitate to express them. Allow yourself to be vulnerable with your child; let him know that you have faults and they sometimes cause problems. When you do this you allow internalized anger to melt into compassion, and you establish a bond with your child. I have seen many, many cases in which gut-to-gut communication after a family crisis has brought parents and children much closer together and allowed them to understand one another as "people" for the first time.

Eighteen and Over

An eighteen-year-old, in spite of his lack of experience in life, is a full-fledged adult and must be treated as one. Depending on the range of his sexual activity, he has either firsthand or secondhand knowledge of the problems couples experience, and he is certainly aware of how common marital infidelity is—who knows, he may even have been involved in an affair himself. In any case, there is a very good chance he has guessed that your marital problems were caused by infidelity.

Although I don't recommend you come right out and tell your child that an affair took place, if he gives you strong indications that he knows, don't deny it. If he figures out what happened and you lie to him, he will most certainly resent you for it and may even carry away from the experience a dangerous notion that it is better to lie about problems than to confront them.

But how can you tell whether or not your child knows your secret? Explain the underlying problems that caused the affair—the unfulfilled needs, the childhood roots, and so on. Since you are speaking to another adult, you can go into great detail and make it clear what happened. If you carefully gauge his reactions, you should be able to tell whether or not he suspects an affair. If he suspects it but is afraid to bring it up, make it clear that it's okay to talk about anything that might be bothering him. Rather than volunteering the information, let your child bring it up. Unless he doesn't suspect anything—in which case you should say nothing at all—he will ask you about it if he feels confident that it *is* permissible to do so.

What do you do if your eighteen- or twenty-year-old finds out about the affair? In such a case the unfaithful partner had better be prepared for some intense hostility. All of what I discussed earlier about handling hostility applies here. Interpret, don't react. Allow whatever feelings come up to be expressed. The faithful partner must intervene at this point and make it clear to the child that all is forgiven. Tell him that you have accepted the reality of the affair and still want to continue living with your partner. Explain in your own words the unfulfilled needs that led to the affair and articulate your own responsibility for creating it. Make it clear that you are entirely complete and that you harbor no anger. Demonstrate physical affection for your partner and make your child understand that you are ready to carry on with life anew. When he sees the emotional bond that now exists between you and your partner, his anger will quickly exhaust itself, and he will participate in the good feelings you create.

Of course an assumption is being made here that is worth dwelling on. For the faithful partner to be so supportive, she (or he) must have successfully completed Reconstructive Dynamics. If any anger has not been vented, and if both partners have not been through the successive stages of Vulnerability, Communion, Acceptance, and Reunion, your attempt to communicate with your child will lack authenticity and sabotage the results you wish to achieve. Don't even attempt to communicate with your children until you are confident that a tight bond exists between you and your partner and that you will be able to convey sincerely the love you feel for one another. Your child, no matter what his age, has to genuinely understand that the wounds of the affair have been healed and that his parents are back together for good.

To sum up this section of "How to Handle the Children," let me repeat that you want to explain the underlying conflict that caused your marital crisis but not actually reveal the affair. The more information you give your child—that is, the more open and honest you are with him—the more complete he will feel and the more quickly he will regain his emotional balance. Disclose the affair *only* if your child specifically inquires about it and you think he is emotionally strong enough to handle it.

For the most part, children will respond beautifully to the new cohesiveness in the family. When they understand the reasons why their mother and father weren't getting along, and when they see that the breach has been repaired, they can move on with their lives and be normal, happy kids.

HOW TO HANDLE THE OTHER WOMAN/OTHER MAN

The burden of dealing with the third party falls, quite obviously, on the unfaithful partner. It is impossible to genuinely *be* with your spouse if you still have residual feelings for a third party, so you must, as soon as possible, put a definite end to the relationship with your extramarital lover. If you fail to do that immediately, you will (1) provide fuel for your own fantasies about that person and (2) prolong your partner's struggle to "compete" with the third party. Only by giving your former lover the unequivocal message that you are going back to your spouse can you truly be free in your marriage.

The Party's Over

But how do you drop such a bomb? It is not easy; you have to be very sure of yourself, and you have to be confrontive yet supportive. In breaking off with the third party, you can use many of the skills you developed reuniting with your spouse through Reconstructive Dynamics. I don't recommend you break the news by letter or by telephone; neither of these media will get your message across with the force and conviction required. Afterward you may very well feel incomplete or, worse yet, that there is still some chance to get back together.

The best thing to do is to meet the person in a restaurant, a bar, a park, or some other neutral ground. If you expect a scene, you might want to suggest a more private (but not too private) place where you won't disturb anyone. Sit down and explain to the person what has happened. Quite obviously you can't just say, "Well, I'm back with my spouse. I'm sorry. Goodbye." You owe a much more detailed explanation to your former lover. A sample opening might be: "I'm back with my spouse and things are working out. You're free now to get on with your life. It's not fair for you to stay with me because I can't give you what you need. I care about you very much, but it's just not meant to be between us."

That explanation may be all it takes, but I suspect it won't be. Be prepared to encounter some anger and hurt. Common reactions are: "But I thought you loved me." Or, "You used me!" You can't let the person walk away with these feelings. In Reconstructive Dynamics I insisted very strongly that you explain to your spouse precisely what you got out of the affair, precisely what unfulfilled needs caused you to stray. In the previous section on handling the children I emphasized the importance of explaining the roots of your marital crisis to your child. Now you have to explain to the third party precisely why you are choosing to go back to your spouse. Once more you are going to have to let yourself be open, honest, and vulnerable.

Be very brief and to the point but explain in some detail what you learned about yourself through Reconstructive Dynamics. Here is an example of how one explanation might go: "I really care about you, and I assure you that every moment we spent together was absolutely authentic and real, but I've discovered some things about myself and about my relationship with my spouse that made me realize I should stay married. I sought you out primarily because of some very fundamental insecurities I have about myself. You made me feel great, and I loved being with you, but our relationship prevented me from confronting my problems and overcoming them. Now that I have confronted these things, I realize how important I am to my spouse and how important she is to me, and I'm not willing to give that up." Notice that the speaker has made himself vulnerable by admitting his own faults. You might even be more specific, explaining what your insecurities were (e.g., unfulfilled social needs, dominating mother, expectations from childhood, weak communication skills, etc.). When you explain your conflict and make yourself vulnerable, you allow the third party an opportunity to interpret rather than react, and you give her room to feel compassion for you. If the person really loved you, she will want what's best for you, even if it will be painful for a while.

The third party may, however, react with violent anger. Just as you did with your spouse in Reconstructive Dynamics, allow the third party to ventilate feelings. Tell the person, "It's okay to be angry. I know if I were in your position I would be. I certainly feel a lot of anger at myself for putting you in this predicament, for hurting my spouse and children as I've messed up a lot of people's lives." Explain again why this happened, and encourage the person to talk about her own reasons for getting involved with you. Perhaps that person is locked in a destructive pattern of behavior and your presence merely camouflaged a problem that needed to be confronted. Encourage your former lover to vent her feelings thoroughly so that you can both walk away from one another feeling complete.

Sometimes the third party may react not by exploding but by internalizing feelings. Very often people respond to rejection by saying, "No big deal," and they walk away with their head in the air and their heart in their stomach. If you can help it, don't let your former lover get away with this act. Neither of you will feel in any way complete unless you confront your true feelings and *choose* to end your relationship.

Of course, I'm assuming here that you have successfully worked through Reconstructive Dynamics and that you are *absolutely* sure of what you are doing. If you are not sure of yourself, don't even make this final rendezvous because it could rekindle your feelings for your former lover, in which case you might destroy all the progress you have made and set yourself back to square one. Your uncertainty is caused by fear that your former lover can still fulfill a need that your spouse cannot; you feel that the affair provides you with something you can't give up. If that is the case, go back to the point in Reconstructive Dynamics that will allow you to confront your unfulfilled needs and try to work them out. In order to handle the other man/other woman, you must first be able to handle yourself. You can only do that when you are complete with your spouse.

Why is it so important to have this confrontation with the third party? Thus far I may have given the impression that you confront the third party mostly for her benefit, but you should understand that you are also confronting yourself. If you can end your extramarital relationship with strength, conviction, and compassion, you know that you are complete with yourself and your spouse. How you handle the third party is, in fact, a test of your own integrity. It may be much easier in the short run to keep the affair going; there may very well be an immediate emotional payoff in it for you that is hard to resist. When you choose to end your affair, you are making a courageous decision based not on a whim but on all you learned about yourself in Reconstructive Dynamics and on considerations about what is best for you and your family.

The unfaithful partner faces a thorny problem after he has broken off with his lover. Every time a conflict arises in his marriage, his first impulse may be to run from his problems rather than face them. When things are going well in his marriage, it is easy to forget the affair. But in times of conflict the memory of a comforting, supportive, understanding third party can reemerge. How do you combat the urge to escape?

First of all, ask your partner for support. Tell her that you are having these feelings and that you can't cope with them alone. Whatever you do, don't just hold those feelings in—vent them! Go back to what you experienced in Reconstructive Dynamics when you described what unfulfilled needs were satisfied by your lover. In the moments of bonding after you ventilated your feelings you probably realized that the gratification you received from your lover was very superficial and could never really satisfy your deepest needs. In moments of doubt try to reexperience those moments of lucidity and objectivity when you were able to clearly understand what you really wanted out of life.

Secondly, I suggest that you eliminate any remnants of the affair in your physical environment that may remind you of the third party. If you have letters your lover wrote you, read them to your spouse, then destroy them. If you have pictures, gifts, or other memorabilia of that person, throw them away. You don't want to fill your world with sentimental reminders of someone you had best forget.

One final tip. Before you go to this crucial meeting with your former lover, tell your spouse about it. Let her support you right up to the last minute, not only because you need all the support you can get but because the way you handle this incompletion in your life will strongly affect your partner's ability to overcome the trauma of the affair. Think of yourself as an emissary carrying a message to your former lover from *both* you and your spouse. Your partner has to have complete confidence in you, and by allowing her to support you on your "mission" you create a bond of trust that will allow the wounds of the affair to heal more quickly.

To sum up, your goal is to complete your relationship with your former lover. It is essential that she understand your motivations for ending the relationship and that your decision in no way invalidates anything you experienced together. Ideally, you and the third party should walk away from this meeting feeling that you care for one another but that nothing more needs to be said and that no possibility exists that you will get back together. Close the door on your extramarital affair. Whatever you do, don't slip a spare key into your side pocket and give yourself a means to go back whenever you may be tempted to do so. Complete this relationship—and that means throwing away the key.

HOW TO HANDLE FRIENDS, RELATIVES AND OTHERS WHO KNOW

Friends and Others Who Know

In this section we are going to discuss the problems you will encounter when you and your partner reemerge socially after an affair. As you can imagine, you are going to feel awkward at first around friends and acquaintances who know about your marital problems. You will be wondering: What are they thinking? Are they thinking that we are back together for the wrong reasons? That we'll never make it? That after what happened we have no business being together? It is a sad fact that even after the conflict of the affair has been resolved between you and your partner, other people, by making judgments about you and drawing false conclusions, can reactivate the negative feelings you thought were behind you.

Your friends are a very important part of your lives. You no doubt spend a great deal of time talking about them, discussing their personalities, their strengths, their weaknesses, their careers, their children, and their relationships. You have to believe they spend just as much time talking about you. When personal tragedy strikes you, naturally your friends are going to be interested. No matter how benevolent that interest may be, however, it can cause problems. You and your spouse are trying to put the affair behind you and move on in life. Often, those close to you are not willing to do so. You may find that reestablishing social relations is a real test of how well you have overcome the trauma of the affair.

At some point before you reunited, the faithful partner probably confided in one or a number of people about her problem. She (or he) needed support and naturally turned to her closest friends. This is perfectly normal. Problems can arise afterward, however, when these friends refuse to forgive the unfaithful partner for what he has done. In their zeal to support the wounded faithful partner, they tend to overdo it, creating irrational, angry, moblike sentiments and rallying antagonism against the "rotten bum" who so hurt their friend. Angry and hurt as she was, the faithful partner no doubt encouraged these feelings at first. After Reconstructive Dynamics she has worked them out, but her friends have not. Very often they still view the unfaithful partner as a rotten bum, and they think the faithful partner is a sucker for going back to him.

The Letter "A"

Like Hester in Hawthorne's *The Scarlet Letter*, the unfaithful partner reapproaches friends with a scarlet "A" for adultery. His spouse's confidantes usually despise him, and even his own friends may be uncomfortable in his company. A woman I knew who had had an affair noticed for months after she got back with her husband that her own friends, even close ones, seemed to be avoiding her, presumably because they were afraid she would seduce their husbands. This reaction is extremely common. You too may find that you have a reputation as a wife-stealer (or husband-stealer). At gatherings when you speak to someone of the opposite sex, you may feel very uncomfortable, as if you are being watched by that person's spouse. You may even think everyone has designs on you because you are perceived as someone who "swings." People have all kinds of strange ideas, and you have to learn to deal with them.

Who Knows?

Before you actually begin to socialize after getting back together, I suggest you and your partner sit down and discuss the kinds of reactions you are likely to get. Find out who in particular concerns you. Ask your partner, "How do you feel about such and such? Will he act strangely?" Compare impressions about the people you will encounter. It is also very important that you tell each other how much other people know. The faithful partner must tell her spouse all the people she confided in as well as the extent of their knowledge. The unfaithful partner, of course, must reveal not only whom he confided in but all the people who knew about his affair, right down to the last restaurant waiter. I hope you can see why this is so important. The last thing you need at this point is to walk around town wondering if everyone from cocktail sippers at parties to taxi drivers to flower vendors knows that your spouse cheated on you. That would only create anger, resentment, and pain.

Games People Play

You probably think you frequent a rather enlightened group of people—everyone wants to believe this—but you could be in for a shock when you try to fit in socially after an affair. Issues with deep implications such as adultery can bring out qualities in people that usually remain hidden. My clients often tell me that friends and acquaintances who they thought were quite broad minded became self-righteous and judgmental and draw all sorts of moralistic conclusions about the "infidel" and his spouse. In a sense, you become a soap opera for those around you; you provide excitement in their lives, something to gossip about, a chance to pull out their little bags of petty ready-made judgments and play with them for a while.

When reestablishing contact with your friends, it might be helpful to keep in mind that their attitudes toward you may have to do with their own marital problems. Now that you have vigorously confronted yourself through Reconstructive Dynamics and have observed your own relationship from a clear and objective point of view, you will be much more aware of the games people play. You will see the incompletions between couples, the poor communication, the destructive roles they are stuck in; in sum, all the things you and your partner were willing to confront and work through. If you sense hostility or tension between yourself and others, or if you sense others are making judgments, recognize that people may unconsciously fear you. They may be suppressing a lot of anxiety about their own relationships and wondering if the trauma you experienced may not be waiting at their own doorsteps. Self-righteous judgments and anger are often surface manifestations of our deepest fears—we condemn all the more vehemently patterns of behavior in others that we see in ourselves.

How will you and your partner handle this social pressure? It's sad to think that after you have worked so hard to get where you are, the people around you are trying to destroy all the progress you've made. Having overcome the trauma of the affair through Reconstructive Dynamics, you are much stronger than you were before, and the emotional bonding between you and your partner has no doubt made you resilient enough to handle a certain amount of pressure. But you can't live the rest of your lives with an "us against the world" or a "nation of two" attitude. You need the support of your friends. So at some point you are going to have to ask yourselves, Do we want to sit down and talk with such and such and explain how things really are, or do we want to end our relationship with that person?

Show Them You're For Real

Let's say, for example, that the faithful partner's best friend is unable to reestablish her (or his) rapport with the unfaithful partner. If you feel you can trust that person, and I presume you can, both partners should sit down and explain to her why the affair occurred and what you learned through Reconstructive Dynamics. The unfaithful partner must acknowledge that he hurt his spouse deeply and that anger directed toward him is entirely justified. The real burden, however, falls upon the faithful partner to convince her friend that she has forgiven her partner totally and that she really loves him even though he made a mistake. She must make it clear that she is not motivated by a parasitic need or the fear of being alone but by a genuine desire to be with her partner. Do this with any intimate friend who is having trouble relating to you as a couple after the affair. Convince him or her that the anger is justified—remember that there is no such thing as a *wrong* feeling—but that holding onto it like a sentimental keepsake serves no one's best interest.

With very close friends you can actually sit down and talk. With others you probably don't want to, and, besides, it's none of their business. The best you can do is demonstrate your feelings of togetherness and unification. Work together to show people that a deep emotional bond exists between you and your partner and that you really want to spend the rest of your lives together. Others will be skeptical at first, but when they see that the good feelings between you are real—and they are if you completed Reconstructive Dynamics successfully—they'll get the idea sooner or later.

Relatives

If some of your friends can't accept you after the affair, you can go out and find new ones; but you can't very well go out and find new parents and parents-in-law, can you? You really have no choice but to confront parents and in-laws with any resistance they may be showing toward your reunion. Let's look at some of the problems likely to come up.

The parents of the faithful partner are most likely going to harbor deep resentment for the unfaithful partner. They will have great difficulty forgiving the evil monster who cheated on "daddy's little girl" or "mommy's little boy." Parents are extremely possessive of their children, even after they have grown up. This is no doubt the reason people have so much trouble relating to their parents-in-law; when you marry someone, you assume a position of great power in that person's life and therefore usurp some, if not all, of his or her parents' influence. This can be very threatening. When an affair occurs, two things happen. First, the parents are extremely angry because their son-in-law or daughter-in-law abused his or her power over their child. Second, their own power in their child's life is suddenly restored, and, as we all know, when you have power you generally use it. During the trauma of the affair the faithful partner no doubt leaned heavily upon her family for support, and it is very possible that she kindled embers of antagonism against her spouse. I strongly suspect that her parents fueled the fire.

The unfaithful partner may even have to face the responsibility of having ruined his partner's family name. In this country we no longer have such a strong sense of honor, but an affair can nonetheless do damage to a clannish sense of pride. I know many families, especially close ones, that accept new brides and grooms into the coveted "inner circle" only after very close scrutiny. They make it a great privilege to be allowed in. When that privilege is abused, it can be extremely difficult, if not impossible, to regain one's good standing with one's in-laws.

As with children and friends, you and your partner must create a context in which your parents can vent their feelings about the affair. Very likely they will have a distorted image of what happened, and they will blow things totally out of proportion. Expect this to happen; that way you can interpret, not react. The anger the faithful partner's parents feel is perfectly normal; their child has been deeply hurt. However, holding on to that anger and poisoning your relationship is not normal, and you have to help them reach an understanding of your conflict, which will allow that anger to pass. The first step in that process is allowing them to speak their minds freely.

If at all possible, both partners should sit down and talk with the indignant parents. Once they have vented their feelings thoroughly, you both must explain why the affair occurred. The unfaithful partner must explain that he acted not out of any malicious desire to hurt his spouse but because of his own inadequacies or unfulfilled needs. He must tell his parents-in-law that he loves their daughter (or son) very much, that the affair taught him a great deal about himself and his marriage, and that he wants to be accepted back into the family.

The immediate reaction of the faithful partner's parents will be to blame the unfaithful partner. They don't want to believe their child is in any way responsible, and they will jump at the opportunity to pour their contempt on "what's his name." The faithful partner must explain calmly and clearly her own responsibility in creating the affair. She might say, "Mom and Dad, I'm not excusing my husband for having an affair, but I recognize that he has needs that I wasn't fulfilling. Had I recognized those needs and been willing to fulfill them, I'm sure we could have avoided this problem. I am in part responsible."

You must help your parents see things as they really are. That is the only way to restore the harmony in your relationship with them as a couple. Explain to them as you did with your children and good friends the causes of the affair—the unfulfilled needs, the destructive roles, perhaps even the childhood imprints—that may have contributed. In Reconstructive Dynamics you and your partner struggled very hard through poisonous blame, anger, and resentment in yourselves, and it can be very upsetting to see them recycled in your relationship from the outside. The way to avoid this happening is to give others a clear understanding of why the affair occurred. Be careful, however, when explaining the childhood imprints that contributed to the problems in your marriage. Your parents may feel extremely threatened when you touch upon the way you were raised as a child. Imagine telling your parents that your spouse had an affair because his or her need for physical affection wasn't being fulfilled and that the reason you couldn't fulfill this need was that as a child you lacked physical contact and came to fear it. I once counseled a man who told his parents that because he had been so driven to succeed as a child he had never learned to be satisfied with what he had. He told them he had cheated on his wife not because he didn't love her but because even in his marriage that pattern of dissatisfaction prevailed—he felt he needed more than his wife could give him. His parents never imagined that their behavior could have had such an effect on their children, and they were forced to confront this painful issue long after anything could be done about it. They naturally felt very guilty. I don't think it is necessary to go into such detail with your parents. Of course you wouldn't really be blaming them—you should now recognize that you are responsible for *yourself*—but they could misunderstand your message, and you and your partner could find yourselves in a real quagmire. Use your own common sense in this case.

It is extremely important that you reestablish balance not only in the nuclear family but with all people who are important in your lives. You want to avoid at all cost allowing people to retain their initial judgments and negative feelings about your affair. Judgments and negative feelings are fueled by ignorance. They disappear when you make yourselves vulnerable and explain, from the heart not the head, the origin of your problems. The essential message to convey is that the affair was merely a *symptom* of a problem or series of problems; it was just the tip of the iceberg. Also, make it clear that the unfaithful partner acted not out of malice but out of frustration, and that placing total responsibility or blame on him reflects a superficial understanding of what actually happened.

Having dealt with trauma in my clients' lives for years, I can readily assure you that in many cases people come through hardship understanding themselves much better than before and having created more meaningful relationships with those they love. An affair really is only a symptom of deep, often suppressed conflict, and when it occurs a couple is forced to confront issues they should have confronted years before. Reconstructive Dynamics provided you a structure in which to do that. In this chapter we have discussed how you can take what you learned and apply it to relationships with those close to you. I hope you have succeeded in clearing the air with your children, friends, and relatives, just as you did with yourselves through Reconstructive Dynamics. Your relationships will be much richer for having done so.

Chapter 12

ON SEEKING PROFESSIONAL HELP

ON SEEKING PROFESSIONAL HELP

What does it mean to seek professional counseling? On one level it looks like an admission of failure. All people try to work their problems out alone, and only if they "fail" to do so would they turn to a professional. But the hundreds of people I've counseled over the years are anything but failures. For the most part they are highly successful, interesting, dynamic people who, at one point in their lives or another, recognize that their problems are bigger than they are. There is no shame in admitting that. It doesn't mean that they are psychologically fragile or in any way neurotic. We live in a very complex world in which people are not always in control of the circumstances of their lives. When things get out of hand, it takes courage to stop and observe that and to call in a third party who can use his expertise to work things out with you.

No counselor can solve all your problems *for* you. A lot of people, once they make the decision to go into therapy, think of it as some kind of panacea. But counselors are not magicians who can solve people's problems with a wave of the wand. They are *moderators* who can help couples understand one another better. When you are deeply involved in a relationship, you can't see things that are crystal clear to an outsider. A therapist is a trained outsider, a third party who you and your partner allow to penetrate your relationship in order to describe objectively what behavior may be causing problems. A therapist can make you aware of negative behavior patterns and can point you in a direction that will allow you to change them. Obviously, he can't do that *for* you.

REASONS FOR SEEKING PROFESSIONAL HELP

I would like to think that after Reconstructive Dynamics no one would need professional help. But I recognize that some people need a third party to structure their communication, to guide them through the process of self-discovery. When left on our own, it is very easy to lose our motivation to communicate feelings, and you may tend to let things slide; you become complacent. When you decide to see a therapist, you consecrate a specific period of time to focus on the problems of your marriage, which eliminates the possibility of letting communication remain incomplete.

Even people with the best of intentions fall into manipulative behavior every now and then. If one partner is extremely dominant, his manipulation can go unchecked for a long period of time and retard the reconstructive process. In such cases a professional therapist can be of great value. He is trained to moderate between couples and to recognize and make people aware of destructive behavior patterns. After years of marriage, couples are often not even vaguely conscious of the patterns they have developed together. As an outsider, a therapist can easily interpret messages that are incomprehensible to a couple themselves.

The process of reconstructing a marriage can be very trying, even when it seems to be working. If you and your partner go through Reconstructive Dynamics and manage to purge yourselves of all the emotional garbage you have been living with for years, you may still have difficulty adjusting to your new relationship. I once counseled a couple who had been in therapy before and had confronted a lot of emotional issues, but the woman had managed to open up much more easily than her husband, and their rates of emotional growth were very different. Consequently, the man felt threatened. The fact that his wife was extremely supportive made him feel even more threatened. He saw in his wife's emotional growth the reflection of his own inadequacy. This couple clearly needed marital counseling, a third party to mediate between them.

Sexual problems are perhaps the most difficult to work out alone. The trauma of an affair can create sexual disfunctions such as premature ejaculation, impotence, and frigidity, all of which can be cured in therapy.

Most people, when they confront the emotional garbage that has been poisoning their lives, manage to eliminate it. It may be recycled occasionally, but they have the tools to handle it. Others cannot. Certain behaviors are so deeply imprinted that it takes constant maintenance to keep them from running our lives. These people generally need counseling. Even after Reconstructive Dynamics you can find that patterns of behavior persist in spite of your efforts to eliminate them. You may, for example, have arrived at an understanding intellectually that you have been acting like a Victim, yet this destructive pattern continues. In such a case a counselor could help you work out the problem on an emotional level and possibly eliminate it.

Many couples have great difficulty handling the anger and hurt that result from an affair. If you sense that a prolonged gap in communication with your partner may be due to repressed anger or pain, and you don't think you can handle it, call a therapist. Try to work out the problem yourself, and be sure that it isn't due to some situational conflict (e.g., job stress, menstrual period, death in the family, etc.) that will pass in time. I recommend therapy only for some ongoing problem due to internalized feelings that create destructive patterns of behavior. Don't necessarily get one right away. Give yourself a few weeks or months and try to work things out yourselves. But if your problems persist, don't be afraid to admit that you need marital counseling.

I like to think of a therapist as a translator. He (or she) has to moderate an exchange of messages and make sure that both parties are understanding one another. When two people attempt to confront a painful issue together, communication can lose its focus and become manipulative. It's much easier to let yourself go off on a tangent than it is to confront a feeling. And it's much easier to shirk responsibility by manipulating than it is to accept responsibility. A therapist can keep you focused and prevent both conscious and unconscious manipulation.

Frustration, anger, and hurt can get in the way of meaning. When a person is in a highly emotional state, his message is often transmitted ambiguously in a package of excess wordage. A good therapist can cut through that package and deliver the message in simple terms. When people get emotional they also tend to "tune out"—quite clearly a defense mechanism—and they don't even hear what their partner is saying. Again, an objective third party can see that and reopen the lines of communication. A therapist can also identify ulterior motives for presenting feelings in a particular way; he can intervene when one partner becomes accusatory and starts to dump on the other; in sum, he can usually get to the truth much more quickly than you can.

REASONS PEOPLE GIVE FOR NOT SEEKING HELP

I find that the reasons people come up with to avoid seeking help are often linked to the very problems that disrupt their lives. For example, if someone were to obstinately deny that he needs professional counseling in spite of hard evidence that he does, I would immediately suspect that many of that person's marital difficulties are caused by denial or the unwillingness to confront problems of many levels.

We have discussed at great length throughout the book the nature of denial mechanisms. They serve to protect us from the truth, and they allow us to avoid taking responsibility. If you have a problem, the first step in overcoming it is to admit that it exists and take responsibility for it. A phone call to a professional counselor is a courageous step that amounts to an acknowledgment that you have a problem and are willing to confront it. When you do that, you are already well on the road to recovery.

What do you do if you recognize the need for marital counseling but your partner does not? If your spouse is unwilling to risk seeking help to save your marriage, you have to be confrontive yet supportive. Use some of the tools you learned in Reconstructive Dynamics. Explain to your partner in a nonthreatening way, using "I" language, that you feel it would be helpful to enlist an objective third party who would mediate between you and help you strengthen your marriage. In a very understanding, supportive way, present your spouse with evidence that things are not working and that you are both missing out on the joy your marriage could bring you. Make it very clear to your partner that the counseling is for *both* of you and that you feel you will personally get value out of it. Take responsibility for *your* role in creating the problem and create a context in which your spouse can admit his own. If he needs time to think about it, that's fine, but don't let the subject drop. Too much is at stake.

Or you might have to confront your partner with your belief that he is locked into a destructive role that prevents him from seeing the truth. I once encountered a man who would throw up his arms and tell his wife, "We'll never work things out; it's hopeless!" When she suggested therapy he of course said that it would be a waste of time and money because it would certainly fail. In therapy it became clear that the man had always been very comfortable being a Victim and that his refusal to improve his marriage, either himself or with the help of a counselor, merely fell in line with the destructive pattern of behavior that ran his life.

Perhaps the most common obstacle to seeking professional help is the fear of being vulnerable. This fear exists on two levels. First there is the fear of placing yourself in a subordinate role. When you seek professional help you are allowing someone else to *help* you, which implies you can't help yourself, which places you in a position of vulnerability. Second, when you decide to get marital counseling, you decide to discover the truth about yourself, to expose that part of you that you have been protecting. Therapists, because of their training and the objectivity they have as third-party observers of your relationship, are able to see through the games people play in order to avoid vulnerability. That can be extremely frightening.

If in the course of therapy a person demonstrates his unwillingness to open up and be vulnerable, a good therapist will be able to recognize that many of his marital problems are no doubt caused by his efforts to "protect" himself. Curiously enough, once therapy has actually begun, I find that such people are much less afraid of me, the counselor, than they are of their partners. It is by then quite clear that a lot of emotions have been suppressed and a lot of communications left incomplete in that relationship.

The willingness to seek professional help, when it is sought for the right reason, is an affirmation of your commitment to make your marriage work. Rather than thinking of yourself as a failure for seeking therapy, think of yourself as taking a dynamic step to reinforce everything you have accomplished so far in your marriage.

WHAT KIND OF THERAPY IS RIGHT FOR YOU?

There are many different therapeutic approaches available to you once you decide to seek professional help. Rather than tell you which ones I prefer, I would encourage you to do some research and draw conclusions yourself. Certain types of people will respond better to one therapeutic approach than another. Psychoanalysis, for example, is clearly not for everybody. There are many books on the market* that offer a general overview of the various types of therapy: psychoanalysis, transactional analysis, Rogerian psychology, Gestalt, reality therapy, rational emotive therapy. Each one has its strong and weak points, and I can't tell you which one would be best for you. That depends on your emotional makeup and the special problems you have in your relationship.

The best way to choose an approach is through a combination of research and advice from others. Describe to your doctor the nature of your problem and see if he can't suggest a therapist. You have to be careful, though, not to let one personal judgment determine your choice. Just because your friend had a bad experience with, say, Gestalt, doesn't mean you will. Get lots of feedback from people, but use your judgment in making a final decision. If you should begin one therapy and find you don't care for it, don't hesitate to change. There are lots of options.

Here I offer you a very brief, admittedly incomplete, description of several different therapeutic approaches. I strongly encourage you to do more reading on them all before you choose one.

Reality Therapy

Reality therapy was developed by William Glasser in the 1960s as an alternative to psychoanalysis, which Glasser feels

---

*I recommend Joel Kovel, *A Complete Guide to Therapy: From Psychoanalysis to Behavior Modification*, (New York: Pantheon Books, 1976).

discourages the patient from taking responsibility for himself. Reality therapy focuses on the patient's conscious behavior, encouraging him to take responsibility for his own actions, and helps him better handle life situations.

Gestalt Therapy

Gestalt is a very directive, or confrontive, approach to behavior. It emphasizes the organization of experience into patterns that, when confronted, can be broken. Some refer to Gestalt as a marriage between psychoanalysis and psychodrama. In Gestalt you attempt to get at the core of a problem and then "act out" or "experience" your conflict.

Psychoanalytic Therapy

Most people know essentially what Freud's psychoanalytic approach was about. Psychoanalysis is a rather complex approach to behavior whose general design is to reconstruct the personality by eliciting and interpreting the patient's unconscious mental contents and processes and by establishing a therapeutic relationship, or transference, with the analyst.

Transactional Analysis

Transactional Analysis, or TA, is a form of group psychotherapy formulated by Eric Berne that studies the interactions between individuals in everyday situations. Berne holds that at any given moment each person in a social aggregation will exhibit a parental, adult, or child ego-state and that social interaction is a series of games played by various combinations of ego states. This method of therapy was popularized first by Berne's *Games People Play* and later by Thomas Harris's *I'm OK, You're OK.*

Rational Emotive Therapy

This is a highly directive approach developed by Albert Ellis that holds that emotional difficulties are due to faulty, illogical attitudes that can be altered by controlling the thought processes. Simply stated, it is the curing of unreason by reason.

Rogerian Psychology

Often referred to as "client-centered" therapy, this approach developed by Carl Rogers is nondirective, which means that the therapist allows the patient to draw conclusions himself. Rogers views psychotherapy as an opportunity for the patient to grow and "become a person" by realizing his own inner potential. This client-centered approach holds that human nature is fundamentally good and that we all have the capacity for self-actualization but that we are blocked by emotional conflicts, distorted perceptions, and a poor self-image.

How do you actually choose a therapist? I don't recommend you let your fingers do the walking through the Yellow Pages. A marital counselor becomes an intimate part of your relationship when you allow him access to your most hidden dreams and fears, so I think it is wise to choose him or her more carefully than you might, say, a dentist. You have to look at a variety of factors in making a choice: your emotional needs and wants, your attitudes, your personality, your value system, your financial situation. It is extremely important to find a person whom you can trust.

Again, I suggest you talk to your doctor or friends and try to get a referral. There is no guarantee that you will be compatible with someone recommended to you, but it is nonetheless better than choosing randomly. Either way, your therapist's personality may conflict with your own. He or she could remind you of someone in your past who made you uncomfortable or hurt you, and you may very well have a barrier to communicating with that person. You may not be able or willing to give that person the power he or she needs to help you in your marriage.

If you begin therapy and after some time decide that the counselor isn't right for you, find a new one. Always give it a try, though, for at least a month. It is not uncommon to have a very negative reaction toward someone the first few times we meet him and to discover good things as we get to know him more intimately. Give your therapist time to develop a rapport with you. He or she may surprise you. You may, on the other hand, find that that person will not be able to help you. Don't be afraid to change.

If you can't get a referral, you might try calling a therapist on the phone and talking to him briefly. See how you react to his (or her) voice, manner, and ideas. It's difficult to make a reasonable judgment on the basis of a single conversation, but often gut reactions are correct.

Perhaps you went through Reconstructive Dynamics and you still think some things have to be worked out. Does that mean that the process was a failure? No! Any attempt to communicate, even if it doesn't lead to "enlightenment" is nonetheless worthwhile and will make therapy much easier. A lot of things come out through Reconstructive Dynamics, and even if you don't feel you can handle the problems in your relationship without professional help, you will be closer to a solution than if you were to start therapy cold.

Let me conclude this chapter by repeating that there is no reason to fear seeking professional help. Sometimes the circumstances of our lives create problems that we can't handle ourselves. It takes integrity to recognize that. Think about the couples you know personally. How many of them could benefit from a little more self-awareness? How many of them refuse to seek marital counseling for the wrong reasons: fear of vulnerability, fear of social stigma, fear of being thought crazy? They just live with their problems and miss out on many of the true joys of marriage. I hope that you can use the tools of self-awareness you have acquired in Reconstructive Dynamics to resolve the issues that come up between you and your partner. If you should find that you can't solve all your problems, I hope you now have the courage to seek professional help.

CONCLUSION

Successfully completing Reconstructive Dynamics is a great accomplishment for any couple. You should now recognize that even if you had not had an affair, the self-knowledge you gained in this process would still have been helpful and strengthened your marriage. Many of the problems you overcame in reuniting after the affair are identical to those that can create erosion in any marriage. Most people allow problems to simmer for years and years without confronting them; their marriages survive, but they lack vitality, spontaneity, and true intimacy. In a sense, you and your partner were lucky. Your problems reached a boiling point and you had to either resolve them or end your marriage. You decided that your marriage was worth saving, so you vigorously confronted yourself and opened the door to a *better* relationship with your spouse than you had before.

Look around you and ask yourself how many couples you know portray a semblance of normalcy and stability but are nonetheless stagnating. How many of them are stuck in destructive roles that lock them into the same kind of mechanical behavior patterns that led to an affair in your marriage? Observe such negative behavior in others, not in order to make judgments but to increase your awareness of yourself and to eliminate these patterns in your own relationship. As I pointed out in Reunion, from this point on in your marriage, you will recycle negative feelings about the affair and about dozens of other issues. Now, however, you can control them rather than allowing them to control you.

Reconstructive Dynamics provided you and your partner with a structure to work through your marital problems and the tools with which to do so. The ultimate goal of this book, however, is to allow you to transcend the need for a formal structure. I said at one point that Reconstructive Dynamics never really ends; in your marriage you will be continually confronted with new and challenging problems to overcome, using, of course, the tools provided in this book. Every time you work through a problem, you grow as a person, and when you work together as husband and wife, you grow as a couple. Like a body constantly rebuilding its cellular structure, your relationship must constantly renew itself if it is to remain dynamic and alive.

If you are dissatisfied in your work, it is perfectly acceptable to change jobs. If you are tired of living in the same city, no one thinks it particularly unusual when you pack your bags and decide to move "just for a change of air." Filet mignon eaten five days a week would make you long for a piece of celery; even the best joke in the world isn't funny after you have heard it three or four times. It is one of the facts of life that repetition is boring and unsatisfying to human beings. We need new challenges in our careers, new landscapes to rest our eyes on, a variety of tastes to stimulate our palates, and fresh, novel humor to keep us sane. And yet, strangely enough, in spite of the tremendous variety of interesting people around us, we are expected to stay with the same marital partner all of our lives, to bounce ideas off the same person every morning at breakfast, to forever function socially as a member of the same couple, to make love to the same body over and over again. It just doesn't make sense.

And yet it does. Your relationship with your spouse is different from your relationship to a job, a town, a joke, or a piece of meat. First of all, you feel needed by your partner, whereas Chicago or your latest ethnic joke couldn't care less about you. Next time you sit down to a good meal, ask yourself, How will this dish feel if I don't eat it? Second, your spouse can change, and perhaps more importantly, you can help him or her change. When both partners in a relationship evolve and grow as people, when they both remain excited about life, their relationship will work, provided they are compatible. I hope you can now see that I wrote this book to help people break out of behavior problems that cause them to stagnate as individuals and cause their relationships to get stuck like a scratched record repeating the same phrase over and over again. Relationships need not be like this; I sincerely hope that yours no longer is.

In a landmark work called *Laughter*, French philosopher Henri Bergson attempts to explain what makes people laugh. Among his conclusions are mechanical behavior and lack of awareness of the world around us. According to Bergson, the repetition in slapstick comedy—for example, Charlie Chaplin falling out of the same chair several times in a row or running into the same door time and again—is funny because it is mechanical. When we laugh at Chaplin's hapless character, we are punishing him for acting like a machine. When a man strolling dreamily down the street slips on a banana peel and falls, we laugh because he was not paying attention to his environment. He was so absorbed in his own thoughts that he didn't see that reality had placed a banana peel in his path. Our laughter is his punishment for not being aware.

In this book my goal has not been to keep you from getting laughed at. But I have insisted that mechanical behavior and lack of awareness are the enemies of a dynamic and meaning-ful relationship. The punishment for repetitious, mechanical behavior and lack of awareness in a marriage is not laughter but tears—your own.

Author's Note

Dr. Ronnie Edell's research into the issues that concern today's couples is an ongoing process. To this end, he welcomes input from his readers. If you have had any experience with this program you would like to share, or if you have comments, questions or suggestions that may be addressed in a follow-up book, you may write to Dr. Edell at:

Dr. Ronnie Edell
P.O. Box 3718
La Mesa, California 91944-3718